Publisher's Note

The Hawaiian language is alive and well and flourishing. After being confined to scholarly publications, a handful of Hawaiians and for naming streets, its written and spoken use expands every day. Most of the credit goes to a heightened cultural awareness that began with the Hawaiian Renaissance movement of the 1970's and accelerated with the sovereignty movement of the 1990s.

Today, there is growing attendance in Hawaiian language immersion programs that teach youngsters how to converse and communicate in Hawaiian. More and more programming in Hawaiian—newscasts, church services, discussions—is heard on the airwaves. Many public announcements are now bilingual, and books on how to speak Hawaiian or teach children the Hawaiian language are crowding bookstore shelves.

This expertly prepared vocabulary dictionary handbook will help introduce the casual reader to the beautiful, poetic Hawaiian language. Hopefully it will continue the expansion of the daily use of Hawaiian in homes, schools, office and everyday conversations.

ISBN-10: 1-56647-112-5
ISBN-13: 978-1-56647-112-1

Library of Congress Catalog Card Number: 95-81196

Cover design by Courtney Young
Cover photo © Douglas Peebles

Fourteenth Printing, October 2018

Mutual Publishing, LLC
1215 Center Street, Suite 210
Honolulu, Hawaii 96816
Ph: (808) 732-1709
Fax: (808) 734-4094
email: info@mutualpublishing.com
www.mutualpublishing.com

Printed in Taiwan

HANDY
HAWAIIAN DICTIONARY

with English-Hawaiian Dictionary
and Hawaiian-English Dictionary

Over five thousand of the commonest and
most useful English words and their
equivalents, in modern Hawaiian speech,
correctly pronounced, with a complementary Hawaiian-English Vocabulary.

Compiled by

Henry P. Judd
Former Professor of the Hawaiian Language
at the University of Hawaii

Mary Kawena Pukui
Hawaiian Translator at the
Bishop Museum

and

John F.G. Stokes
Former Curator of Polynesian Ethnology
of the Bishop Museum

Mutual Publishing

Preface

The purpose of this little work is to assist the English-speaking person so desiring to acquire readily a working knowledge of the Hawaiian language. We learn best to speak by speaking, whether it be our own language or another tongue, so the plan is to furnish the reader with a verbal equipment sufficient to enable him to converse accurately in Hawaiian with those who still use the language as their own. The equipment offered is, in addition to grammatical notes, a careful selection of five thousand of the most used and most useful English words, with their various equivalents as spoken by present-day Hawaiians among themselves. The whole is contained in a small booklet, especially limited as to size so that it may be conveniently carried for ready reference.

We recommend to the reader or student sincerely desiring to learn the language, attendance at classes in Hawaiian. Failing this we expect that he will practice speech with Hawaiians wherever he may find them, and so accustom his ear to the native enunciation.

It might be noted that the brusque approach of some haoles to Hawaiians is resented. Hawaiians are naturally polite and deferential, and appreciate such qualities in their friends.

We feel confident that the English list will prove extensive enough for ordinary wants. For frequency of use it has been checked by the word-counts of Edw. L. Thorndike (1921 and 1932).

W. F. Tidgman (1921), Ernest Horn (1926), and Buckingham and Dolch (1936). On the point of utility, it was found to contain practically all of the 850 English words which C. K. Ogden (Basic English, 1934) considered sufficient to cover the needs of everyday life. However, since the vocabularies of individuals, as well as of localities and classes, vary greatly, we felt that the range of synonyms should not be too closely restricted, and the usefulness of the present work is thereby enhanced.

The Hawaiian translations are based on H. R. Hitchcock's English Hawaiian Dictionary (1887) modified, where desirable, after reference (1) to the following English-Hawaiian vocabularies: J. S. Emerson (1845), Lorrin Andrews (1865), F. E. Midkiff and J. H. Wise (about 1929), Mary H. Acherley (1930), an anonymous manuscript used in Hawaiian classes at the University of Hawaii by F. W. Beckley in 1925 and by J. F. Woolley in 1928, and subsequently published for the Hawaiian Language League (1936), the Hawaii Tourist Bureau (1937) and O. Shaw (1939), and, (2) to L. Andrews' Hawaiian-English lists (vocabulary, 1836 and dictionary, 1865), and their revisions by H. H. Parker (1921).

For elision of archaic or obsolete terms, and particularly for the Hawaiian pronunciation, main dependence has been placed on the second member of the compilers who, in her early life, received special training on the subject from the old masters of chanting. Debatable points were referred to many Hawaiian scholars, in particular to Mr. David Piimanu, translator at the

Archives of Hawaii, and the Reverends S. K. Kamaiopili, Edward Kahale and H. K. Poepoe, to all of whom, and to the many others consulted, we make our grateful acknowledgment.

Special thanks are due to Dr. Denzel Carr, the accomplished linguist, for guidance in evaluating basic sounds.

For the Hawaiian portion, emphasis is laid on the fact that the words selected are those currently used by the present generation between its members. Some native terms, recorded when the language was first written over a century ago, have become obsolete and are omitted as unheard today. Also avoided, but for another reason, is the "pidgin," "haole" or "pake" Hawaiian, frequently mistaken for real Hawaiian by foreigners.

In another class is the introduction of terms necessitated by the changes in modern Hawaiian living conditions. The Hawaiian met the requirements by various methods: (1) Adapting its original terms. (2) Direct borrowings of foreign words and clothing them in Hawaiian garb. (3) Combining (1) and (2).

The subject of communications furnishes examples of all the groups. For the first, we may follow the evolution of the terms moku and ka'a. Formerly and today, moku means "severed," and hence also a "district" or "island," namely, "something cut off." When foreign ships were first seen, on account of their size they were thought to be floating islands, and therefore called moku. From this, steamers became mokuahi (fire ships), airplanes, mokulele (flying ships), and submarines, mokulu'u (diving boats).

Ka'a means "to roll," "to ·revolve," "move round about," etc. Hence, when introduced, wheeled vehicles were termed ka'a. From this, railroad trains became ka'aahi (fire cars), and street-cars, ka'auwila (lightning or electric cars) a term also applied at first to automobiles.

However, the equivalent for the word "automobile" was soon included in the second group, dressed in Hawaiian fashion as okomopila. Other terms, such as kelepona, kelekalapa, uwea, etc. will be recognized readily as native pronunciation of the English, "telephone," "telegraph," "wire," etc. The Hawaian status of adaptations of this class is sometimes questioned, but they have as good standing in Hawaiian as have "telephone," "tea," "canoe," etc. in English.

The third group includes such interesting hybrids as uwea'ole, literally "wireless," and kalaiwaka'a, "chauffeur." The term ka'a, as already indicated, had a native origin, while kalaiwa is merely the Hawaiian pronunciation of "driver."

We have adherred to the work of earlier writers on the Hawaiian language, with two exceptions:

(1) The glottal closure, known to the early Hawaiians as 'u'ina, we recognize as a consonant and include in the alphabet. It is represented by an inverted comma ('), as is done regularly for the Samoan dialect, and is being done now by the Bishop Museum in its Ha-

waiian manuscripts. It represents the Polynesian (not the Hawaiian) "K," attenuated until almost completely elided. Not only by the Hawaiians was this Polynesian "K" so treated, but also by the Samoans and Tahitians, while it was retained in full volume by the other Polynesians in New Zealand, Tonga, Cook, Marquesas, Tuamotu and Easter Islands.

The 'u ina is still part of Hawaiian speech, but has not previously been indicated in writing except to distinguish between a'u "my" and au "thy" and in a very few other words. It has been treated largely as a diacritical mark, although Alexander noted in his grammar: "This gutteral is properly a consonant, and forms an *essential* part of the words in which it is found." Its presence or absence in Hawaiian words marks distinct terms. For instance, three such words have been written ai, although pronounced differently. The correct forms would be 'a'i, meaning "neck," 'ai, "food," and ai, "sexual intercourse."

For clarity, we believe that the 'u'ina should be indicated when writing. But, whatever the student may choose to do, we afford him the opportunity of knowing the words he uses, and thus of avoiding possible slips.

(2) The second exception is the allowance of three values to the Hawaiian vowels, instead of the two, "long" and "short," previously given. We added an "intermediate" after endeavoring in vain to reconcile some of the pronunciations in the latest dictionary with the spoken Hawaiian.

Since this work is intended for use by English-speaking people, it would be well to list the main points in which Hawaiian differs from English.

Hawaiian articulation is based very largely at the back of the tongue, while that of English is nearer the tip.

In Hawaiian, vowels are of primary importance, and many words have no consonants; all vowels and consonants are sounded, and semi-vowels are absent. In English, many vowels and consonants are silent, and semivowels are present; the consonants are all-important, numbering about twenty-five and represented (omitting "c, q and x") by eighteen characters, only seven of which occur in Hawaiian.

In Hawaiian, all syllables end with a vowel, and no two consonants adjoin.

Generally, nouns precede their adjectives, and verbs their subjects.

The same word may very often appear as a noun, adjective, verb or adverb, without change in pronunciation.

The verbs "to be," and "to have," and the auxiliaries are not represented in Hawaiian by verbs, but by construction of the sentence or by particles.

In Hawaiian, personal pronouns cover a wider field and are more precise than in English.

Grateful acknowledgment is made to the Director and Staff of the Bishop Museum of their suggestions and guidance in the work, and of the use of the Museum's facilities.

The Compilers.

Grammatical Notes

This is not the place for a complete grammar of the Hawaiian language, copies of which are for sale in the book stores. However, the following notes will be helpful to the English-speaking student.

ALPHABET

The Hawaiian alphabet is comprised of thirteen letters, the vowels **a, e, i, o, u,** and the consonants **h, k, l, m, n, p, w** and the **'u'ina** represented by an inverted comma (').

The vowels are given pure sounds based on the Italian, unlike the English in which four of the long vowels are really diphthongs. Such will be realized after slowly pronouncing the English long "a, i, o, u." Thus, "a" closes to "ee"; "i" begins with "ah" and closes to "ee"; "o" closes to "oo" or to "u" as in "rule," and "u" is pronounced "iu" or "yu." Omitting the vanish, Hawaiian vowels are pronounced as follows:

Long	Short
ā, as in father.	ă, as in republican.
ē, as in obey, fete.	ĕ, as in nicety.
ī, as in marine, pique.	ĭ, as in mariner, charity.
ō, as in rose, vote.	ŏ, as in democrat, eulogy.
ū, as in rule.	ŭ, as in pull.

As indicated, the long vowel is marked with the macron, and the short vowel with the breve. One other value, at least, may be noted between the long and the short. We have termed it the "intermediate," and written it without diacritical marks: a, e, i, o, u. However, we have not so far been able to find English words to illustrate the value, unless, perhaps, for the a, as in "flora." When accented the vowel seems to acquire additional strength.

In Hawaiian the short vowels as in the English, "at, net, it, not, nut" are lacking, although the vowel in the last word is approximated by the Hawaiian ā.

The Hawaiian ends his syllable with a vowel, without carrying it to the consonant following.

VOWEL COMBINATIONS

Two adjoining vowels generally coalesce as a diphthong, when the second is light or unaccented. Andrews combines all the vowels in this manner, but the following are more common:

Ae and ai, like "i" in "line," but closing to ĕ and ĭ respectively

Ao and au, like "ow" in "how," but closing to ŏ and ŭ respectively.

Ea, near "ea" in "pear."

Ei, like "ai" in "raiment," or "a" in "lay."

Ia, as in "pier."

Oa, near the "a" in "all" or "aw" in "awl."

Oe, oi, as in "oil" or "coy," but closing to ĕ and ĭ respectively.

Ou, like the English long "o," closing to "oo."

Other combinations are present, with the first vowel light or unaccented, and particularly when the second vowel is strong and accented: The initial i is pronounced like "y," so for ia we hear "yah," for iu, "you," etc. The medial i, is split into very light i and "y," so that mikioi, is not pronounced "micky-oy" but mi-kiyoi. Similar conditions apply to Hawaiian e, but in a lesser degree.

After o and u, the sound of "w" creeps in, and in many words, for clarity, the w is so written. Thus, the words in each of the following couples are the same: oa', owa'; oi' owi'; ua'hi, uwa'hi; aue', auwe'; ui'la, uwi'la; uo', uwo'.

Many words contain more than two vowels together, especially with compounds, the pronunciations of which are followed. In other words, a division is generally made into pairs of vowels, one heavy and one light, or the pronunciation may be ascertained by observing the accent. In this connection, it would be well to remember that the 'u'ina is a consonant and that such a word formerly written hauoli is hau'oli, and is thus at once divisible into hau-'o-li for pronunciation.

CONSONANTS

The consonants are pronounced as in English, with some exceptions:

K. As in English, with some variation towards "t," and to "tch" before iu. For chanting, it is pronounced "t." It represents the Polynesian "t" which predominated in the Hawaiian Islands between 1778 and 1809 according to the dozen vocabularies made in those years. By the time the present Hawaiian orthography was established in 1825, the "k" sound had become so general that the character "k" was adopted.

L. An unstable consonant, now pronounced as in English, but formerly spoken as a soft

"r" and (though rarely) as "d." In the various
lists and writings of 1778-79, the sound was
"r" (totals, "r" 126 times, "l" once and "d,"
four times). By 1792-94, from this percentage
of 0.7, the "l" sound had increased to 8%, and
by 1804, to 16%. In 1826, the missionaries
voted six to two in favor of retaining "l" for
the Hawaiian alphabet, and rejecting "r." In
some words, "l" alternates with "n"; for instance, the Hawaiian for "charcoal" is **nanahu**
or **lanahu**.

W. This consonant ranges between soft "w"
and soft "v," inclining however to "w." The
sound "w" is heard (1) when an initial: (2)
when a medial, (a), preceded by o or u; (b)
when followed by an accented or strong vowel;
(c), when an initial of parts of compounds.
The "v" sound is heard when preceded by **a,
e, i,** and followed by a short vowel.

Some speakers consistently use the soft "v"
for w, except after o and u. Such usage was
regarded by missionary orthographers as mere
affectation. It were better to regard it as a local
dialectical variation of limited range. However, some foreigners today are pronouncing
it as though a strong "v" in the mistaken idea
that such is correct.

' The 'u'ina is the vestige of the Polynesian
"k," and is sounded, somewhat like a grunt,
by a brief stoppage of the glottis. It has been
called the "glottal stop," "gutteral break," and,
from its employment in Arabic, the "hamzah."
Its close relationship to the Polynesian "k"
will be realized by sounding "ah" with the
open glottis, and then with the temporary

closure, followed by "kah" sounded in the throat. This Polynesian "k" has, as in Hawaii, been reduced by the natives of Samoa and Tahiti. In Samoa it is regarded and written as a consonant.

Although seldom written in Hawaiian, as it should be, nevertheless it has been preserved in speech—in most instances correctly, as may be ascertained from the Polynesian prototypes of the words. The following are examples:

Hawaiian		Other
Previously		Polynesian
Written	Pronounced	
aa	aa	
aa	a'a	aka
aa	'aa	
aa	'a'a	kaka
ahu	ahu	ahu
ahu	'ahu	kahu
koe	koe	toe
koe	ko'e	toke
kai	kai	tai
kai	ka'i	taki

The first four words, although similarly written, are shown by their pronunciation to be distinct from each other. The same applies to the pairs which follow them.

The accent occurs on the syllable next to the last in most Hawaiian words. Some are unaccented.

By changing the accent, or the length of the vowel, or both, a word will take on an entirely different signification. The word poho, if po'ho, means "to patch"; if pohō', "to sink."

Kŏ'kŏ means blood, and kōkō, netted bag.
Kŏhŏ'lă, "reef flats" and kŏhŏlā', "whale."
Kă'lă, "proclamation" and kālā, "dollar."
Lŭ'lŭ, "calm, still" and lūlŭ', "to shake."

In emphasis, the vowel is sometimes lengthened, as for instance, kŏlŏ'hĕ, "mischief," has
been pronounced, kōlō'hĕ. Similarly, today,
the 'u'ina may be heard where it is out of
place. Măŭă and kĕĭă are two examples ob-
served, which some people pronounce mă'ŭă
and kĕ'ĭă.

ARTICLES

The definite article "the" is represented in
Hawaiian by ke or ka in the singular, and by
na in the plural. Ke is used before all words
beginning with the letter k, while, in general
ka precedes the rest. However, ke also precedes some other words, particularly among
those beginning with a, o, p and '. which will
be indicated in the lists by (ke). The plural
form na is also a common plural sign.

The indefinite article "a" or "an" is expressed by he, and sometimes by kahi, kekahi
or ho'okahi, meaning "one." Kekahi is also
the equivalent of the expression "a certain."

"He" is used only in the nominative case,
for in other cases the word "kekahi" is used.
Example—I see a horse. Ke ike nei au i kekahi lio.

NOUNS

Gender is indicated by the terms kane,
"male," and wahine, "female" following the
noun. Rarely, distinct whole terms are found
as 'elemakule, "old man," and luahine, "old
woman."

The plural is indicated (1) by the **na**, as **na kamaliʻi**, "the children." (2) By the collective nouns, **mau, poʻe, pae** and **puʻu**. Mau has a general, but limited application as **he mau lio**, literally, "many horses," hence "some horses." **Poʻe** is generally used for animate objects, **puʻu** for inanimate and **pae** for lands, as **kela poʻe kanaka**, "those people," **he puʻu pohaku**, "a heap of stones," or "many stones," **keia pae moku**, "these islands." (3) By the addition of **ma** to a person's name, as **Hanale ma**, "Henry and his group," or "the Henrys." (4) By lengthening a syllable in a few words, terms for persons as **kănăʻkă**, "person," **kāʻnăkă**, "people"; **ʻĕlĕmăkŭʻlĕ**, "old man," **ʻĕlĕmāʻkŭlĕ**, "old men."

Except for this class of examples Hawaiian has no inflections.

Declensions are by prepositions or particles.

PREPOSITIONS OR PARTICLES

"Of" as the sign of the genitive case is expressed by **a** or **o**. A implies that the object is created, initiated or intimately connected and controlled by or with the subject when a living person. O is general. **Na hale a Keoki**, means "The houses built by George"; **Na hale o Keoki**, "The houses owned or occupied by George." Thus, the son of George would be indicated by the use of **a**, but the father of George, by **o**. "The bow of the ship," is expressed as **Ka ihu o ka moku**.

A possessive case is expressed by **ka** or **ko**, "of," in the use of which the rules are similar for **a** and **o**, although the order of the possessor and possessed is changed. Thus, while

"George's house," may be expressed in Hawaiian in two ways, **Ka Keoki hale,** and **Ko Keoki hale,** the first indicates that George was the builder, and the second, the occupant.

A wider possessive is contained in **na** or **no** (which also follow the rule for a and o) and is translated as "of, for, concerning, on account of." **No Keoki he mau hale,** literally "Of or for George a few houses," would be translated as "George has or possesses some houses." **No ko Keoki hale,** . . . means "Concerning or on account of George's dwelling..." An obligation is also implied by **na** as **Na Keoki e kukulu i kona hale,** "George should build his house."

No is also translated as "from," as is **mai,** when used with the directives **aku,** "thither" and **mai,** "hither," after the place-name affected. **No** indicates origin and **mai** separation, thus, **No Kauai mai** implies that one belongs to Kauai, and **Mai Kauai mai,** merely an arrival from Kauai. **Mai Honolulu aku,** implies a departure from Honolulu.

I, ia, io, "to," "at" or "in" of time, and "by" with adjectives and neuter verbs. The form **ia** is used before pronouns and proper names, as is **io** when also followed by **nei** or **la.**

I is also a word, not translatable in English, but important in Hawaiian and used to connect the verb and the object. It might be termed the sign of the accusative case. It becomes **ia** and **io** before pronouns, etc. as mentioned in the preceding paragraph.

In brief speech it implies a request or command, through the elision of the verb, as **i wai,** "bring water."

Ma, "at" or "in" of place, and "by" before pronouns and names of persons when it takes **o** immediately following and later **nei** or **la.** Other equivalents include: through, unto, alongside of, by means of, according to.

Me, "with." **E helepu me ia,** "Go together with him."

E, "by," after passive verbs, as **Ua hana'ia e Keoki,** "It was done by George."

The vocative case, used in address, is indicated by **e,** as **E Keoki!** "O George!"

The "o emphatic," so termed, is the word **'o,** appearing as a sign of the nominative always before proper names and pronouns, as: **Holo aku la o Lono,** "Lono sailed off." **O lakou no na kanaka,** "They are the people."

PERSONAL PRONOUNS
First Person

Singular, I, **aŭ, waŭ.**

Dual,   We, { inclusive, I and you, **kāŭā.**
             { exclusive, I and he, **māŭā.**

Plural, We, { inclusive, I and you many, **kākŏŭ.**
            { exclusive, I and they many, **mākŏŭ.**

Second and Third Persons

Singular, You, **'ŏĕ.**   He, she or it, **iă.**

Dual,   You two, **'ŏlŭă.**   They two, **lăŭă.**

Plural, You many, **'ŏukoŭ.**   They many, **lākoŭ.**

DECLENSION, PERSONAL PRONOUN, SINGULAR NUMBER

Case No.	Case Sign	Equivalent	First Person	Second Person	Third Person
1. 2. 3.	ʻo { a { o	. . of:	au — I ʻowau, wau — I	ʻoe — you ʻo ʻoe — you	ia — he, she or it ʻoia — he
		of:	{ a'u { o'u — of me, my, mine	au ou — your	ana, { a ia la / a ia nei } — his ona, { o ia la / o ia nei }
4.	{ ka, { ko	of:	ka'u, ku'u ko'u, ku'u — of me, my, mine	kau, ko kou, ko — your	kana, { ka ia la / ka ia nei } — his kona, { ko ia la / ko ia nei }
5.	{ Na { No	{ for, of, belong- { ing to:-	na'u no'u — mine	nau nou — yours	nana, { na ia la / na ia nei } — his nona, { no ia la / no ia nei }
6.	{ ia { io	to, and objec- tive:	ia'u io'u la io'u nei — me	ia ʻoe i ou la i ou nei — you	ia ia — him
7.	ma	through or by:	ma o'u la ma o'u nei — me	ma ou la ma ou nei — you	iona la ma ona la — him
8.	mai	from:	mai o'u aku mai o'u mai — me	mai ou aku mai ou mai — you	{ mai ona aku { mai ona mai } — him
9.	me	with:	me au — me	me ʻoe — you	me ia — him
10.	e	by:	e au — me	e ʻoe — you	e ia — him

ADJECTIVES

Attributive adjectives follow their nouns, and are not modified for gender, number or case.

Comparisons are formed by the addition of adverbs;

Positive degree,   anu, cold
Comparative "   anu a'e, anu aku, colder
Superlative "   anu loa, coldest, very cold.

The comparative is also indicated (1) by contrast, as: nui kela, 'u'uku keia, "that is greater than this," lit. "that is large, this is small." (2) by the verb 'oi, "to excel," or the adverb mamua o, "before," or by both. The statement "This is sweeter than that," may be variously rendered: Ono a'e keia i kela; Ono aku keia mamua o kela; 'oi aku ka ono o keia mamua o kela; etc.

NUMERALS

The cardinal numbers used today are:

1	ka'hi	20	iwăkălu'ă
2	lu'ă	30	kănăko'lŭ
3	ko'lŭ	40	kănăhă'
4	hă	50	kănălĭ'ma
5	lĭ'mă	60	kănăo'nŏ
6	(ke) o'nŏ	70	kănăhĭ'kŭ
7	hĭ'kŭ	80	kănăwă'lŭ
8	wă'lŭ	90	kănăĭ'wă
9	ĭ'wă	100	hane'lĭ
10	'ŭ'mĭ	1,000	kăŭkă'nĭ
11	'ŭmĭkūmamaka'hĭ	1,000,000	mĭlĭo'nă

In general, the units are prefixed by 'a when counting. At other times the prefix is e, except for "one," which is ho'oka'hi. The tens and larger numbers are preceded by an article.

The units are connected with the higher numbers by **kuma'ma** (as with "11" above), and the tens by **me**. Thus 968 becomes **eiwa haneli me kanaonokumamawalu.**

The numbers following "40" are introductions complementing the ancient native system, which continued with

400 lău	40,000 kĭ'nĭ
4,000 mă'nŏ	400,000 lĕ'hŭ

and rendered the number 968 as **elua lau me eha kanahakumamawalu,** lit. "two four-hundreds and four forties and eight." "Four" was also expressed by **kăŭnă,** and "forty" by **ka'ăŭ.** Apparently Hawaiian numeration was a blending of the quarternary and decimal systems.

The ordinals are formed by placing the distinguishing articles (**ke** or **ka**), before the cardinal, except for "the first," which is **ka mua.** Thus, "the sixth time" becomes **ke ono o ka wa,** lit. "the six of the time."

Distributive numbers are indicated by the prefix **pa,** as **pakahi,** "one apiece," **palua,** "two apiece."

Fractions are expressed by the prefix **ha'pa,** as **hapakolu,** "one-third."

VERB
Conjugation, Active Voice

Indicative mood

Primitive tense	**hana au**	I worked
Present tense	**ke hana nei au**	I work
Present tense	**e hana ana au**	I am working

Past tense	i hana au	I worked*
Perfect tense	ua hana au	I have worked
Pluperfect tense	ua hana e au	I had worked
Future tense	e hana au	I shall work

Subjunctive and conditional

Present tense	ke hana au	if I work
Future tense	ina e hana au	if I shall work
Past tense	ina hana au	if I worked
Preterite tense	ina i hana au	if I should work
Preterite tense	i hana au	if I should work
Imperative	e hana 'oe	work you
Prohibition	mai hana 'oe	don't you work
Infinitive	e hana	to work

Participles

Present	e hana ana	working
Past	i hana	worked

In the primitive or indefinite tense, the past is generally understood; more rarely the present or the future may be represented.

The passive voice is formed by suffixing ia (euphonic variants, hia, lia, mia, 'ia) to the verb, or by inserting ia after a following adverb. Occasionally the i of the suffix is elided.

---

*I hele au—is correct but conditional—I went (because of something). Ua hele au—I went (no condition).

The verb "to be."

A term for the verb "to be" is lacking from Hawaiian, wherein the association of the object and its name is generally sufficient to make a term unnecessary. In the simplest form of statement, the verb is indicated by the article **he**, "a or an," as **he ilio**, "it is a dog," lit. "a dog," and is sometimes followed by the strengthening particle **no**, as **he wai no**, "there is water," lit. "a water indeed."

It is also understood with words in apposition, as **'Owau ke ali'i**, "I am the chief," lit. "I, the chief," in which case the subject is generally preceded by the **'o** emphatic.

The sentence "So it is in Hawaii here," would be rendered "So in Hawaii here," namely **Pela no ma Hawai'i nei**. "Who is that?" in Hawaiian idiom becomes "Who that?" namely **'Owai kela?** the answer to which may be **'o Keoki no**, "it is George," or simply "George."

Thus it may appear that a term for the verb is not essential to the language.

The verb "to have."

A term for this verb indicating ownership is also lacking, but to express its meaning, the possessive case is used. For instance, "John has a horse," would be rendered **No Keoni he lio**, lit. "John's (or of John) a horse." "He has a land" would be **He 'aina kona**, lit. "A land his." "He has no land," **'A'ole ona 'aina**, "Not of him land."

The passive verb **loa'a**, "to be obtained, to get" approximates the equivalent of "possess." "I received the book," would be rendered **Loa'a**

ia'u ka puke, lit. "Received by me the book"
in which "the book" becomes the subject of
the sentence.

As an auxiliary verb, "have" is translated
by ua.

Directives and locatives

Following the verb (or the adverb if present)
but not expressed in English, are the directives aku, "outward," mai, "hither," a'e, "up-
wards or sideways," and iho, "down." These
directives are followed by the particle nei,
meaning "nearness" in place or time, or by la,
indicating remoteness. When la is combined
with aku, a'e and iho, the accent is moved forward, as follows: aku'la, a'e'la and iho'la.

Relative particle ai

This particle followed the verb, either di-
rectly, or after the adverb and directive. Following a vowel, it is sometimes abbreviated
to 'i. It is translatable by "which," "in which,"
"when," "where," depending on the context.

Order of words in a simple sentence.

The tense sign.
The verb itself.
The qualifying adverb.
The passive sign ia.
The verbal directive.
The locatives nei or la, or the particles ana
    or ai.
The strengthening particle no.
The subject.
The object.

Of course it is seldom that all are found
together in the one sentence.

WORD ADAPTIONS and CONTRACTIONS

As mentioned previously, the same word may be a noun, adjective, verb or adverb in Hawaiian. At other times we may see a noun, adjective or adverb made into a verb by pre-fixing the causative **hoʻo** or **haʻa**. Before certain vowels, these have been contracted to **hoʻ** or **haʻ**.

Inversely, nouns are formed from verbs by use of the present participial form **ana**, "ing." "Contraction," for instance is translated in Hawaiian as "contracting," and has practically the same meaning. In addition, many words may be found with the participle reduced to **na**, after a vowel and joined to its verb. For instance, **hanauna**, "a generation," or "the group of brothers and sisters," was derived from **hanau ana**, **hanau** meaning "to bear" or "be born."

Example of Hawaiian narrative

From Alexander we adapt the following analysis of a passage from the Hawaiian romance of Laieikawai:

```
    1    2                3
Iloko o ko Laieikawai mau la ma Waiapuka,
During Laieikawai's    days at Waiapuka,
```

ua hoʻomauia ka pio ana o ke anuenue ma
was continued the arch -ing of the rainbow at

```
                1
kela wahi, iloko o ka manawa ua a me ka
that place,  in    the  time rainy and the
```

4
malie, i ka po, me ke ao; aka, 'a'ole
fair, in the night, and the day; but not

5   6
nae i ho'omaopopo na mea a pau i ke 'ano
yet - understood the persons all - the nature

o keia anuenue; aka, ua ho'omauia keia mau
of this rainbow; but were continued these

                    5
ho'ailona ali'i ma na wahi i malamaia
signs chiefly at the places were guarded

7   8   3   8
'i   ua   mau mahoe nei.
where these   twins

                    9
I   kekahi   manawa   ia   Hulumaniani
On a certain   time   to   Hulumaniani

10   10 6
e ka'ahele ana ia Kaua'i a puni ma kona
travel-   -ing - Kauai around in his

                            9
'ano   makaula nui no Kauai, a ia ia
character prophet great of Kauai, and to him

5   11 12   12
i hiki ai iluna pono o Kalalea, 'ike mai
arrived - upon right - Kalalea, saw hither

13   6   4
la 'oia i ka pio a keia anuenue i Oahu
then he - the arch of this rainbow on Oahu

nei; noho   iho   la 'oia malaila he
here; dwelt accordingly - he there   a

                14   15
iwakalua la i kumu e 'ike maopopo ia
twenty day as means to seen clearly be

  16   17   18
  'i   ke 'ano o kana mea e 'ike nei.
by which the nature of him thing to see which.

Translation: In the days when Laieikawai
was at Waiapuka, the arching of the rainbow
was continued at that place in rainy weather
and in fair weather, by night and by day; but
yet, all persons did not understand the nature
of this rainbow; but these tokens of a chief
were continued in the places where these twins
were guarded.

On a certain time while Hulumaniani was
traveling around Kauai, in his capacity of
great prophet of Kauai, when he arrived at
the very summit of Kalalea, he saw the arch
of this rainbow on Oahu here; he accordingly
dwelt there twenty days in order to discern
more clearly the nature of what he saw.

Notes:

1. Iloko o is a compound preposition like
   "inside of" in English.

2. Ko, the preposition "of" indicating the
   genitive case.

3. Mau, sign of the plural.

4. I, and before proper nouns and pronouns,
   ia, a widely used preposition meaning, "to,
   towards, in, at, unto, by, for, in respect

of, above, more than, on account of, etc."
according to Andrews. It is also the sign
of the objective case.

5. I, the sign of the past tense.

6. I, sign of the objective case; ia (sometimes io) before proper nouns and pronouns.

7. 'I, abbreviation of the relative particle ai,
referring back to wahi. It should be joined
to the verb.

8. Ua ... nei together mean "this" or "these."

9. I, ia, in this connection is referred to the
preposition in No. 4 above, and thus might
be translated as "upon." However, Andrews regards it as an adverb meaning
"while" or "when," which is clearly its
application in the places used.

10. E . . . ana, the participial form indicating
continuance.

11. Ai, the relative particle.

12. Iluna . . . o, "on top of," paralleling No. 1
above.

13. La, here implying past time.

14. I, here denotes purpose.

15. Ia, form of the passive separated from its
stem by an adverb.

16. 'I, relative particle referring to kumu (see
Nos. 7, 11).

17, 18. Kana, "his" and nei, a relative particle
substituted for ai; a common construction
of a relative clause.

English-Hawaiian
Vocabulary

In the word-list which follows, the synonyms are separated by commas, the definitions by semi-colons and the parts of speech by colons. When a word in English represents more than one part of speech, the noun is given first.

A

a, an, kekă'hĭ, kă'hĭ, hŏ'ŏkă'hĭ, he.

abandon, (desert), hă'ălě'lě lŏ'ă; (give up), waĭhŏ lŏ'ă.

abdicate, (vacate), hă'ălě'lě; (resign), waĭhŏ.

abdomen, 'ŏpū'.

ability, mă'nă hŏ'ŏkŏ', 'ĭ'kě hă'nă.

able, (competent), makăŭkăŭ, ăkămăĭ; (potential, hi'kĭ.

aboard, mālu'nă: go aboard, 'ě'ě.

abode, wă'hĭ no'hŏ pa'ă.

abolish, hŏ'ŏpăŭ, hŏ'ŏnŏ'ă.

about, mā kăŭwă'hĭ; (at), mā; (almost), 'ă'ně-'ă'ně, kokŏ'kě; (concerning), e pi'lĭ ă'nă nŏ.

above, mālu'nă, ĭlu'nă, kĭ'ěkĭ'ě a'ě.

abroad, (widely), lă'hă; (in foreign lands), i nă 'ăĭnă 'ē; (out-of-doors), māwa'hŏ.

abrupt, (rough), kă'lăkă'lă; (brief), okĭ 'ē; (as land), pa'lĭ lŏ'ă.

absent, mā kă'hĭ 'ē, hĭ'kĭ 'o'lě măĭ: to absent, hŏ'ŏkă'ăwa'lě.

absolute, kūkă'hĭ, mă'nă lŏ'ă.

absolutely, maolĭ, kūakă'hĭ.

absolution, hūĭkă'lă.

absolve, kă'lă.

absorb, (imbibe), o'mŏ; (be engrossed) lĭ'lŏ lŏ'ă.

abstain, kaohĭ, 'ă'ŏ'lě e hŏ'ŏpă'.

abstract, (summary), mŏ'ole'lŏ i hŏ'ŏpokŏlěĭ'ă: (to withdraw), unu'hĭ; (steal), kă'ĭ'lĭ.

absurd, lăpŭwa'lě.

abundant, la'wă po'no, nu'ĭ wa'lě.

abuse, abusive, ho'omaĭ'nŏ'ĭ'nŏ, ha'nă 'ĭ'nŏ.

academy, 'ăhăhŭ'ĭ 'ĭ'mĭ nā'ăŭaŏ.

accelerate, 'āwīwī, hŏ'ŏhikīwa'wĕ.

accent, kālĕ'lĕ lĕ'ŏ.

accept, (receive), a'pŏ, la'wĕ măĭ; (agree to),
aĕ.

accessible, (attainable), hi'kĭ; (friendly), lăŭle'ă.

accessory, (accomplice), kŏkŭ'ă; (adjunct), hŏ-
'u'lŭ'u'lŭ.

accident, ulĭ'ă.

accommodate, (receive), hŏ'ŏkĭ'pă; (supply),
hŏ'ŏlă'kŏ; (help), kŏkŭ'ă.

accompany, he'lĕ pū; —(as on piano), kŏkŭ'à
pū.

accomplish, hŏ'ŏkŏ', ho'lŏ po'nŏ.

accord, kūlĭ'kĕ, lŏka'hĭ.

according to, māmu'lĭ o.

account, (narrative), mŏ'ole'lŏ; (reckoning),
he'lŭ, pi'lă wăĭwăĭ: to account, hŏ'ĭ'kĕ,
hŏ'ăkā'kă.

accumulate, (amass), hŏ'a'hŭ; (collect), hŏ-
'ĭ'lĭ'ĭ'lĭ.

accurate, pololeĭ lŏ'ă.

accuse, hŏ'ahe'wă, hŏ'ŏpĭ'ĭ.

accustom, hŏ'ŏmă'ămă'ă.

ace, ĕ'kĭ; (flyer), meă lĕ'lĕ pŏ'ŏke'lă.

ache, 'ĕ'hă; (sharp), hŭ'ĭ; (dull), nălŭ'lŭ.

achieve, hŏ'ŏkŏ', hă'nă.

acid, wăĭ ăki'kă, meă 'ă'wă'ă'wă.

acknowledge, (admit), aĕ; (verify), hŏ'ŏ'ĭă.

acquaintance, hoălaŭnă; (knowledge), 'ĭkĕ.

acquire, lŏa'a.

acquit, hŏ'ŏkŭ'ŭ, kă'lă.

acre, e'kă.

across, mā kĕlă 'ăŏ'ăŏ, măĭ kekă'hĭ 'ăŏ'ăŏ a
kekă'hĭ 'ăŏ'ăŏ: to step across, măŭ'ă'ĕ; to

lay across, kăŭ kĕ'ă.

act, (deed), hă'nă; (legislative), kānāwăĭ o
kā 'ăhă'ōle'lŏ: (to do), hă'nă; (carry out),
hŏ'ŏkō'; act in drama, hă'nă kĕă'kă; act
for, pă'nĭ hă'kăhă'kă.

action, (court), hŏ'ŏpĭ'ĭ; (naval) kăŭă ĭwăĕnă
o nā mo'kŭ kăŭă; man of action, kănă'kă
'ĕlĕ'ŭ.

active, 'ĕlĕ'ŭ, mi'kĭ hă'nă.

actor, kănă'kă hă'nă kĕă'kă.

actual, maolĭ, 'o'ĭaĭ'ŏ.

acute, (sharp), 'oĭ; (pain), hŭ'ĭ; (shrewd),
mă'ălĕă.

add, (numbers), hŏ'u'lŭ'u'lŭ; add on, pakŭ'ĭ.

additional, hŏ'ŏpĭ'lĭ hoŭ.

address, hă'ĭ'ōle'lŏ; (abode), wă'hĭ no'ho; to
address, (as a person), kămă'ĭlĭ'ŏ; (as a
letter), kakăŭĭnŏă.

adieu, ālo'hă.

adjourn, hŏ'ŏpănŏ'ŏ.

adjust, hŏ'ŏpo'nŏpo'nŏ.

adjutant, lu'nă kŏkŭ'ă, ho'pĕ; adjutant-general,
ho'pĕ kĕnĕlă'lă.

administer, (as public affairs), lă'wĕlă'wĕ; (as
estates), hŏ'ŏpo'nŏpo'nŏ; (as oaths), hŏ-
'ŏhĭ'kĭ; (impart), hăă'wĭ.

admiral, akĭmală'lă.

admiration, măhā'lŏ, măkăhe'hĭ.

admire, măhā'lŏ, 'ăpŏ'nŏ.

admit, (let in), hŏ'ŏkŏ'mŏ; (acknowledge), aŏ.

adobe, pōhakŭle'pŏ, wăĭmă'nŏ.

adopt, (as own child), hănăĭ; (as god-child),
hŏ'ŏkă'mă; (approve), 'ăpo'nŏ; (as opinion), 'ă'pŏ.

adore, (worship), hŏ'ŏmă'nă; (glorify), hŏ-'ŏnă'nĭ.

advantage, kūlă'nă i 'oĭ a'ĕ.

adversary, ĕnĕ'mĭ, meă kū'ē', hoăpaĭŏ.

adversity, pō'ĭ'nŏ, pōpilĭki'ă, ne'lĕ.

advertise, advertisement, hŏ'ŏlĕ'hă.

advice, 'ōlelŏă'ŏ.

advise, ā'ŏ.

affair, hă'nă, 'ă'nŏ hŏ'ŏĭ'pŏĭ'pŏ.

affect, (influence), hŏ'ŏhŭ'lĭ mană'ŏ; (pretend), hŏ'ŏkămă'nĭ.

affectation, (ke) 'ă'nŏ hŏ'ŏĭŏ.

affection, (love), (ke) alo'hă; (disease), mă'ĭ.

affidavit, hŏ'ŏhi'kĭ, hŏ'ō'ĭai'ŏ.

affirm, hō'ō'ĭă.

afford, (give), hāă'wĭ; can afford, hĭ'kĭ.

afloat, lă'nă, lĕ'wă.

afraid, makă'ŭ.

Africa, Apeli'kă.

after, māho'pĕ, māmu'lĭ.

afternoon, 'aŭĭ'nă lā.

afterward, māho'pĕ ă'kŭ, ĭho'pĕ ă'kŭ.

again, hoŭ.

against, kū'ē' a'kŭ.

age, (period), aŭ; (years), măkăhi'kĭ: aged,
(ancient), kăhi'kŏ; (full of years), nu'ĭ nă
măkăhi'kĭ.

agent, (one who acts), ākĕ'nă, ho'pĕ: (power
or cause), mă'nă, kŭ'mŭ.

aggressive, hō'u'kă wa'lĕ, hă'nă wa'lĕ.

aggressor, meă he'wă mu'ă.

agile, māmā, kă'ŭkă'ŭlĕ'lĕ.

agitate, (shake), hŏ'ŏlŭ'lĭlŭ'lĭ; (incite), hō'a'lă

ago, māmu'ă a'kŭ nĕĭ; wā i ha'lă.

agree, mană'ŏ li'kě; (consent), aě li'kě; (cove-
nant), kŭ'ĭka'hĭ; (harmonize), kŏ'hŭ li'kě.
agreeable, 'o'lŭ'o'lŭ.
agreement, 'ōle'lŏ aě li'kě.
agriculture, 'oĭhă'nă măhĭ'ăĭ.
aground, (as a ship), ĭ'lĭ, (canoe), măŭ.
ah, kăhăhă, ăŭwě'.
aha! (serves you right), 'ăĭkŏ'ĭă.
ahead, ĭmu'ă, māmu'ă a'kŭ.
aid, kŏkŭ'ă; (cooperate), a'lŭ.
aim, kăŭlo'nă pololeĭ; (intend), mană'ŏ.
aimless, lălăŭ wa'lě.
air, ěă, lě'wă; (melody), le'ŏ me'lě: to air,
kăŭlă'ĭ; to put on airs, hŏ'ŏkŏ'hŭkŏ'hŭ.
airship, mokulě'lě.
alarm, pū'i'wă, hikĭle'lě: to alarm, hŏ'ŏpū'i'wă.
alas, ăŭwě'.
albacore or tuna, (ke) 'ă'hĭ.
albatross, (goony), ŭă'ŭkewăĭ; (black-footed),
ka'upŭ.
alcohol, ălěkŏho'lă, wăĭ kŭ'lŭ.
alert, măkăa'lă.
alga, lĭ'mŭ.
alias, (false name), ĭnŏă kă'păkă'pă: (namely).
'ō'ĭă ho'ĭ.
alibi, mā kă'hĭ 'ē.
alien, kŭ'pă nŏ kă 'ăĭnă 'ē; (stranger) mălĭhĭ'nĭ.
alienat- hŏ'ŏhu'lĭ kŭ'ē', hŏ'ŏmokuahă'nă.
alight, (dismount), le'lě ĭla'lŏ; (on branch).
kăŭ: (lighted), mălă'mălă'mă.
alike, li'kě a li'kě.
alive, o'lă; (lively), hŏĭhŏĭ.
all, păŭ lō'ă, āpăŭ, hŭĭ'nă păŭ.
allegiance, kŭpă'ă măho'pě.

alley, (ke) a'lă 'olŏlī'; bowling alley, kăhŭ'ă
    'olŏhū'.

alliance, kŭ'ĭka'hĭ; (group), hŭ'ĭ.

allow, aĕ.

allowance, hăăwi'nă, māhe'lĕ.

allure, kūlă'nă măkăhe'hĭ: to allure, hŏ'ŏwă'lĕ-
    wă'lĕ.

ally, hoă, kōkŭ'ă.

almighty, mă'nă lō'ă: The Almighty, Kē Akŭ'ă
    Mă'nă Lō'ă.

almost, 'ă'nĕ'ă'nĕ, kokŏ'kĕ, măĭ.

alms, manawăle'ă.

aloft, ĭlu'nă, mālu'nă.

alone, wa'lĕ nŏ, me'hăme'hă, hŏ'ŏkă'hĭ wă'lĕ
    nŏ.

along, mă; along with, pū; (onward), a'kŭ.

alongside, mă kă 'ăŏ'ăŏ.

aloud, lohe'ă.

already, ānŏ' ĭ'hŏ nĕĭ.

also, ho'ĭ, nŏ ho'ĭ, kekă'hĭ.

altar, kūă'hŭ.

alter, (change), hŏ'ŏlŏ'lĭ; (castrate), pŏ'ă.

alternate, (substitute), ho'pĕ: alternate colors,
    păŭkūkū: to alternate, 'ă'lŏ kekă'hĭ a o
    kekă'hĭ a'kŭ.

although, 'oĭaĭ, ĭnă' nŏ pa'hă, 'e'ĭă nă'ĕ, akă'.

altitude, kĭ'ĕkĭ'e'nă.

altogether, păŭ pū, hu'ĭ li'kĕ.

always, măŭ, i nă wă a păŭ.

amazing, kupăĭăna'hă, kăhăhă.

ambassador, 'ĕlĕ'lĕ aŭpu'nĭ.

ambition, (urge), (ke) ā'kĕ; (aspiration), ĭkăĭ-
    kă kā mană'ŏ e lōa'a.

ambush, hālu'ă, to ambush, hŏ'ŏhālu'ă.

amen, āmĕ'nĕ, āmă'mă.

amend, hŏʻŏpo'nŏpo'nŏ hoŭ: amends, hŏʻŏmai-
ka'ĭ ă'nă.

America, Amĕli'kă.

amiable, ʻo'lŭ'o'lŭ.

amid, ĭwaĕnă, māwaĕnă.

amidships, māwaĕnăko'nŭ o kā mo'kŭ.

ammunition, pōkā'.

among, amongst, ĭwaĕnă, māwaĕnă.

amount, hŭĭ'nă, helu'nă.

ample, la'wă po'nŏ.

amuse, hŏʻŏlĕʻălĕʻă.

amusement, lĕʻălĕʻă, pă'a'nĭ.

an, kă'hĭ, hŏʻŏkă'hĭ, kekă'hĭ, hĕ.

anarchy, hŏʻŏmă'lŭ ʻo'lĕ, kănăwăĭ ʻo'lĕ.

ancestor, kŭpu'nĭ; ancestors, kŭ'pună.

anchor, helĕu'mă, hĕkăŭ.

anchorage, wă'hĭ kŭ mo'kŭ.

anchovy, nĕ'hŭ.

ancient, kăhĭ'kŏ.

and, ā, ă mĕ.

angel, ănĕ'lă.

anger, angry, hŭhŭ', ĭnăĭnă.

angle, hŭĭ'nă.

angler, kănă'kă kāmŏkŏĭ.

animal, holŏhŏlo'nă.

ankle, pŭʻŭpŭʻŭwawaĕ.

anklet, kŭpe'ĕ wăwaĕ.

annex, pakŭ'ĭ, hŏʻŏkŭ'ĭ.

anniversary, lā hŏʻŏmană'ŏ.

announce, (proclaim), kūkă'lă; (publish), hŏ-
ʻŏlă'hă.

annoy, hŏʻŏnau'kĭu'kĭ, hŏʻŏulŭhu'ă.

annual, pō'ăĭ măkăhi'kĭ.

anonymous, ĭnóă ʻo'lĕ.

another, (additional), hoŭ; (different), oko‘ă,
    ‘ē: another person, ha‘ī.

answer, pa‘nĕ, hă‘ĭ‘nă: to answer, pa‘nĕ, hă‘ī.

ant, no‘năno‘nă, naŏnaŏ.

antique, meă kăhi‘kŏ.

antiquity, wā kăhi‘ko.

anus, ‘ōko‘lĕ.

anvil, kŭ‘ă, kŭăhăŏ.

anxiety, anxious, piholhoī, hŏ‘pŏhŏ‘pŏ.

any, kekă‘hī.

anybody, anything, kekă‘hĭ meă.

anyhow, mă kekă‘hĭ ‘ă‘nŏ.

anywhere, mă nā wă‘hĭ li‘kĕ ‘o‘lĕ.

apart, kă‘ăwa‘lĕ.

apartment, keĕ‘nă no‘hŏ.

ape, ke‘kŏ, măpŭ: to ape, hŏ‘ŏmahŭ‘ī.

apiece, pă-; one apiece, păka‘hĭ.

apologize, mi‘hĭ.

apparatus, pa‘ăha‘nă, la‘kŏ ‘oīhă‘nĕ

apparent, moakă‘kă.

appeal, (to plead), nonoī; (urge), kŏĭ; (as a
    decision), hŏ‘ŏpī‘ī.

appear, hō‘ĕă măĭ, hi‘kĭ măĭ.

appearance, nanăĭnă, hĭ‘ōhĭ‘ŏnă.

appease, hŏ‘ŏnă‘, hŏ‘ŏmă‘ălĭ‘lĭ, hŏ‘ŏmă‘lĭmă‘lĭ.

appeasement, (modern), a‘ĕ wa‘lĕ ă‘nă i kā
    ha‘ī kŏĭ.

appendix, (book), ‘ōle‘lŏ pakŭ‘ī; (human), nă-
    ‘ăŭ moă.

appetite, ‘o‘nŏ kā ‘ăĭ; without appetite, kăne‘ă.

applaud, māhā‘lŏ.

applause, pă‘ĭpă‘ī.

apple, āpă‘lă.

apply, (as an object), hŏ‘ŏpī‘lĭ; (as the mind),
    hŏ‘ŏpă‘ă; (as for work), noī.

appoint, hŏʻŏkŏʻhŭ.

appraise, hŏʻŏhoʻlŏ wăīwăī.

appreciate, (rise in value), hŏʻŏmāhŭʻăhŭʻă; (esteem highly), hŏʻŏmaīkaʻī.

April, Apeliʻlă.

approach, hŏʻŏkokŏʻkĕ.

appropriate, kŭpoʻnŏ: to appropriate, hŏʻŏkăʻă-waʻlĕ.

appropriation, hăăwiʻnă.

approve, ʻāpoʻnŏ, hōʻapoʻnŏ.

approximate, ʻăʻnŏ liʻkĕ, ʻăʻnĕʻăʻnĕ pololeī: to approximate, hŏʻŏkokŏʻkĕ.

apron, epăʻnĕ.

apt, (fit), kŭpoʻnŏ; (ready), makăŭkăŭ; (ac-customed), măʻă, wălĕa.

aquarium, wăʻhī hŏʻīʻkĕʻīʻkĕ īʻă.

arbitrary, (capricious), māmuʻlī o kă manăʻŏ īʻhŏ; (despotic), măwaʻhŏ o kĕ kănăwăī.

arbitrate, ŭwaŏ.

arch, pīʻŏ; (chief), kīʻĕkīʻĕ: to arch, hŏʻŏpīʻŏ.

archery, pănăpŭʻă.

archipelago, paĕmoʻkŭ.

archives, waīhoʻnă mōʻoleʻlŏ aŭpuʻnī.

area, (size), nuʻī; (surface), ʻīʻlī.

argue, wĕʻhĕwĕʻhĕ kŭmumanăʻŏ; (dispute), hŏ-ʻŏpăʻăpăʻă; (use repartee), hŏʻŏpăpă ʻoleʻlŏ.

arise, aʻlă, ʻĕŭ, kū.

aristocratic, kŏʻīkŏʻī, hăʻnŏhăʻnŏ.

arithmetic, alīmăkīʻkă, nā heʻlŭ.

ark, paʻhŭ; Noah's Ark, Halĕlăʻnă a Noă.

arm, līʻmă, lālā; arms, meă kăŭă: to arm, hŏ-ʻŏlăʻkŏ i nā meă kăŭă.

armament, laʻkŏ kăŭă.

armchair, noʻhŏ nuʻī.

armistice, hŏʻŏmaʻhă kĕ kăŭă.

armory, ha′lĕ waĭho′nă la′kŏ kăŭă, ha′lĕ paĭ-
    kaŭ.

armpit, pō‘aĕ‘aĕ.

army, pū‘ă′lĭ koă.

around, pu′nĭ.

arouse, hö‘ĕŭ‘ĕŭ, pāĭpāĭ.

arrange, hŏ‘ŏpo′nŏpo′nŏ, hŏ‘ŏno′hŏno′hŏ.

arrest, (apprehend), hŏ′pŭ; (check), kĕ‘ăkĕ‘ă.

arrive, (here), hi′kĭ măĭ; (there), kū măĭ; (in
    sight), hō‘ĕă.

arrogant, hŏ‘ŏkĭ‘ĕkĭ‘ĕ, hă‘ăkĕĭ, hŏ‘ŏkă′nŏ.

arrow, pu‘ă pă′nă.

arrowroot, pi‘ă.

arsenal, wă‘hĭ la′kŏ kăŭă.

art, hă′nă no‘ĕaŭ; (skill), (ke) ăkămăĭ.

artful, mă‘ăleă.

article, (thing), meă; (clause), păŭkū′ ‘ōle′lŏ;
    (essay), mană‘ŏ i kakăŭ ĭ‘ă.

artificial, hă′nă ĭ‘ă e kă lĭmă o kănă′kă;
    (feigned), hŏ‘ŏkămă‘nĭ, ‘o‘ĭai‘ŏ ‘o‘lĕ.

artillery, nă pūkŭnĭa′hĭ.

artisan. kănăkă ăkămăĭ i kă′nă hă′nă.

artist, meă i wălĕa i kā′nă hă′nă.

as, lĭ′kĕ, e lĭ′kĕ mē; (since), ‘oĭaĭ; (as if), mĕ
    hē meă la; (such as), pēnĕĭ.

ascend, pĭ′ĭ; (as smoke), pūnō′hŭ.

ascent, pĭ′ĭ′nă.

ascertain, hŏ‘ŏmaŏpŏ′pŏ lō′ă, ‘ĭ′kĕ lĕ′ă.

ash, ashes, le′hŭ.

ashamed, hi′lăhi′lă.

ashore, i kăpăkăĭ: to go ashore, (to land), le′lĕ
    ĭŭ′kă, paĕ; (to ground), ĭ′lĭ.

Asia, Aki‘ă.

aside, mă kă ‘ăŏ‘ăŏ, mă ka′hĭ kă‘ăwa′lĕ.

ask, (request), noĭ; (invite), kŏ'nŏ; (inquire),
   ninaŭ; just ask questions, niĕ'lĕ.
asleep, hiămoĕ.
aspect. hĭ'ŏhĭ'ŏ'nă, nanāĭnă.
ass, kekă'kĕ, 'ĕkă'kĕ.
assassinate, kĭmŏpō', kī pū wa'lĕ.
assault, (military), hō'ŭ'ka; assault and battery, hăkăkā' a mē kā lĭ'mă nu'ĭ pū.
assemble, 'ākŏăkŏă.
assembly, 'ă'hă, ānăĭnă.
assert, (affirm), hō'ŏ'ĭă; (state), hă'ĭ.
assess, (tax), 'aŭhăŭ; (compute), he'lŭ.
assets, wăĭwăĭ.
assign, (give), hăă'wĭ; (as property), waĭhŏ.
assist, kŏkŭ'ă.
assistant, kokŏ'ŏlu'ă, ho'pĕ.
associate, hoă, kokŏ'ŏlu'ă: to associate,, lăŭnă
   pū.
association, 'ăhăhŭ'ĭ, hŭ'ĭ.
assort, hŏ'ŏkakă'ăwa'lĕ.
assortment, kĕlă mē kĕ'lă meă.
assume, (take for granted), kŏ'hŏ; (as power),
   la'wĕ; (pretend), hŏ'ŏkămă'nĭ, pĭ'ĭkoĭ.
assurance, 'ŏnĭpă'ă; (impudence), maha'ŏĭ.
assure, hō'ŏ'ĭă; (insure), pănă'ĭ o'lă.
astern, ĭho'pĕ.
astonish, kahahā, hŏ'ŏpu'ĭ'wă.
astonishing, kupăna'hă, kămăhă'ŏ.
astride, kĭ'ĭhelĕĭ.
astrologer, kĭ'lŏ hōkū'.
astronomer, ā'ŏhōkū'.
at, mă, i.
athlete, ĭkăĭkă.
athletic, hŏ'ŏikăĭkă kĭ'nŏ.
atmosphere, lĕ'wă, (ke) ĕă.

atoll, mokŭpu'nĭ 'ākŏ'äkŏ'ă.

atom, hŭ'năhŭ'nă.

attach, hŏ'ŏpi'lĭ, hŏ'ŏpa'ă; (as for debt), hŏ'pŭ; (be enamored), pi'lĭ ālo'hă.

attack, (person), lĭ'mă nu'ĭ; (army), hŏ'ŭ'kă.

attempt, hō'a'o.

attend, (heed), hŏ'ŏlo'hĕ; (serve), mālă'mă, lă'wĕlă'wĕ; attend meeting, he'lĕ i kā hālā-wăĭ.

attention, (heed), hŏ'ŏlŏ'hĕ, nānā; (to study), hŏ'ŏhŏ'ŏ; (civility), mali'ŭ: stand at attention, kū māli'ĕ.

attitude, 'ā'hŏ.

attorney, lō'ĭŏ, ho'pĕ: attorney-general, lō'ĭŏ kuhi'nă.

attract, 'u'mĕ.

attractive, 'ăŭlĭ'ĭ, meă hiăăĭ ĭ'ă.

auction, kūkālā'.

audience, (ke) ānăĭnă.

auditor, lu'nă hŏ'ŏ'lă.

August, (month), Aŭka'kĕ: (grand), hă'nŏ-hă'nŏ lŏ'ă.

aunt, makuăhi'nĕ hanaŭnă.

Australia, Aŭkakūlĭ'ă.

authentic, 'o'ĭai'ŏ.

author, (source), kŭ'mŭ, meă hŏ'ŏkŭ'mŭ; (composer), meă hă'kŭ.

authority, (official), mă'nă kăŭo'hă; (expert), meă 'ĭ'kĕ.

authorize, hŏ'āmă'nă.

autocracy, mă'nă hŏ'ŏkă'hĭ.

autograph, hăpăpūlĭ'mă.

automatic, meă hă'nă nŏ'nă ĭ'hŏ.

automobile, ŏkŏmopi'lă.

Autumn, Ha'u'lĕlăŭ.

auxiliary, kokŏʻŏluʻă.

avenue, (ke) alănŭʻĭ ăke'ŏ

average, awĕliʻkĕ.

aviation, lĕʻlĕ ă'nă.

aviator, meă lĕʻlŏ.

avocado pear, peă.

avoid, 'ă'lŏ, lăŭnă 'oʻlĕ.

await, kă'lĭ, kăkă'lĭ.

awake, (sleepless), hĭăʻă: to awake, a'lă; awake suddenly, puoʻhŏ.

award, (judgment), 'ŏleʻlŏ hŏʻŏhoʻlŏ; (prize), maka'nă.

aware, hŏʻŏmaŏpŏʻpŏ.

away, mă kă'hĭ 'ĕ, a'kŭ: go away, he'lĕ pĕlă'.

awful, wĕʻlĭwĕʻlĭ.

awhile, lĭʻŭlĭʻŭ ĭ'kĭ.

awkward, hĕ'măhe'mă.

awning, (ke) ănĭ'nĭ, lo'lĕ pa'lĕ lă.

ax, kŏʻĭliʻpĭ.

axis, ĭ'hŏ.

axle, paĕpaĕkŏʻmŏ.

B

babble, wălăʻăŭ.

baby, pēpē.

bachelor, kănă'kă i ma'lĕ 'oʻlĕ.

back, ku'ă: to back, e'mĭ ku'ă: at the back, măho'pĕ a'ĕ.

backbone, ĭwĭkŭămŏʻŏ.

backward, ĭho'pĕ; (slow), lŏlo'hĭ.

bacon, pūa'a ha'mĕ, 'ĭ'ŏ pua'a ŭa'hĭ.

bad, (sinful), 'ĭ'nŏ, kŏlŏ'hĕ; (worthless), wăĭwăĭ 'oʻlĕ, măkĕhe'wă; (decayed), pŏpŏ'pŏ, pălăhŏ'.

badge, hŏʻăĭlo'nă.

bag, 'ĕ'kĕ.

baggage, ukă'nă.

bail, (of bucket), 'ău pākĕ'kĕ; police bail, pe'lă: to bail water, kā.

bait, măŭnŭ.

bake, hŏ'ŏmo'ă 'o'mă, hŏ'ō 'o'mă.

baker, kănă'kă pŭ'hĭ pala'oă.

balance, kŏĕnă: to balance, kăŭlĭ'kĕ; (as accounts), hŏ'ŏhālĭ'kĕ.

bald, 'ohu'lĕ, nĭ'ă.

bale, pū'o'lŏ nu'ĭ; (as of hay), pū'ā'.

ball, kĭnĭpōpō; cannonball, pōkā'; (dance), (ke) ānăĭnă hŭ'lăhŭ'lă.

ballet, hŭ'lăhŭ'lă pĕ'kŭpe'kŭ.

balloon, pālu'nă.

balloon-fish, 'ō'opŭhuĕ.

ballot, pālo'kă.

bamboo, 'o'hĕ.

banana, măĭ'a.

band, (girdle), (ke) a'pŏ; (company), hŭ'ĭ, 'ăhăhŭ'ĭ; (group), po'ĕ; (musicians), ba'nă: to band, hŭ'ĭ.

bandage, wăhĭ' 'ĕ'hă.

bank, (stream), kă'pă; (earth), ahu'ă; (finance), banăkō'.

bankrupt, panăkălu'pă.

banner, haĕ.

banquet, 'ăhă'aĭnă hŏ'ŏhă'nŏhă'nŏ.

baptism, papeki'kŏ.

bar, 'ăŭkā', păŭkū'; (saloon), pākaŭkaŭ; (in court), pā; (lawyers), pă'pă lō'ĭŏ; (harbor), wă'hĭ pāpă'ŭ; (obstruction), pa'lĕ: to bar, pă'nĭ, pa'ă.

barbarous, hihĭ'ŭ, hūpō; (cruel), lŏkŏ'ĭ'nŏ.

barber, kănă'kă 'ă'kŏ lăuŏ'hŏ.

bare, (empty), nĕ'ŏ; (naked), 'ōlo'hĕlo'hĕ, kō-
    hä'nă; bare reef, kūä'ăŭ, kŏhŏ'lă; (mere),
    wa'lĕ nō
bargain, (good), măkĕpo'nŏ; (bad), pŏhŏ'; to
    bargain, kū'äĭ.
bark, (tree), 'ĭ'lĭ; (dog), 'äŏă; (vessel), kĭăpä'.
barn, halĕpāpă'ă, ha'lĕ holŏhŏlo'nă.
barnacle, pio'ĕo'ĕ.
barracks, ha'lĕ no'hŏ koă.
barracuda, kākū.
barrel, pa'hŭ pāle'lă.
barren, (of animals), pā; (of land), păno'ă; (of
    tree), hu'ă 'o'lĕ.
barrier, pākū, meă kĕ'äkĕ'ă.
base, (foundation), kŭ'mŭ, kăhŭ'ă: (vile), haŭ-
    mi'ă: baseball, kĭnĭpōpŏ.
bashful, hi'lăhi'lă.
basin, (hand), pā kĭ'nĭ; (land), pŏ'hŏ 'äĭnă;
    (pond), lŏkŏwăĭ.
basis, mŏ'lĕ, kŭ'mŭ.
basket, 'ĭ'ĕ, paĭkĭ.
bat, (mammal), 'ōpe'äpe'ă; bat for ball, lā'äŭ
    kĭnĭpōpŏ.
bath, bathe, 'aŭ'aŭ.
batter, (baseball), meă hi'lĭ kĭnĭpōpŏ; (cake),
    mea'ŏ'nŏ mo'ă 'o'lĕ.
battery, hŭĭ'nă pūkŭnĭa'hĭ; (electric), mĭkĭ'nĭ
    hă'nă ŭwi'lă.
battle, hō'ŭ'kă kăŭă.
battleship, mo'kŭ kăŭă, manŭwā'.
bay, ku'o'nŏ, kăĭku'ŏ'nŏ.
bayonet, 'ĕlăŭĕkĭ'.
bazaar, ha'lĕ kū'äĭ, fĕă.
be, bē (see p. 24)
(see p. 24)

beach, (wash of waves), aĕkăĭ; sand beach, kă'hă o'nĕ; (shore), kăhăkăĭ.

beacon, lă'mă.

bead, hu'ă a'nĭa'nĭ, pūpū lĕĭ.

beak, nŭ'kŭ, nŭ'kŭ mă'nŭ.

beam, kao'lă; (breadth), lăŭlă'; (light), kū-kū'nă: (to shine), mălă'mălă'mă.

bean, pāpă'pă.

bear, peă: to bear, (reproduce), hānaŭ, hŏ'ŏ-hu'ă; (carry), hăă'wĕ; (support), kŏ'ŏ; (endure), āhŏnu'ĭ.

beard, 'ŭ'mĭ'ŭ'mĭ.

bearer, (carrier), meă la'wĕ; (messenger), 'ĕlĕ'lĕ.

bearing, (mien), 'ă'nŏ; (of ship), hŏ'ăĭlo'nă nānā.

beast, holŏhŏlo'nă.

beat, (patrolman's), 'āpă'nă: (to strike), ha-haŭ, pĕpe'hĭ; (vanquish), lănăki'lă; beat to windward, hŏ'ŏpĭ'ĭpĭ'ĭ.

beauty, beautiful, nă'nĭ.

because, nŏ kā meă; (since), 'oĭaĭ.

beckon, (with head), kunōŭ; (with hand), pe-'a'hĭ.

become, (befit), kŏhŭpo'nŏ, kūpo'nŏ; (come to be), lĭ'lŏ.

bed, moĕ, pe'lă moĕ; flower-bed, mă'lă pu'ă; (as of river), kōwă': bedroom, lŭ'mĭ moĕ.

bee, nalŏme'lĭ.

beef, 'ĭ'ŏ pĭ'pĭ.

beer, pĭ'ă.

beetle, pŭ'ŭ.

before, mămu'ă, ĭmu'ă o kĕ a'lŏ.

beg, māki'lŏ; (entreat), kŏĭ ĭkăĭkă; (request), noĭ.

begin, hŏ'ŏkŭ'mŭ; (start), hŏ'ŏmă'kă.

behalf, (sake), po'nŏ; (for), nō.

behave, no'hŏ po'nŏ, no'hŏ māli'ĕ.

behind, ĭho'pĕ, māho'pĕ, mā kē ku'ă

being, (human), kănă'kă; (viable), meă o'lă.

belief, believe. mănă'ŏĭ'ŏ: (trust), hilĭnă'ĭ.

bell, pe'le.

bellow, 'ŭwō'.

bellows, 'ŭpāmaka'nĭ.

belly, 'ōpū'.

belong, pi'lĭ ĭ'ă, nā, nō.

beloved, meă ālo'hă.

below, māla'lŏ, ĭla'lŏ.

belt, kŭă'pŏ, kā'ĕĭ.

bench, (seat), no'hŏ lō'i'hĭ; (work), pă'pă
    hă'nă.

bend, pe'lŭ, pĭ'ŏ: to bend, pe'lŭ, hŏ'ŏkekĕ'ĕ;
    bend knee, kūku'lĭ; bend neck, kūlŏŭ.

beneath, māla'lŏ.

benefactor, meă lokomāĭkă'ĭ, maku'ă.

benefit, po'nŏ, pōmaĭka'ĭ.

bent, (tendency), a'kĕ o kā nă'ăŭ; (bias), pa'e'-
    wă'e'wă: (crooked), kăpăkă'hĭ; (folded),
    pelŭĭ'ă, lākĕ'ĕ.

berry, hu'ă lĭ'ĭlĭ'ĭ.

beside, mā kā 'ăŏ'ăŏ; beside the mark, halăhĭ';
    beside oneself, hehe'nă.

besiege, hŏ'ŏpŭ'nĭ.

best, 'oĭ lō'a, măĭkă'ĭ lō'ă.

bet, pi'lĭ, pilĭwăĭwăĭ.

betray, kūmakaĭă.

better, măĭkă'ĭ a'ĕ.

between, māwaĕnă, ĭwaĕnă.

beware, ākăhĕ'lĕ, mālă'mă.

beyond, māŏ' a'kŭ, ĭō' a'kŭ.

bias, hiŏ'; (diagonal), lǎ'lǎ.

Bible, Kā Pǎ'lǎpǎ'lǎ Hemŏlě'lě.

bicycle, paĭkĭka'lǎ, kǎ'ǎ he'hĭ wāwa'ě.

bid, (order), kǎŭo'hǎ, kēnā'; (at auction), kŏ'-
    hŏ.

big, nu'ĭ, nunu'ĭ.

bill, pi'lǎ, pǎ'lǎpǎ'lǎ; (beak), nǔ'kǔ mǎ'nǔ.

bind, pū'ā', nākĭ'ĭ; (as books), hǔ'mǔhǔ'mǔ.

bird, mǎ'nǔ.

birth, hānaǔ.

birthday, lā hānaǔ.

biscuit, pele'nǎ.

bishop, piho'pǎ.

bit, hǔ'nǎhǔ'nǎ, hākĭ'nǎ; drill bit, nǎŏ wĭ'lĭ;
    bridle bit, hāŏ.

bite, na'hǔ; (nip, insect bite), 'ǎ'kĭ.

bitter, mǔ'ěmǔ'ě, 'ǎ'wǎ'ǎ'wǎ.

black, 'ě'lě'ě'lě.

blacksmith, (ke) āmǎ'lǎ.

bladder, 'ōpū' mĭ'mĭ, pǔ'ǔ mĭ'mĭ.

blade, (as of knife), mǎ'kǎ; grass blade, lǎǔ.

blame, 'ahě'wǎ: to blame, hō'ahe'wǎ.

blank, hǎ'kǎhǎ'kǎ.

blanket, hǔ'lǔhǔ'lǔ, kǎ'pā hǔ'lǔhǔ'lǔ.

blast, (explode), hŏ'ŏpahū'; (wither), mǎě.

blaze, lǎ'pā a'hĭ: to blaze, 'a'a'.

bleach, hŏ'ŏkě'ŏkě'ŏ; bleach clothes, hŏ'ŏhěǔ.

bleed, (lose blood), kǎhěkŏ'kŏ; (extract blood),
    hŏ'ŏkǎ'hě kŏ'kŏ.

blend, hǔĭpū', kāwĭ'lĭ pū.

bless, hŏ'ŏpōmaĭka'ĭ.

blessing, pōmaĭka'ĭ.

blight, kǎkǎ'ně, pōna'lŏ: (to wither), mǎě, mĭ-
    mĭ'nŏ; (frustrate), hŏ'ŏho'kǎ.

blind, (in one eye), măkăpă'ă; (wholly), mă-
 kăpŏ'.

blister, 'olŏpŭ'.

block, păŭkŭ'; (pulley), pala'kă hi'ŭ: to block,
 păpă'nĭ a pa'ă, kĕ'äkĕ'ă.

blond, (ke) o'hŏ hākĕäkĕă.

blood, kŏ'kŏ.

bloom, blossom, pu'ă: to bloom, moha'lă.

blot, hāpa'lă, kŏ'hŭ: to blot, pă'ĕ'lĕ, hŏ'ŏhāpă'-
 lă; remove blot, holoĭ a na'lŏ.

blotter, pĕ'pă 'o'mŏ inĭ'kă.

blouse, pala'kă, pălăŭkĭ, lake'kĕ.

blow, haŭă, kŭ'ĭ: to blow, pŭ'hĭ; (pant), păŭ-
 păŭă'hŏ; (as the nose), hŏ'ŏkē'.

blow-hole, (ke) pŭ'hĭ.

blue, polŭ', u'lĭu'lĭ.

bluff, pa'lĭ, nŭ'ŭ: (gruff), 'okă'lăkă'lă: to bluff,
 hō'ă'ă'nŏ.

blunt, (as a tool), 'oĭ 'o'lĕ, kūmūmū; (abrupt),
 okă'lăkă'lă.

blush, pĭ'ĭ kā 'u'lă.

boar, pua'a ka'nĕ.

board, pă'pă; (food), 'äĭ: to board, (feed),
 hānăĭ: (go on board), 'ĕ'ĕ.

boast, kăĕnă, ākĕ'nă; boast and strut, li'kĭ.

boat, mo'kŭ; rowboat, wă'äpā; steamboat, mokua'hĭ.

body, kĭ'nŏ.

boil, mă'ĭ hēhē: to boil, paĭlă, kŭ'pă.

boiler, ĭ'pŭ ma'hŭ.

boisterous, hăŭwală'äŭ; (stormy), ĭ'nŏ nu'ĭ,
 kūpĭ'kĭpĭ'kĭ'ŏ'.

bold, 'ă'ă, wiwo'o'lĕ.

bolt, măki'ă; (of cloth), ăpă': to bolt, (fasten),
 hŏ'ŏpă'ă; (flee), măhu'kă.

bomb, pōkā' păhū'.

bond, po'na, pă'lăpă'lă hŏ'ŏpă'ă.

bondsman, ho'pĕ mā kă po'nă.

bone, ĭ'wĭ.

bone-fish, 'o'i'ŏ.

bonito, (ke) ă'kŭ.

booby, loĭe'lĕ; (gannet), ā.

book, pu'kĕ.

bookkeeper, kupakā'kŏ.

boom, (in river), (ke) pă'nĭ; (of sail), pū'mĭ;
    (noise), kă'nĭ; market boom, pĭ'ĭ'nă o kē
    kŭmŭkū'ăĭ.

boot, kāmă'ă pu'kĭ: to boot, pĕ'kŭ.

border, kă'ĕ, pale'nă, lĭ'hĭ.

bore, (to drill), wĭ'lĭ, hoŭ; (to weary), hŏ'ŏulŭ-
    hu'ă: bored, hŏĭhŏĭ 'o'lĕ.

borrow, nonoĭ nō kă mănā'wă.

bosom, po'lĭ.

boss, hă'kŭ hă'nă, lu'nă: to boss, no'hŏ hă'kŭ.

bossy, hŏ'ŏhă'kŭ.

both, nă meă elu'ă; laŭă elu'ă.

bother, hŏ'ŏpĭlĭkĭ'ă.

bottle, 'ōmo'lĕ; (gourd), hŭĕwăĭ.

bottom, kō la'lŏ lō'ă, păpākū', kă'hĭ măla'lŏ:
    (rump), lĕ'mŭ.

bough, lālā.

bound, lĕ'lĕ; (limit), kăŭpale'nă.

boundary, pale'nă.

bouquet, pokē' pu'ă.

bow, (of ship), ĭ'hŭ; (salute), kunōŭ: to bow,
    kunōŭ.

bow, (weapon), pă'nă; cross-bow, kăkă'kă;
    (ribbon), pō; rainbow, (ke) ānu'ĕnu'ĕ: (to
    curve), pĭ'ŏ.

bowels, nā'ăŭ, ŭ'hă.

bowl, po'lă: to bowl, 'olŏkă'ă 'olŏhū'.

box, pa'hū: to spar, pălēpălĕ', mŏ'kŏmŏ'kŏ.

boy, ke'ĭkĭ, keĭkĭka'nĕ: boys, kămălĭ'ĭ ka'nĕ.

brace, kŏ'ŏ.

bracelet, kūpĕ'ĕ lĭ'mă, (ke) apŏlĭ'mă.

braid, hĭ'lŏ: to braid, ulă'nă, hĭ'lĭ, hĭ'lŏ.

brain, lŏ'lŏ.

brake, pĕlĕ'kĭ, meă hŏ'ŏpă'ă.

branch, lālā: to branch, mă'nămă'nă.

brand, hŏ'ăĭlo'nă pă'ĭ; to brand, kŭ'nĭ, hŏ'ăĭlo'nă.

brandy, pala'nĭ.

brass, kĕlĕă'wĕ.

brave, ʞoă, wiwo'o'lĕ.

brawl, hăkăkā', hăŭnaĕlĕ.

bread, pala'oă.

breadfruit, 'ŭ'lŭ.

breadth, lăŭlă', (ke) ăke'ă.

break, (to fracture), uhă'kĭ, hă'ĭ; (demolish), wăwa'hĭ; (sever), mo'kŭ; (as waves), po-pŏ'ĭ; break open, kĭpŏ'; (shatter), 'ulŭpă'; (as glass), năhă'; (tame), hŏ'ŏlă'kălă'kă; (rend), haĕhaĕ; (as day), wĕ'hĕwĕ'hĕ.

breaker, po'ĭ'nă na'lŭ; (high surf), kăĭkŏŏ'.

breakfast, 'ăĭnă kakăhĭă'kă.

breast, ū, umăumă, wăĭū': to breast, paĭŏ.

breath, hă'nŭ, (ke) a'hŏ, (ke) ĕă.

breathe, hă'nŭ, hă.

breed, (reproduce), hănăŭ; (spread), hŏ'ŏlă'-hă; (arouse), hŏ'ŭ'lu.

breeze, a'hĕa'hĕ, maka'nĭ a'nĭa'nĭ.

brethren, nă hoăhănăŭ.

bribe, kĭpē.

brick, ŭwĭnĭhă'pă.

bride, wăhi'nĕ ma'lĕ hoŭ.

bridge, ŭa'pŏ; (as of nose), ĭ'wĭ.

bridle, kăŭlăwă'hă: (to restrain), kaohĭ.

brief, pă'lăpă'lă hō'ăkă'kă: (short), poko'lĕ.

bright, (brilliant), 'owă'owă'kă; (shining), hŭ-
    lă'lĭ; (as moon), kōnă'nĕ; (clever), holŏ-
    mu'ă lō'ă.

brim, brink, kă'ĕ, nĭaŏ, kă'pă.

bring, hōmăĭ, la'wĕ măĭ; prefix ĭ- as in ĭwăĭ,
    "bring water."

British, Pĕlĕka'nĕ.

brittle, hă'kĭhă'kĭ wa'lĕ, pă'ăpă'ă'ĭnă.

broad, lăŭlā', akeă.

broadcast, 'ōle'lŏ hŏ'ōlăŭla'hă.

broil, hăŭnaĕlĕ: to broil on coals, kōă'lă;
    (broil undressed), pūle'hŭ; (broil in
    leaves), lawa'lŭ.

broken, hă'kĭ, năhă'.

broker, ākĕ'nă.

broom, pūlu'mĭ.

brother, hoăhănăŭ ka'nĕ; older brother, kăĭ-
    kŭa'ă'nă; younger brother, kăĭkăĭnă; bro-
    ther of sister, kăĭkunā'nĕ.

brow, laĕ; eyebrow, kŭ'ĕmă'kă; (brink), kă'ĕ.

brown, u'lĭu'lĭ, hă'ĕ'lĕ'ĕ'lĕ.

brownie, menĕhū'nĕ.

bruise, pălăpū': to bruise, hō'ĕ'hă.

brunette, hāu'lĭ.

brush, pala'kĭ: to brush, kahĭ'lĭ, pūlu'mĭ.

brute, (beast), holŏhŏlo'nă; (human), kănă'kă
    lŏkŏ'ĭ'nĕ.

bubble, hŭ'ă, hŭ'ăhŭ'ă.

bucket, pākĕ'kĕ.

buckle, pĭ'hĭpĭ'hĭ: to buckle, hŏ'ŏpă'ă.

bud, (flower), 'ōpu'ŭ: leaf-bud, (formation),
    mŭ'ŏ; (opening), li'kŏ.

Buddhist, **Bu'dă, Hŏ'ŏmă'nă Kĕpănī'**.

budget, **pi'lă hăăwi'nă**; (as of news), **pū'o'lŏ:** to budget, **hŏ'ŏlālā i kā hŏ'ŏlĭ'lŏ ă'nă**.

bug, **pū'ŭ, 'ŭ'kŭ, mū**; bedbug, **'ŭ'kŭ li'ŏ**.

bugle, **pū kĕlĕă'wĕ**.

build, (as house), **kūku'lŭ**; (as ship), **kăpĭ'lī**.

building, **ha'lĕ**.

bulb, **hu'ă kă'nŭ**; (electric), (ke) **a'nĭa'nī kūku'ĭ**.

bulk, **nu'ĭ, hapănu'ĭ**.

bulkhead, **pākū**.

bull, **pĭpĭ ka'nĕ**.

bullet, **pŏkā'**.

bulletin, **pă'lăpă'lă hŏ'ŏlă'hă**.

bully, **hŏ'ŏma'ăŭ**.

bulwark, **palĕkăĭ**.

bump, **pū'ŭ:** to bump, **hŏ'ŏkŭ'ĭ**.

bumper, **pa'lĕ hŭi'lă**.

bunch, (as grapes), **huhu'ĭ**; (as bananas), **'āhu'ĭ,**

bundle, **pū'o'lŏ,** (ke) **'o'pĕ**; (sheaf), **pū'ā'**; bundle of poi, **pa'ĭ'ăĭ**.

bunk, **wa'hĭ moĕ**; (bosh), **'ŏpă'lā**.

buoy, **poĕ**; (float), **mo'ŭo**.

buoyant, **lă'nă**.

burden, **hăă'wĕ, ukă'nă hă'lī:** to burden, **hŏ'ŏkăŭmă'hă**.

bureau, (office), **'oĭhă'nă, māhe'lĕ**; **pahŭ'u'mĕ**.

burial, bury, **kă'nŭ:** (funeral), **hŏ'ŏlĕ'wa**.

burn, **wĕ'lă a'hĭ:** to burn, **'a, ho'ā', kŭ'nĭ**; (scorch), **papă'ă**; (destroy by fire), **pū'hĭ i kē a'hĭ**.

burr, **hu'ă kă'lăkă'lă**.

burst, **păhū', pŏhā'**.

bus, **kă'ă 'ohu'ă**.

bush, laălā'ăŭ, lā'ăŭ hă'ăhă'ă.

business, 'oĭhă'nă.

busy, pa'ă i kā hă'nă.

but, (otherwise), akā'; (furthermore), 'eĭă nă'ĕ; (except), kŏĕ nă'ĕ; (only), wa'lĕ nō.

butcher, meă lo'lĕ pĭ'pĭ.

butter, wăĭŭpă'kă.

butterfly, pūlĕlĕhu'ă, lepĕlepĕohi'nă.

butterfly-fish kikaka'pŭ.

buttocks, lĕ'mŭ.

button, pĭ'hĭ.

buy, kū'ăĭ măĭ.

by, e, mā: by and by, māmu'lĭ, kokŏ'kĕ, ma-ho'pĕ.

C

cabbage, kāpĭ'kĭ.

cabin, keĕ'nă mo'kŭ, pūpŭ'pŭ ha'le.

cabinet, (political), pă'pă kuhi'nă; (case), pa'-hŭ waĭho'nă.

cable, kăŭlă nunu'ĭ; (anchor chain), kăŭlăhaŏ helĕu'mă; telegraph cable, ŭwe'ă kĕlĕkălă'-ma.

cactus, pāpi'pĭ, pāni'nĭ.

cafe, ha'lĕ 'ăĭnă.

cage, wă'hĭ hŏ'ŏpă'ăhaŏ; bird-cage, pa'hŭ mă'-nŭ.

cake, meă'ŏ'nŏ.

calabash, 'umĕ'kĕ; water gourd, hŭĕwăĭ.

calendar, ălĕmăna'kă.

calf, pĭ'pĭ ke'ĭkĭ; (of leg), 'o'lŏ'o'lŏ wāwaĕ.

California, Kalĕpo'nĭ.

call, kāhĕă; (name), kă'pă; (visit), kĭ'pă.

calm, māli'ĕ, lă'ĭ; dead calm, pō'hŭ: to calm, hŏ'ŏmāli'ĕlĭ'ĕ, hŏ'ŏnā'.

camera, pa'hŭ pă'ĭ kĭ'ĭ.

camouflage, hŏ'ŏpĕ'ĕpĕ'ĕ.

camp, wă'hĭ hŏ'ŏmoă'nă: to camp, hŏ'ŏmoă'nă.

campaign, (political), pāĭpāĭ kalăĭ'ăĭnă.

can, kĭ'nĭ: (be able), hi'kĭ; to can, hŏ'ŏkŏ'mŏ ĭlo'kŏ o kē kĭ'nĭ.

Canada, Kanaka.

canal, ăŭwā'hă, ăŭwăĭ.

cancel, hŏ'ŏpăŭ.

cancer, mă'ĭ 'a'ăĭ.

candidate, mŏ'hŏ.

candle, ĭ'hŏĭ'hŏ.

candle-nut, hu'a kūku'ĭ.

candy, kănăkē', kō 'o'mŏ'o'mŏ.

cane, kŏ'ŏkŏ'ŏ; sugar-cane, kō.

cannery, ha'lĕ hŏ'ŏkŏ'mŏ kĭ'nĭ; pineapple cannery, ha'lĕ hă'nă halăkahi'kĭ.

cannibalism, 'ăĭ kănă'kă.

cannon, pūkŭnĭa'hĭ.

canoe, wă'ă.

canvas, kāpolĕ'nă; (sails), nă pĕ'ă.

canvass, (for funds), noĭ; (for votes), pāĭpāĭ.

cap, păpalĕkă'pŭ.

capable, mākăŭkăŭ.

cape, (headland), laĕ; (garment), kĭheĭ, kŏlo'kă; feathered cape, 'ahŭ'ŭ'lă.

capital, (money), kŭmŭpă'ă; (seat of government), kapĭka'lă.

captain, kāpĕ'nă.

captive, pi'ŏ.

capture, hŏ'pŭ, lăwĕpī'ŏ.

car, kă'ă; railroad car, kă'ă alăhaŏ.

carbon, 'ĭ'ŏ o ka nană'hŭ.

card, pĕ'pă ĭnŏă; cardboard, pĕ'pă mānoănŏă;

(playing), pĕ'pă hahaŭ; (business), pă'lă-
pä'lă hŏ'ŏlä'hă.

care, mălă'mă a'na: to care, mană'ŏ nu'ï; care
for, mālä'mă, kiă'ï; be careful, ākăhĕ'lĕ.

career, 'oïhă'nă.

careless, kāpŭ'lŭ, hŏ'ŏhe'măhe'mă.

cargo, ukă'nă.

carnation, ponïmōï'.

carnival, fĕa.

carpenter, kămănă'.

carpet, moĕnă wĕlĕwĕ'kă.

carriage, kă'ă; (the act), hă'lï ă'nă.

carry, la'wĕ, hă'lï, hă'lïha'lï, hāpaï, 'a'wĕ (obsolete); (on shoulder), 'ăŭă'mŏ, ā'mŏ (archaic); (with yoke), 'ăŭă'mŏ; (on back),
hăă'wĕ, wa'hă (archaic); (as a child in
arms), hï'ï; (in hands), kă'ïkă'ï, la'wĕ; (on
stick between two), kŏï, kă'ïkă'ï; (as
corpse), hŏ'ŏlĕ'wă.

cart, kă'ă la'wĕ ukă'nă, kă'ă kăŭwŏ'.

carve, (as meat), 'o'kï'o'kï; (as wood), kalăï.

case, pa'hŭ, wăhï'; court case, hïhï'ă.

cash, kālă kūi'ke.

cashier, meă mālă'mă kālă.

cast, (throw), kiŏ'lă, hŏ'ŏlĕï, nŏŭ; cast for fish,
kāmŏkŏï; (as metal), hŏ'ŏhehĕ'ĕ.

castaway, n., 'ōlu'lŏ.

caste, kūlă'nă ïwaĕnă o kănă'kă.

castle, kākĕ'lă.

cat, popŏ'kï, 'ōwaŭ.

catalog, (of names), pă'pă ïnŏă; (of goods),
pu'kĕ meă kū'ăï.

catch, hŏ'pŭ, 'ă'pŏ: (as a cold), lŏa'a.

caterpillar, pĕ'ĕlu'ă, enŭ'hĕ.

Catholic, Kākōlï'kă, ăkeă wa'lĕ, pi'lï lăŭlă'.

cattle, pĭ′pĭ.

cause, kŭ′mŭ; (in law), hĭhĭ′ă: to cause, hŏ′ŏkŭ′mŭ.

caution, (ke) ākăhĕlĕ: to caution, ā′ŏ.

cavalla or pompano, (large size), ulu′ă; (medium), pā′u′u; (small), pāpĭ′ŏpĭ′ŏ.

cavalry, koă kăŭ li′ŏ.

cave, (ke) ā′nă, lu′ă.

cease, o′kĭ, hō′o′kĭ, hŏ′ŏpăŭ; (stop!), 'uō′kĭ!

ceiling, pă′pă pa′lĕ.

celebrate, hŏ′ŏkŭlăĭă.

celebrity, meă kăŭlă′nă.

cell, (room), lŭ′mĭ haĭkĭ; (cavity), pu′kăpu′kă.

cellar, keĕ′nă māla′lŏ o kă ha′lĕ.

cement, (mortar), pu′nă pōha′kŭ, (gum), pila′lĭ; to cement, hŏ′ŏpĭpĭ′lĭ.

cemetery, ĭlĭ′nă, pā ĭlĭ′nă.

censer, ĭpŭkŭ′nĭ 'ă′lă.

censor, lu′nă 'āpo′nŏ.

censure, 'ōle′lŏ hō′ahe′wă.

census, păpăhē′lŭ kā′nākă.

cent, kĕnŏ′kă.

center, kĭkŏwaĕnă, waĕnăko′nŭ.

centipede, kănăpĭ′.

century, kĕnĕkulĭ′ă, hăne′lĭ măkăhi′kĭ.

ceremony, hă′nă hŏ′ŏhă′nŏhă′nŏ.

certain, (sure), maopŏ′pŏ lō′ă; (some) kekă′hĭ.

certainly, ĭ′ŏ; (in response), aĕ nō pa′hă, pēlă′ ĭ′ŏ nō, pēlă′ nō.

certificate, pă′lăpă′lă hō′ō′ĭă.

chain, kăŭlăhaŏ.

chair, no′hŏ.

chairman, lunăhŏ′ŏma′lŭ.

chalk, pŏ′hŏ.

challenge, 'ă′'ă

chamber, keĕ'nă, lŭ'mĭ; (association), 'ă'hă,
'ă'hăhŭ'ĭ; chamber of gun, (ke) a'pŏ.

champion, pŏ'ŏke'lă.

chance, (opportunity), wă kŭpo'nŏ; (happen-
ing), meă ulĭ'ă wa'lĕ.

change, lŏ'lĭ; small change, ke'nĭke'nĭ lĭ'lĭlĭ'ĭ: to
change, lŏ'lĭ, hŏ'ŏlŏ'lĭ; change appearance,
hŏ'ănŏ'ĕ; (become), lĭ'lŏ; (exchange), kŭ-
ă'pŏ; change form, hŏ'ŏmălŭ'lĕ; change
money, wăwa'hĭ kălă.

channel, kōwă'.

chant, (recite), o'lĭ; chant and dance, hŭ'lă.

chapel, halĕhălăwăi hŏ'ŏmă'nă.

chapter, moku'nă.

character, (ke) 'ă'nŏ, 'ă'nŏ maolĭ; (symbol),
hŏ'ăilo'nă.

charcoal, nănă'hŭ, lănă'hŭ.

charge, (command), kăŭo'hă; charge a debt,
kă'kĭ, hŏ'ăi'ĕ'; (accuse), hŏ'ŏpĭ'ĭ; charge a
gun, hŏ'ŏpĭ'hă; (in battle), hō'ŭ'kă.

charity, manawăle'ă, ălo'hă.

charm, 'onŏŭ; (trinket), meă hŏ'ŏhĭ'wăhĭ'wă:
(to delight), hŏ'ŏlĕ'ălĕ'ă: charming, nă'nĭ.

chart, (diagram), pă'lăpă'lă hō'ĭ'kĕ; (map),
pă'lăpă'lă 'ăĭnă.

chase, a'lŭa'lŭ, hăhăĭ.

chaste, ma'ĕma'ĕ, haŭmĭ'ă 'o'lĕ.

chat, kămă'ĭlĭ'ŏ hŏ'ŏnănĕ'ă.

chatter, wălă'ăŭ.

chauffeur, kalăĭwă, kalăĭwă kă'ă.

cheap, măkĕpo'nŏ, e'mĭ.

cheat, 'apŭ'kă, kĭkĭ'kĭ.

check, (draft), pi'lă kĭkŏ'ŏ kălă; (pattern), pă-
pămŭ': to check, kĕ'ăkĕ'ă, kaohĭ; (as list),
kă'hă.

checkers, kōnă′nĕ, păpămū′.

cheek, pāpāli′nă.

cheer, hăŭ′o′lĭ: (to gladden),hŏ′ŏhŏĭhŏi; (encourage), pāĭpāĭ; (hurrah), hūlō′.

cheerful, o′hăo′hă, hŏĭhŏĭ.

cheese, wăĭūpăkăpă′ă.

chemical, wăĭ lā′ăŭ.

chemistry, pă′ĭ lā′ăŭ, hŏ′ŏhŭ′ĭhŭ′ĭ lā′ăŭ.

chest, umaumă, kĕ′ăpă′ă: (box), pa′hŭ nu′ĭ.

chew, năŭ; chew the cud, hŏ′ŏlŭălŭă′ĭ.

chicken, (fowl), moă; (chick), moă ke′ĭkĭ.

chief, ălĭ′ĭ; (head man), (ke) pŏ′ŏ.

child, ke′ĭkĭ, kă′mă: children, kămălĭ′ĭ.

chill, (cold and damp), kŏ′ĕkŏ′ĕ, hŭ′ĭhŭ′ĭ;
    (shivering), hă′ŭkĕ′kĕ; (cramps), ′ŏpĭ′lĭ;
    chills and fever, lĭ mē kă wĕ′lă.

chimney, pu′kă ŭa′hĭ.

chin, ′ăŭwaĕ.

China, (country), Kĭ′na; (people), Pă′kē′;
    (crockery), pā.

chisel, kĭ′lă.

chocolate, kŏkŏle′kă.

choice, meă kŏ′hŏ, wae: (exquisite), mi′lĭmĭ′lĭ.

choir, pă′pă hĭme′nĭ.

choke, (throttle), ′u′mĭ, ′u′u′mĭ; (from food),
    pu′u′ă, lăŏwă.

choose, kŏ′hŏ, waĕ.

chop, po′kĕpo′kĕ: to chop firewood, kākā;
    (fell), kŭ′ă; chop up, ′o′kĭ′o′kĭ.

Christian, Kalĭkĭă′nŏ.

Christian Science, Hŏ′ŏmă′nă Nă′ăŭaŏ.

Christmas, Kalĭkĭmă′kă.

church, (building), luăki′nĭ, halĕpu′lĕ; (organization), ekalĕai′ă.

cigar, kĭkă′.

cigarette, kikălĭ'kĭ.

circle, pō'ăĭ; (of friends), pōhăĭ.

circuit, kă'ăpŭ'nĭ.

circulate, (as blood), lă'nă; (publish), hŏ'ŏlă'hă; (move around), ho'lŏ kă'ăvŭ'nĭ.

circumcise, 'okĭpoĕpoĕ.

circumstance, (ke) 'ă'nŏ: circumstances, kŭlă'nă.

circus, hă'nă kĕă'kă.

citizen. kŭ'pă, măkă'ăĭnănă.

city, kūlănăkăŭha'lĕ.

civil, (polite), 'ă'nŏ 'o'lŭ'o'lŭ, wăĭpăhē'; (civic), kiwi'lă.

civilization, mălă'mălă'mă o kă lăhu'ĭ.

claim, kūleă'nă: to claim, kŏĭ.

clam, 'ōlĕ'pĕ.

clan, 'oha'nă.

clap, (as hands), pă'ĭpă'ĭ; (as of thunder), kŭ'ĭ.

clasp, (as hands), a'pŏ; (embrace), pūlĭ'kĭ.

class, pă'pă, kălă'nă.

clause, (paragraph), păŭkū' pă'lăpă'lă; (of sentence), mămă'lă o kă hōpună'ōle'lŏ oko'ă.

claw, mĭkĭaŏ.

clay, pālŏ'lŏ.

clean, ma'ĕma'ĕ: (to weed), waĕlĕ: (cleanse), hŏ'ŏmă'ĕmă'ĕ, (purify), hŭĭkă'lă.

clear, moakă'kă, maopŏ'pŏ; (as water), 'a'ĭa'ĭ; (as weather), măli'ĕ: (to free), hŏ'ŏpăkĕ'lĕ, hŏ'ŏkŭ'ŭ; (to clarify), wĕ'hĕ.

clerk, (secretary), kakăŭ'ōle'lŏ; (salesman), meă kū'ăĭ.

clever, ăkămaĭ, no'ĕaŭ.

cliff, pa'lĭ.

climate, (ke) 'a'nŏ o kē ĕă o kă 'ăĭnă.

climb, (ascend), pǐ'ǐ; (as a tree), pīnă'nă.

clip, meă hŏ'ŏpă'ă; 'umǐ'ǐ: to clip, 'ă'kŏ.

clipper, mokŭlĕ'lĕ.

cloak, kŏlo'kă; (feathered), 'ahŭ'ŭ'lă: to cloak, u'hǐ.

clock, ŭwa'kǐ nu'ǐ.

close, (tight), pa'ă; (stingy), pǐ; (sultry), ǐkǐ-ǐ'kǐ: to close, (shut), pă'nǐ; (cover), po'ǐ; (terminate), hŏ'ŏpăŭ: (near), 'ă'nĕ li'kĕ, kokŏ'kĕ, pi'lǐ.

closet, waǐho'nă.

cloth, lo'lĕ.

clothe, hŏ'ŏkŏ'mŏ lo'lĕ, hō'ă'ă'hŭ: clothes, lo'lĕ ko'mŏ, 'ă'ă'hŭ.

cloud, ăŏ; to cloud over, hŏ'ŏmă'lŭmă'lŭ.

club, (weapon), ne'wă; (social), kălă'pŭ, 'ăhă-hŭ'ǐ.

clumsy, he'măhe'mă, hāwăwă'; (lumbering), pepĕ'ĕku'ĕ.

cluster, hŭ'ǐhŭ'ǐ.

clutch, 'ă'pŏ.

coach, kă'ă; (tutor), kŭ'mŭ; to coach, ā'ŏ

coal, nănă'hŭ pǐkǐmă'nă.

coarse, (as material), mānoănoă, ŏpŭ ŭpŭ'ŭ; (uncultured), kuă'ăǐna.

coast, kăpăkăǐ: to coast, (toboggan), hĕ'ĕho-lu'ă.

coat, kŭ'kă; coat of arms, hō'ăǐlo'nă nō kē kŭ-lă'nă; (as of paint), hŏ'ŏkă'hǐ ha'mŏ ă'nă.

cobweb, pūnawĕ'lĕwĕ'lĕ.

cock, moă ka'nĕ: cock the gun, hō'a'lă i kĕ kǐ'kŏ.

cockroach, 'ĕlĕlū'.

cocktail, meă ǐ'nŭ i awǐ'lǐ ǐ'ă.

coconut, nǐ'ŭ; coconut palm, kŭ'mŭ nǐ'ŭ.

code, (legal), pu'kĕ kānāwăĭ; (secret), ka'kĕ.

coffee, ko'pĕ.

coffin, pa'hŭ kūpāpa'ŭ.

coil, 'ōwĭ'lĭ.

coin, kālā pa'ă.

coition, ăĭ.

cold, coldness, (ke) a'nŭ; (a chill), ĭĭ; cold in
    head, punĭ'ă: (chilly), a'nŭa'nŭ, hŭ'ĭhŭ'ĭ;
    (reserved), laŭlaŭnă 'o'lĕ.

collar, 'ă'ĭ kă'lă.

collect, (assemble), hō'akoăkoă, hō'a'hŭ;
    (glean), noĭ'ĭ; collect taxes, 'o'hĭ.

collection, hō'a'hŭ ă'nă, hō'ĭ'lĭ'ĭ'lĭ ă'nă; (heap),
    ahu'ă.

collector, meă 'o'hi; (tax), lu'nă 'aŭhăŭ; (cus-
    toms), lu'nă 'o'hĭ đu'tĕ.

college, ku'lă nu'ĭ.

collision, hō'ŏkŭ'ĭ.

colonel, kŏne'lă, kolone'lă.

colony, panălā'ăŭ.

color, hō'ŏlŭ'ŭ, wăĭ hō'ŏlŭ'ŭ; (stain), kŏ'hŭ.

colorless, 'a'ĭa'ĭ.

column, kōlă'mŭ, kĭ'a nu'ĭ; (as of figures),
    lāla'nĭ.

comb, kă'hĭ; hair-comb, kă'hĭ lăŭō'hŏ.

combat, hō'ŭ'kă kăŭă, hākăkā'.

combine, hŭ'ĭ pū, hō'ŏhŭ'ĭ; (cooperate), a'lŭ
    pū.

come, he'lĕ măĭ; (approach), hō'ŏkokŏ'kĕ.

Come! Măĭ!

comet, hōkūwe'lŏwe'lŏ.

comfort, comfortable, 'o'lŭ'o'lŭ, ma'hă: to com-
    fort, hō'ō'lŭ'ō'lŭ.

comic, hō'ŏmăkĕ'ă'kă, hō'ă'kă'ă'kă.

command, kăŭo'hă: to command, kăŭo'hă, ke-nā'.

commander-in-chief, ălĭhĭkăŭă.

commence, hŏ'ŏmă'kă, hŏ'ŏkŭ'mŭ.

commencement, (graduations), pu'kă.

commend, 'āpo'nŏ, hō'apo'nŏ.

comment, 'ōle'lŏ wĕ'hĕwĕ'hĕ; (criticism), lŏĭ-lŏĭ.

commerce, 'oĭhă'nă kālĕ'pă.

commission, (warrant), pă'lăpă'lă hŏ'ŏkō'; (pay), 'ŭ'kŭ nō kē kū'ăĭ ă'nă: to commission, hŏ'ŏkŏ'hŭ, hŏ'āmă'nă.

commissioner, kōmĭkĭ'nă, 'ĕlĕ'lĕ aŭpu'nĭ, lu'nă aŭpu'nĭ.

commit, (do), hă'nă; (consign), hŏ'ŏĭ'lĭ; (to memory), hŏ'ŏpă'ă nā'ăŭ; (to prison), hŏ-'ŏpă'ăhaŏ.

committee, kōmĭ'tĕ.

common, pi'lĭ lĭ'kĕ; common report, lăŭla'hă; common sight, măŭ; common sense, no-'ŏno'ŏ po'nŏ, (ke) āŏ kănă'kă.

commonwealth, aŭpu'nĭ măkă'ăĭnă'nă.

commotion, pĭ'ŏlo'kĕ.

communicate, hă'ĭ mană'ŏ.

community, po'ĕ.

compact, (agreement), 'ōle'lŏ aĕ lĭ'kĕ; lady's compact, hŏ'ŏnă'nĭnă'nĭ: (condensed), pa'ă, pa'ăpū.

companion, hoă.

company, măŭ hoă; (association), hŭ'ĭ, 'ăhă-hŭ'ĭ; military company, pū'ă'lĭ koă.

compare, hŏ'ŏhālĭ'kĕ.

comparison, hŏ'ŏhālĭ'kĕ ă'nă.

compass, pănănă.

compel, kŏĭ, hŏ'ŏkĭkĭ'nă.

compete, hŏ'ŏkūkū.

competent, makăŭkăŭ.

complain, hŏ'ŏha'lăha'lă; (grumble), 'ohu'mŭ.

complaint, (bodily), mă'ĭ; (legal), kŭ'mŭ hŏ-
'ŏpĭ'ĭ.

complete, păŭ po'nŏ: to complete, hŏ'ŏkŏ' po'-
nŏ, pa'ă po'nŏ.

complex, pohĭhi'hĭ

complexion, (ke) 'ă'nŏ o kă 'ĭ'lĭ kănă'kă.

complicate, hŏ'ŏhĭhĭ'ă, hŏ'ŏhŭĭkaŭ.

compliment, 'ŏlɛ'lŏ măhă'lŏ.

comply, aĕ a'kŭ.

compose, hă'kŭ; (to quiet), hŏ'ŏmă'ălĭ'lĭ.

compound, hŏ'ŏhŭ'ĭ, kă'ăwĭ'lĭ pū.

comprehend, hŏ'ŏmaŏpŏ'pŏ.

compromise, aĕ lĭ'kĕ.

comrade, hoă.

conceal, hūnă'; conceal self, pĕ'ĕ; conceal
corpse, hūnăkĕ'lĕ.

conceited, hŏ'ŏkă'nŏ, hŏ'oĭ'oĭ, hŏ'ŏĭŏ.

conceive, (physically), hăpăĭ; (mentally), hŏ-
'ŭ'lŭ i kă mană'ŏ.

concern, (interest), kūleă'nă, po'nŏ; (business),
'oĭhă'nă: to concern, pi'lĭ: concerned, pilĭhu'ă: concerning, nŏ.

concert, 'ă'hă me'lĕ: act in concert, a'lŭ lĭ'kĕ.

conclude, (close), hŏ'ŏ'kĭ; (as a treaty), hŏ-
'ŏho'lŏ.

conclusion, hopĕ'nă, pānĭ'nă mană'ŏ.

concrete, kămĕ'kĭ: (not abstract), kuăpă'pă.

condemn, hŏ'ahe'wă.

condescend, hŏ'ŏhă'ăhă'ă a'kŭ, mali'ŭ măĭ.

condition, (state), 'ă'nŏ; (terms), kānăwăĭ.

conduct, 'ă'nŏ o kă hă'nă ă'nă: to conduct
(lead), alăkă'ĭ; (direct), hŏ'ŏkĕ'lĕ.

confer, (give), hāā'wǐ; (converse), kūkā pū.

conference, 'ă'hă kūkā, (church), 'ă'hă nu'ĭ, hŭ'ĭ nu'ĭ.

confess, mi'hǐ.

confide, wĕ'hĕwĕ'hĕ mană'ŏ.

confidential, (trustworthy), păŭlĕ'lĕ ĭ'ă, hilǐnă'ĭ ĭ'ă; (secret), meă hūnā'.

confine, (boundary), pale'nă: to confine, hŏ-'ŏpă'ă.

confirm, (ratify), hŏ'ō'ĭă; (strengthen), hŏ'ŏ-kupă'ă.

conflict, hăkăkā', paĭŏ: to conflict, kū'ē'.

conform, hŏ'ŏkulĭ'kĕ, kūlĭ'kĕ.

confound, hŏ'ŏkăhu'lĭ.

confuse, hŭĭkăŭ, hŏ'ŏhĭlĭkăŭ.

confusion, (tumult), hăŭnaĕlĕ, pĭ'ŏlo'kĕ; (disorder), hŭĭkăŭ.

congenial, kŏ'hŭ, 'o'lŭ'o'lŭ.

congratulate, congratulation, māhă'lŏ.

congregate, 'ākŏăkŏă, hŭ'ĭ.

congregation, (ke) ānăĭnă pu'lĕ.

Congregationalist, Kalăwĭ'nă.

congress, 'ăhă'ōle'lŏ lăhu'ĭ; Congress of U. S. A., 'A'hă Kăŭkānăwăĭ o Ameli'kă Hŭĭpŭĭ'ă.

connect, hŏ'ŏhŭ'ĭ.

connection, pi'lĭ ă'nă.

conquer, lănăki'lă, la'wĕ pi'ŏ.

conqueror, na'ĭ.

conscience, lună'ĭkĕhă'lă.

conscious, 'ĭ'kĕ maopŏ'pŏ.

consecrate, hŏ'ŏlă'ă.

consent, aĕ.

consequence, hopĕ'nă.

consequently, nolăĭlă.

consider, no'ŏno'ŏ.

consideration, mali'ŭ ă'nă; (pay), u'kŭ.

consign, hŏ'ŏĭ'lĭ.

consignment, wăĭwăĭ i hŏ'ŏĭlĭĭ'ă.

consist, hŏ'ŏhŭ'ĭ, hŭĭĭ'ă.

consistent, kūpă'ă.

console, hō'ŏ'lŭ'ŏlŭ, hŏ'ŏnā'.

consolidate, hŏ'ŏhŭ'ĭ a hŏ'ŏpă'ă.

conspicuous, (visible), ahŭwă'lĕ; (distin-
    guished), hă'nŏhă'nŏ.

conspire, 'ohu'mŭ.

constant, (firm), kūpă'ă; (continuous), kūmăŭ,
    măŭ.

constitute, (appoint), hŏ'ŏkŏ'hŭ; (compose),
    hŏ'ŏlĭ'lŏ.

constitution, (laws), kŭmŭkānāwăĭ; (body),
    (ke) o'lă kĭ'nŏ.

constrain, (impel), kŏĭ; (restrain), kaohĭ.

construct, kūku'lŭ.

construe, wĕ'hĕwĕ'hĕ 'ōle'lŏ.

consul, kanĭkĕ'lă.

consult, kūkā pū.

consume, (use up), hŏ'ŏpăŭ; (destroy), lŭ'kŭ;
    (eat), 'ăĭ.

consumption, hŏ'ŏpăŭ ă'nă; (T. B.), mă'ĭ hŏkĭ'ĭ.

contact, hŏ'ŏpi'lĭ ă'nă: to contact, hŭ'ĭ pū.

contain, pa'ă kūlo'kŏ, pa'ă ĭlo'kŏ.

contemplate, no'ŏno'ŏ.

contemporary, o'lă lĭ'kĕ.

contempt, hŏ'ŏwăhăwăha'.

contend, 'ā'ŭ'mĕ'ŭ'mĕ.

content, 'o'lŭ'o'lŭ, lua'nă.

contention, paĭŏ.

continent, māhe'lĕ 'ăĭnă nu'ĭ.

continual, măŭ.

continue, hŏ'ŏmăŭ.

contract, aĕ lĭ'kĕ, ukŭpăŭ: to contract, (agree upon), hŏ'ŏho'lŏ; (shrink), mĭmi'kĭ; (as disease), lōa'a.

contraction, hŏ'ŏpokŏ'lĕ ă'nă.

contradict, hŏ'ŏkŭ'ĭkŭ'ĭ 'ōle'lŏ.

contrary, (opposed), kŭ'ē'; (stubborn), pa'ă-kīkī'.

contrast, lĭ'kĕ 'o'lĕ, 'ă'nŏ oko'ă: to contrast, hŏ'ŏkūkū.

contribute, hăă'wĭ, hŏ'ŏkŭ'pŭ; (charitably), hăă'wĭ manawăle'a.

control, kaohĭ pa'ă.

controversy, hŏ'ŏpă'ăpă'ă.

convene, hō'ăkoăkoă.

convenient, makăŭkăŭ, kūpo'nŏ.

convention, 'ă'hă, 'ă'hăhŭ'ĭ.

converse, kămă'ĭli'ŏ pū.

conversion, lŏ'lĭ ă'nă, hŭ'lĭ ă'nă.

convert, hŏ'ŏhŭ'lĭ mană'ŏ; (transmute), hŏ'ŏ-lŏ'lĭ.

convey, (carry), la'wĕ; convey property, hŏ-'ŏlĭ'lŏ.

convict, pa'ăhaŏ: to convict, 'ahĕ'wă.

convince, hŏ'ŏmaopŏ'pŏ, hŏ'ŏ'ĭai'ŏ.

cook, kŭ'kĕ: to cook, kŭ'kĕ, hŏ'ŏmo'ă.

cool, hŭ'ĭhŭ'ĭ: to cool, hŏ'ŏmă'ălĭ'lĭ.

cooperate, a'lŭ.

cooperation, lăŭlĭ'mă.

copper, kĕlĕă'wĕ.

copy, ko'pĕ, meă lĭ'kĕ: to copy, kakăŭ ko'pĕ.

coral, 'ăkŏ'ăkŏ'ă; coral-rock, pu'nă; coral-reef, pūko'ă.

cord, kăŭlă lĭ'ĭlĭ'ĭ; (of wood), paĭlă wăhi'e.

cordial, (manner), pūmaha'nă, hŏ'ŏ'lŭ'ŏ'lŭ.

core, hă'kŭ; breadfruit core, pikoĭ.

cork, 'ŭmo'kĭ.

corn, kŭli'nă.

corner, hŭĭ'nă; (outer), kĭ'hĭ; (inner), kū'o'nŏ.

coronation, po'nĭ mōĭ'.

corporal, kōpa'lă: (bodily), pi'lĭ i kē kĭ'nŏ.

corporation, hŭ'ĭ; (protruding abdomen), kē-kē.

corps, po'ĕ, pă'pă.

corpse, kŭpāpa'ŭ.

correct, pololeĭ, po'nŏ: to correct, hŏ'ŏpōlolĕĭ.

correspond, (write), kakăŭ lĕ'kă; (agree), kŏ'-hŭ.

corrupt. (depraved), haŭmi'ă: (to bribe), kĭpē.

cosmetic, meă hŏ'ŏu'ĭu'ĭ.

cost, kŭmŭkŭ'ăĭ: to cost, hŏ'ŏlĭ'lŏ.

costly, nu'ĭ kă lĭ'lŏ.

cot, moĕ 'o'pĭ'o'pĭ.

cottage, ha'lĕ 'u'u'kŭ.

cotton, pŭ'lŭpŭ'lŭ.

couch, (movable), pūnĕ'ĕ; (fixed), hikĭĕ'ĕ.

cough, kŭ'nŭ.

council, 'ă'hă kūkă; privy-council, 'ă'hă kūkă malū'.

counsel, (lawyer), lō'ĭŏ; (advice), 'ōlelŏă'ŏ.

countenance, helĕhĕle'nă.

count, he'lŭ.

counter, (in store), pākaŭkaŭ; (in games), hŏ'ăĭlo'nă.

counterfeit, hŏ'ŏhăl'ĭ'kĕ kŏlŏ'hĕ, kălă 'apŭ'kă.

country, paĕ'ăĭnă; (rural parts), kuă'ăĭnă.

county, kălă'nă.

couple, păpălu'ă: to couple, hŭ'ĭ pālu'ă.

courage, wiwo'o'lĕ.

course, (ke) a'lă, moĕ ă'nă; (of time), (ke) aŭ; watercourse, ăŭwăĭ, kăhăwăĭ.

court, pā; law-court, 'ā'hā hŏ'ŏkŏ'lŏkŏ'lŏ; (of
　　house), pāha'lĕ; royal court, po'ĕ o kē a'lŏ
　　ălĭ'ī.

courteous, lăŭle'ă, 'ă'nŏ 'o'lŭ'o'lŭ.

courtesy, kūlă'nă wăĭpăhē'.

cousin, hoăhānăŭ.

cover, (lid), (ke) pă'nĭ, (ke) po'ī; (cloth),
　　u'hĭ.

covet, kŭ'kŏ, 'alŭ'nŭ.

cow, pĭ'pĭ wăhĭ'nĕ.

coward, hohē wa'lĕ, makă'ŭ wa'lĕ.

cowboy, panio'lŏ.

cowherd, kă'hŭ pĭ'pĭ.

cowrie, le'hŏ.

crab, papa'ī; rock-crab, 'ā'a'mă; sand-crab,
　　'ohĭ'kĭ.

crack, (small), nakă'kă; (large), 'owa'owă',
　　mawaĕ: to crack, 'owă'.

cracker, (food), pele'nă; (firework), hŏ'ŏpă-
　　hupăhū'.

craft, (trade), 'oĭhă'nă hănăli'mă; (boat), mo'-
　　kŭ lĭ'ĭlĭ'ī; (cunning), mă'ălcă.

cramp, 'opĭ'lĭ, ma'ĕ'ĕ'lĕ.

crash, hŏ'ŏkŭ'ī.

crater, luăpĕ'lĕ.

crave, li'ă, ĭ'ĭ'nĭ; (beseech), noī hă'ăhă'ă.

crawl, kŏ'lŏ.

crayfish, crawfish, u'lă, u'lă papă'pă.

crazy, pūpu'lĕ.

cream, kălĭ'mă wăĭū': ice-cream, hăŭkalĭ'mă.

create, hŏ'ŏkŭ'mŭ: The Creator, Kē Akŭ'ă.

creature, meă o'lă.

credentials, pă'lăpă'lă hŏ'apo'nŏ.

credit, (honor), kŭ'mŭ măhă'lŏ; trade credit,
　　hŏ'ăĭ'ē': to credit, hilĭnă'ī.

creed, kŭ'mŭ mană'ŏĭ'ŏ.

creek, kăĭkŭ'ŏ'nŏ; (stream), kăhăwăĭ, mulĭwăĭ.

creep, (crawl), kŏ'lŏ; (go secretly), hŏ'ŏmŏ'-
  hŏ.

crest, pi'kŏ; family crest, hŏ'ăĭlo'nă kŭăŭhăŭ.

crew, po'ĕ lui'nă.

cricket, 'ūhĭ'nĭ.

crime, kalăĭmă.

cripple, 'ŏ'ŏ'pă.

crisis, lŏ'lĭ ă'nă.

criticise, criticism, lŏĭlŏĭ.

crooked, kekĕ'ĕ, kăpăkă'hĭ.

croon, me'lĕ hŏ'ŏnă'hĕnă'hĕ.

cross, kĕ'ă: (peevish), 'ă'ă'kă: (to thwart),
  'ălăĭ.

crow, ălălă': to crow, 'ŏ'ŏ'.

crowbar, kŏlŏpă', meă ŭ'nĕ.

crowd, pū'ŭ'lŭ: to crowd, hŏ'ŏkē': crowded,
  pa'ăpū'.

crown, kalăŭnŭ, lĕĭ ălĭ'ĭ; (as of head), pi'kŏ.

crude, mă'kă.

cruel, hŏ'ŏma'ĭ'nŏ'ĭ'nŏ.

cruise, ho'lŏ mōa'nă.

cruiser, mo'kŭ manŭwă'.

crumb, hŭ'nă.

crumble, hŏ'o'kăo'kă.

crush, hŏ'ŏpēpē: crushed, pēpē.

crust, papă'ă.

crusty, 'ă'ă'kă.

crutch, kŏ'ŏkŏ'ŏ.

cry, (weep), ŭwē'; (call), kăhĕă.

crystal, pōha'kŭ 'a'ĭa'ĭ: (clear), moakă'kă.

cube, pa'ă'ĭlĭo'nŏ.

cucumber, kă'ŭkă'mă.

cue, (billiards), lā'ăŭ pa'hŭpa'hŭ; (line), lāla'nĭ; (reminder), kŭ'mŭ ho'omănă'ŏ.

cultivate, mă'hĭ.

culture, mă'hĭ ă'nă; kūlă'nă nā'ăŭaŏ.

cunning, mă'ăleă.

cup, po'lă.

cupboard, pa'hŭ pā.

curb, (street), kă'ĕ alănŭ'ĭ; to curb, kaohĭ.

cure, hō'o'lă.

curio, meă pakŭwā' 'o'lĕ.

curious, 'ă'nŏ 'ĕ'; (prying), maha'ŏĭ.

curl, mĭmi'lŏ: to curl, mi'lŏ.

curlew, kĭŏĕă.

curly, pĭ'ĭpĭ'ĭ.

currency, kālā aŭpu'nĭ.

current, (ke) aŭ; air current, (ke) a'hĕa'hĕ;
  current time, he'lĕ nĕĭ; current report, lo-
  nŏĭ'ă.

curse, to lay a curse, 'ănăĭ; (revile), hă'ĭ'lĭ-
  'ĭ'lĭ, kŭă'mŭă'mŭ.

curve, pĭ'ŏ.

cushion, kūkĭ'nĭ, ulu'nă.

custody, (care), mălă'mă ă'nă; (arrest), hŏ-
  'ŏpă'ăhaŏ ă'nă.

custom, meă mă'ă măŭ.

customary, kulu'mă, mă'ă măŭ.

customer, meă kū'ăĭ.

customhouse, ha'lĕ đu'tĕ aŭpu'nĭ.

cut, 'o'kĭ; (carve), 'o'kĭ'o'kĭ; (chop), po'kĕ-
  po'kĕ; (fell), kŭ'ă; (whittle), kŏ'lĭ; to be
  cut, mo'kŭ.

cute, (shewd), mă'ăleă; (attractive), 'ăŭlĭ'ĭ;
  (in speech), pōwe'kŏ.

cycle, (period), (ke) aŭ, wā; (wheel), hŭi'lă.

D

dagger, paho'ă.

daily, kēlā' mē kē'ĭă lā.

dainty, (as food), 'o'nŏ; (in dress), 'ăŭlĭ'ĭ, măĭaŭ.

dairy, wă'hĭ mālă'mă pĭ'pĭ wăĭŭ'.

dam, (ke) pănĭwăĭ; (breeder), kŭmŭlăŭ.

damage, pohō', pō'ĭ'nŏ.

damn, hō'ĭ'nŏ wa'lĕ.

damp, kăwăŭ'; damp and cold, kŏ'ĕkŏ'ĕ.

dance, hă'ă; (foreign), hŭ'lăhŭ'lă; (native), hŭ'lă.

dandy, kănă'kă hŏ'ŏkă'hăkă'hă.

danger, pō'ĭ'nŏ.

dare, 'ă''ă.

dark, pō'ĕ'lĕ'ĕ'lĕ, poŭ'lĭ; dark color, u'lĭu'lĭ.

darling, hĭ'wăhĭ'wă, mĭ'lĭmĭ'lĭ.

darn, pahŏ'nŏhŏ'nŏ.

dart, ĭ'hĕ: to dart, lĕ'lĕ māmā.

dash, (to ground), pākī; (as waves), po'ĭ; (to pieces), wāwa'hĭ.

data, kŭ'mŭ.

date, (time), mana'wă; (fruit), hu'ă pā'mă.

daughter, kăĭkămăhĭ'nĕ.

dawn, wănă'āŏ, (ke) ălăụ'lă.

day, lā; daylight, (ke) āŏ.

dazzle, 'olĭ'nŏlĭ'nŏ.

deacon, kiakŏ'nă.

dead, death, mă'kĕ, mă'kĕ lō'ă.

deaf, ku'lĭ; deaf-mute, 'ă'ā.

deal, (to trade), kālĕ'pă; (apportion), măhe'-lĕ; (as cards), hāă'wĭ.

dear, alo'hă, punăhe'lĕ; (expensive), pipĭ'ĭ: "Dear Sir," "aloha."

debate, hŏ'ŏpāpā, paĭŏ.

debt, 'ăĭ'ē'.

decay, pōpŏ'pŏ, pălăhō'.

deceit, mă'ăleă.

deceive, hŏ'ŏpŭ'nĭpŭ'nĭ.

December, Kĕkĕma'pă.

decent, kūpo'nŏ; (of person), hŏ'ŏpo'nŏ.

decide, hŏ'ŏho'lŏ.

decimal, pāu'mĭ.

decision, mană'ŏ hŏ'ŏho'lŏ.

deck, (ship), one'kĭ; (cards), pŭ'ŭ pĕ'pă.

declare, hă'ĭ, hŏ'ŏlă'hă.

decline, (refuse), hō'o'lĕ; (descend), 'aŭĭ.

decorate, kāhi'kŏ, hŏ'ŏnă'nĭ.

decoration, hō'ăĭlo'nă hă'nŏhă'nŏ.

decoy, pāka'lĭ: to decoy, hŏ'ŏpŭnĭhĕĭ.

decrease, e'mĭ.

decree, kăŭo'hă, kānāwăĭ.

dedicate, hŏ'ŏlă'ă.

deduct, hŏ'ŏlă'wĕ.

deed, (act), hă'nă: to deed, hŏ'ŏlĭ'lŏ.

deep, (as sea), hoho'nŭ; (as pit), pŏ'ŏpŏ'ŏ.

deer, dĭ'ă, kĭ'ă.

defeat, hŏ'aŭhĕ'ĕ; be defeated, (lose), lĭ'lŏ, ha'u'lĕ.

defect, kĭnă'.

defection, kĭ'pĭ.

defective, he'măhe'mă.

defend, defense, pa'lĕ; (court), 'ōle'lŏ pa'lĕ: defenses, pākăŭă.

defer, (postpone), hŏ'ŏpănĕ'ĕ; (to another), mali'ŭ.

defiance, hō'ă'ă'nŏ, 'ă''ă ă'nă.

defile, (ke) alănŭ'ĭ haĭkĭ: to defile, hŏ'ŏhaŭmĭ'ă.

define, wĕ'hĕwĕ'hĕ.

definite, maopŏ'pŏ.

defraud, 'apŭ'kă.

deîy, 'ă''ă.

degenerate, meă 'Ï'nŏ lō'ă: to degenerate, hŏ'ï ho'pĕ.

degree, (rank), kūlă'nă; (measure), kekĕ'lĕ.

dejected, dejection, pilĭhu'ă.

delay, hăkălĭ'ă: (to postpone), hŏ'ŏpăne'e.

delegate, 'ĕlĕ'lĕ: to delegate, hŏ'ŏï'lĭ iă' ha'ï.

deliberate, ākăhĕ'lĕ: to deliberate, no'ŏno'ŏ po'nŏ.

delicate, (health), pă'lŭpă'lŭ; (material), la'hĭ-la'hĭ.

delicious, 'o'nŏ; (tasty), mĭ'kŏmĭ'kŏ.

delight, hăŭ'o'lĭ, o'hăo'hă.

deliver, (give), hăă'wĭ; (save), hŏ'ŏpăkĕ'lĕ.

deluge, wăïkă'hĕ; The Deluge, Kăï-a-Kahină-lĭ'ï: to deluge, kă'hĕ nŭ'ï; (as with work), pa'ă lō'ă.

demand, kăŭo'hă: to demand, kŏï.

democracy, aŭpu'nï a kă le'hŭle'hŭ.

Democrat, Demŏkăla'kă.

demon, kiăpŏlō', kaïmŏnĭ'ŏ, 'ūha'nĕ 'Ï'nŏ.

demonstrate, hŏ'ï'kĕ maopŏ'pŏ a'kŭ.

den, lu'ă holŏhŏlo'nă, (ke) ă'nă.

dense, pa'ăpū'.

dentist, kaŭkă ni'hŏ.

deny, hŏ'o'lĕ.

depart, he'lĕ.

department, māhe'le.

depend, kaŭkă'ï, kă'lï.

deposit, waïhŏ.

depot, (railway), ha'lĕ hŏ'ŏlŭ'lŭ.

depreciate, (lessen), hŏ'e'mĭ; (disparage), hŏ-
    'ĭ'nŏ.
depression, (business), hŏ'e'mĭ 'oĭhă'nă; (men-
    tal), ulŭkū'; (surface), pŏ'hŏ.
deprive, hŏ'ŏnĕ'lĕ.
depth, hoho'nŭ, pŏ'ŏpŏ'ŏ.
deputy, ho'pĕ.
descend, ĭ'hŏ.
descendant, pu'ă, ma'mŏ.
descent, ĭho'nă; (genealogy), pă'pă kūăŭhăŭ.
describe, hŏ'ăkā'kă, hŏ'ĭ'kĕ 'ănŏ.
desert, wăŏăku'ă, pāno'ă: to desert, hă'ălĕ'lĕ.
deserts, hu'ă o kā hă'nă.
design, (purpose), mană'ŏpa'ă; (sketch), (ke)
    ā'nă, kĭ'ĭ kă'hă i hŏ'ĭ'kĕ 'ă'nŏ.
designate, ku'hĭku'hĭ.
desire, (wish), mă'kĕmă'kĕ; (yearn), 'ĭ'ĭ'nĭ;
    (lust), kŭ'kŏ.
desk, pākaŭkaŭ hă'nă.
desolate, nĕ'ŏnĕ'ŏ, me'hăme'hă.
despair, păŭ kā mană'ŏlă'nă.
desperate, pohŏ' lŏ'ă; (rash), 'ă'ă măkĕhe'wă.
despise, hŏ'ŏwăhăwăhā'.
destination, wă'hĭ e he'lĕ a'kŭ ăĭ.
destine, waĕ, kŏ'hŏ.
destiny, hopĕ'nă.
destitute, ne'lĕ, hŭ'nĕ, 'ĭlĭkŏ'lĕ.
destroy, hŏ'ŏpăŭ; lŭ'kŭ.
destroyer, (vessel), mo'kŭ lŭ'kŭ.
destruction, lŭ'kŭ, mă'kĕ.
detach, hŏ'ŏkă'ăwa'lĕ, wĕ'hĕ.
detachment, māhe'lĕ.
detail, (appoint), hŏ'ŏkŏ'hŭ; (relate), hă'ĭ lĕ'ă.
detain, kaohĭ, 'aŭ'ă.
detect, 'ĭ'kĕ.

detective, māka'ĭki'ŭ.

determine, mană'ŏ pa'ă; determined, 'ŏnĭpă'ă.

detest, hŏ'ŏpăĭlŭ'ă.

detour, (ke) a'lă kăpăĕ: to detour, 'ă'lŏ.

deuce, (cards), pă'ălu'ă.

develop, hŏ'ŏmohă'lă.

device, meă ĭ no'ŏno'ŏĭ'ă.

devil, kiăpŏlō'.

devote, mană'ŏ măŭ, hŏ'ŏlă'ă: devoted, pĭ'lĭ
    ālo'hă.

devotion, hŏ'ŏmă'nă, ālo'hă.

devour, 'ăĭ; (voraciously), hŏ'ŏnŭ'ŭ.

devout, hăĭpu'lĕ.

dew, kēhăŭ.

diagonal, lă'lă, hiō'.

diameter, (ke) ānăwaĕnă.

diamond, kăĭmă'nă.

dice, pa'ăo'nŏ, hăĭlo'nă.

dictate, (for writing), hă'ĭ a'kŭ a nă ha'ĭ e ka-
    kăŭ; (order), kăŭo'hă.

dictator, (ke) pŏ'ŏ aŭpu'nĭ na'nă kā mă'nă a
    păŭ lō'ă.

dictionary, wĕ'hĕwĕ'hĕ 'ōle'lŏ.

die, (ke) ā'na: to die, mă'kĕ.

diet, 'ăĭ: to diet, 'ăĭ pākĭ'kŏ.

differ, difference, lĭ'kĕ 'o'lĕ, kū'ē'.

different, oko'ă, 'ănŏ'ē'.

difficult, pa'ăkikĭ', pohĭhĭ'hĭ.

difficulty, kūpĭlĭkĭ'ĭ.

dig, 'ĕ'lĭ; (to loosen ground), pā 'ĕ'lĭ.

digest, (summary), mană'ŏ nu'ĭ: to digest food,
    hŏ'ŏwă'lĭ ĭ kā 'ăĭ; (think over), no'ŏno'ŏ
    po'nŏ.

dignity, hi'ehi'e, kă'pŭkă'pŭ.

dim, pōwe′hĭwe′hĭ; (as twilight), mōle′hŭle′-
hŭ; (as sight), pōhi′nă.

dime, kĕ′nĭkĕ′nĭ.

dimensions, nā ā′nă.

dimple, mĭ′nŏ.

din, hănăkŭ′lĭ.

dine, 'ăĭ: dinner, 'ăĭnă nu'ĭ, pa'ĭ′nă.

dip, hŏ'ōlŭ'ŭ; dip up, kĭŏ'ĕ; (as fingers), hŏ'ō';
(as oars), kŏ′mo; dip the flag, hŭ′kĭ kă haĕ
ila′lŏ a ilu′nă.

diplomacy, kūkā ă′nă mawaĕnă o nā aŭpu′nĭ,
hŏ'ōmă′lĭmă′lĭ.

direct, moĕ pololeĭ: to direct, ku′hĭku′hĭ.

direction, moĕ ă′nă; (medicinal), (ke) ā′nă,
lu′lă.

director, lu′nă hŏ'ōpo′nŏpo′nŏ.

dirt, lĕ′pŏ.

dirty, lĕ′pŏ, păŭma'ĕ′lĕ.

disability, hi′kĭ 'o′lĕ, păŭ kā po′nŏ.

disable, hŏ'ōnĕ′lĕ i kā hi′kĭ.

disagree, kūlĭ′kē 'o′lĕ; (as foods), kūpo′nŏ 'o′lĕ.

disagreeable, 'ă'ă'kă; (unpalatable), 'o′nŏ 'o′lĕ.

disappear, na′lŏ.

disappoint, hŏ'ōho′kă.

disappointment, ho′kă.

disaster, pōpilĭki'ă, pō'ĭ′nŏ.

discard, kiŏ′lă; (give up), hă'ălĕ′lĕ lō′ă.

discharge, (dismiss), hŏ'ōkŭ'ŭ; (freight), hŏ'ō-
lĕĭ ukă′nă; (gun), kĭ pū; (debt), hŏ'ōkă′ă;
(as duty), hŏ'ōkō'; (as water), hŏ'ōkă′hĕ.

disciple, haŭmā′nă.

discipline, ma′lŭ po′nŏ: to discipline, ā'ŏ ĭkăĭkă.

discount, u′kŭ hō'e′mĭ: to discount, hō'e′mĭ.

discourage, discouragement, păŭpăŭa′hŏ.

discover, (uncover), wĕ'hĕ; (reveal), hō'ĭ'kĕ;
(see first), 'ĭ'kĕ mu'ă; (find), lōa'a.

discuss, kūkā, wĕ'hĕwĕ'hĕ.

disease, mă'ĭ.

disgrace, waiă: to disgrace, hŏ'ŏhĭ'lăhĭ'lā.

disgraceful, hi'lăhi'la maolĭ.

disguise, 'ănŏ'ē': to disguise, hō'ănŏ'ē'.

disgust, hŏ'ŏpăĭlŭ'ă.

dish, pā.

dishonest, 'ē'pă.

dislike, mă'kĕmă'kĕ 'o'lĕ.

dismiss, hŏ'ŏkŭ'ŭ; (set aside), waĭhŏ.

disobey, hŏ'ŏkŭ'lĭ, hŏ'ŏlo'hĕ 'o'lĕ.

disorder, (confusion), hŭĭkăŭ; (room), mo-
kakĭ'; (mob), hăŭnaĕlĕ; (disease), mă'ĭ.

dispatch, (send), hŏ'ŏŭ'nă hikĭwa'wĕ; (kill),
pĕpe'hĭ a mă'kĕ.

display, (show off), hŏ'ŏkă'hăkă'hă; (as courage), hō'ĭ'kĕ; (as goods), hō'ĭ'kĕ'ĭ'kĕ.

displease, hŏ'ŏnaŭ'kĭŭ'kĭ.

displeasure, u'kĭu'kĭ.

dispose, (arrange), hŏ'ŏno'hŏno'hŏ; (as property), hŏ'ŏlĭ'lō; (incline), mali'ŭ.

dispute, hŏ'ōpă'ăpă'ă.

disqualify, 'āpo'nŏ 'o'lĕ.

dissolve, hŏ'ŏhehĕ'ē; (terminate), hŏ'ōpăŭ.

distance, mamaŏ, ĭŭ.

distant, mamaŏ.

distinct, (apart), oko'ă lō'ă; (clear), moakā'kă.

distinction, kăŭlă'nă:

distinguish, (discriminate), hŏ'ŏmaŏpŏ'pŏ i kā
lĭ'kĕ 'o'lĕ; distinguish oneself, hŏ'ŏkăŭlă'nă.

distress, (pain), 'ē'hă; (straits), pĭlĭki'ă.

distribute, māhe'lĕ, pŭ'ŭnaŭĕ.

district, 'āpă'nă, 'okă'nă, mo'kŭ.

distrust, kānălŭ'ă, hilĭnă'ĭ 'o'lĕ.

disturb, hōkaĭ, hŏ'ŏpĭlĭkĭ'ă; disturb the peace, hŏ'ŏhaŭnaĕlĕ.

disturbance, hăŭnaĕlĕ; (in class), hăŭwală'ăŭ.

ditch, ăŭwăĭ, ăŭwā'hă.

dive, (submerge), lŭ'ŭ; dive headlong, kŭhoŭpŏ'ŏ.

divide, kuălă'pă: to divide. māhe'lĕ, pŭ'ŭnaŭĕ.

dividend, māhe'lĕ kālā.

divine, (cleric), kăhŭnăpŭ'lĕ: (god-like), 'ă'nŏ akŭ'ă.

division, (sharing), pŭ'ŭnaŭĕ, māhe'lĕ; (faction), mokuahă'nă.

divorce, o'kĭ ma'lĕ, kă'ăwa'lĕ.

dizzy, ponĭ'ŭnĭ'ŭ.

do, (perform), hă'nă, hŏ'ŏkō'. [Not auxiliary.]

dock, (wharf), ŭwa'pŏ; (to reduce), hō'e'mĭ.

doctor, kaŭkă; (native medico), kăhŭ'nă lāpă'-ăŭ.

doctrine, mcă i ā'ŏĭ'ŭ.

document, pă'lăpă'lă.

dodge, a'lŏ.

dog, 'ĭlĭ'ŏ.

doll, kĭ'ĭ pēpē.

dollar, kālā.

dolphin, ma'hĭma'hĭ.

domestic, kănă'kă hă'nă: (not foreign), kŭlo'kŏ.

domesticate, hŏ'ŏlă'kă.

dominate, hŏ'ŏhă'kŭ.

dominion, mă'nă, aŭpu'nĭ.

donate, hāă'wĭ wa'lĕ, maka'nă.

donation, lŭlŭ.

donkey, kekă'kĕ.

door, (ke) pä'nĭ pu'kă; with door-frame, 'ĭpŭ'-
kă; door-way, pu'kă kŏ'mŏ.

dose, māhĕ'lĕ lā'äŭ.

dot, kĭ'kŏ.

double, (duplicate), lu'ă lĭ'kĕ: (twofold), pä-
lu'ă: double-dealing, hă'nă pa'e'wa'e'wă.

doubt, kānălŭ'ă.

dough, pala'oă mä'kă ĭ hŏ'ŏwă'lĭ ĭ'ă; (slang
for money), kālā, mo'nĭ.

dove, (ring neck), ĕhakŏ'; (biblical), mă'nŭ
nūnū.

down, hĕŭ, hĕŭhĕŭ; (downward), la'lŏ, ĭla'lŏ:
go down, ĭ'hŏ.

dozen, kakĭ'nĭ, 'ŭmĭkūmamalu'ă.

draft, (money), pä'läpä'lă kīkŏ'ŏ kālā; (outline), kakăŭ ă'nă, ko'pĕ; (army), waĕ ă'nă;
(of fish), hĕĭ ĭ'ă; (of air), kokŏlŏlĭ'ŏ.

drag, kăŭwŏ'; drag along ground, kăŭalakŏ.

dragon, mŏ'ŏ lĕ'lĕ.

dragon-fly, pīna'ŏ.

drain, ăŭwăĭ; to drain, hŏ'ŏkă'hĕ.

drama, hă'nă kĕă'kă.

draw, (haul), hŭ'kĭ, kăŭwŏ'; (as a picture),
kă'hă; (attract), 'u'mĕ: drawer, pa'hŭ 'u'mĕ.

drawback, kŭ'mŭ kĕ'äkĕ'ă, 'aŭhăŭ đu'tĕ ĭ ho'ĭ-
ho'ĭĭ'ă.

dread, dreadful, wĕ'lĭwĕ'lĭ.

dream, moĕ'uha'nĕ.

dress, lo'lĕ kŏ'mŏ: to dress, (clothe), hŏ'ŏkŏ'-
mŏ lo'lĕ, hŏ'ă'ă'hŭ; (as a wound), wăhĭ';
dress ranks, hŏ'ŏpōlolĕĭ ĭ kā lāla'nĭ; (as
soil), kīpŭ'lŭ; dress fowls, (pluck), ŭ'nŭ-
ŭ'nŭ; (draw), kŭă'ĭ.

drift, (sand), kuălă'pă o'nĕ; drift-wood, pĭ-
hăă': to drift, lă'nă wa'lĕ.

drill, païkaŭ: (to bore), wĭ'lĭ pu'kă.

drink, ĭ'nŭ.

drip, kŭ'lŭ.

drive, (as a car), hŏ'ŏkĕ'lĕ; (as cattle), hŏ'ŏ-
   hu'lĭ, hŏ'ŏā'; (as in work), hŏ'ĕŭ'ĕŭ; (with
   the wind), kă'ălĕlĕ'wă; drive out, kĭpă'kŭ.

driver, kalăĭwă.

droop, lo'hă, lŭ'hĕ.

drop, (as of water), kŭ'lĕ; (of rain), pă'kă u'ă:
   to drop, ha'u'lĕ, hŏ'ŏha'u'lĕ.

drove, pŭ'ā' holŏhŏlo'nă.

drown, pĭho'lŏ, mă'kĕ i kā wăĭ; drown forcibly,
   lŭmă'ĭ.

drowsy, măkăhiamoĕ.

drug, lă'ăŭ lăpăăŭ.

drum, pa'hŭ, pa'hŭ kă'nĭ.

drunk, 'o'nă.

drunkard, kănă'kă 'o'nă măŭ.

dry, malo'ŏ; (barren), păno'ă; (thirsty), măkĕwăĭ: to dry, kăŭlăᵗ, hŏ'ŏmălŏ'ŏ.

duck, kăkā'; wild duck, kolo'ă.

due, (as a debt), 'ăĭ'ĕ'; (suitable), kŭpo'nŏ.

dull, kŭmŭmŭ'; (as sound), kamŭ'mŭ; (stupid),
   lololĕ'lĕ.

dumb, mŭmu'lĕ, 'ă'ă.

dung, kŭkaĕ.

duplicate, lu'ă lĭ'kĕ, ko'pĕ.

durable, pa'ă, măŭ.

during, 'oĭaĭ, i kă wā.

dusk, mōle'hŭle'hŭ.

dust, lĕ'pŏ 'aĕ'aĕ: to dust, kahĭ'lĭ.

duty, po'nŏ; (tax), ду'tĕ wăĭwăĭ, 'aŭhăŭ wăĭwăĭ.

dwell, no'hŏ.

dye, hŏ'ŏlŭ'ŭ.

dynamite, kia'nă păŭkă.

E

each, păka'hĭ, kēlă' meă kē'ĭă meă.

eager, ā'kĕ nu'ĭ, ĭkăĭkă kā mană'ŏ.

eagle, aĕkŏ.

ear, pēpeĭaŏ; (as of corn), huhu'ĭ.

early, hi'kĭ mu'ă; (in morning), wănă'āŏ.

earn, lōa'a māmu'lĭ o kā hă'nă.

earnest, kŭĭ'ŏ, mană'ŏ ĭkăĭkă.

earth, honu'ă; (soil), lĕ'pŏ; The Earth, Kē ăŏ
    nĕĭ.

earthquake, (ke) ola'ĭ, nāŭĕŭĕ.

ease, (comfort), ma'hă, năne'ă.

easily, hi'kĭ wa'lĕ nō, mă'ăla'hĭ.

east, hĭki'nă.

eat, 'ăĭ, pa'ĭ'nă.

echo, kūpina'ĭ, wăwā'.

eclipse, (as of sun, etc.), poŭlĭ.

economize, hŏ'ŏmākăŭlĭ'ĭ.

economy, mālă'mă po'nŏ; (political,, kalăĭ-
    'ăĭnă.

edge, (brink), kă'ĕ; (of implement), mă'kă; (of
    board), nĭaŏ; (border), lĭ'hĭ.

edible, kūpo'nŏ i kā 'ăĭ.

edition, hŏ'ŏpŭ'kă.

editor, lu'nă hŏ'ŏpo'nŏpo'nŏ.

educate, education, hŏ'ŏna'ăŭaŏ.

eel, pu'hĭ.

effect, hu'ă o kā hă'nă; (purport), 'ă'nŏ; effects,
    ukă'nă, wăĭwăĭ: to effect, kō, hŏ'ŏkō'.

efficiency, mikĭoĭ.

efficient, mi'kĭmi'kĭ.

effort, hŏa'o, hŏ'ŏikăĭkă.

egg, hu'ă; hen's egg, hu'ă moă.

Egypt, Aïkupĭ'kă.

eight, wă'lŭ, ewă'lŭ, 'awă'lŭ: eighth, kă wă'lŭ.

eighteen, 'ŭmĭkŭmamawă'lŭ: eighteenth, kă 'ŭmĭkŭmamawă'lŭ.

eighty, kănăwă'lŭ: eightieth, kē kănăwă'lŭ.

either, kekă'hĭ o laŭă.

elastic, lahŏli'ŏ: (springy), hŏ'lŭ, 'ŏ'lŭ.

elation, hŏïhŏï.

elbow, kŭ'ēkŭ'ēlĭ'mă.

elder, kăhĭ'kŏ a'ē: (of brothers), kăïkŭa'ă'nă; (of church), lu'năkăhi'kŏ.

elect, kŏ'hŏ, waē.

election, kŏ'hŏ ă'nă.

electric, electricity, ŭwĭ'lă, ŭĭ'lă.

element, mŏ'lē, kŭ'mŭ; elements, nă meă hŏ'ŏ-kŭ'mŭ.

elementary, kŭ'mŭ mu'ă.

elephant, ĕlĕpă'nĭ.

elevation, (height), kă'hĭ kĭ'ēkĭ'ē; (act), hăpăĭ ïlu'nă.

elevator, elĕwē'kă.

eleven, 'ŭmĭkŭmamaka'hĭ: eleventh, kă 'ŭmĭkŭ-mamaka'hĭ.

eliminate, hŏ'ŏpăŭ.

eloquent, pŏwe'kŏ, makăŭkăŭ i kă 'ŏle'lŏ.

else, (besides), 'ē a'ē; (otherwise), i 'o'lĕ.

elsewhere, mă kă'hĭ 'ē.

embalm, ĭ'ălŏ'ă.

embarrass, hŏ'ŏhĭ'lăhĭ'lă.

embassy, po'ē 'ĕlĕ'lĕ aŭpu'nĭ.

emblem, hō'ăïlo'nă.

embrace, pūlĭ'kĭ, a'pŏ.

emerge, pu'kă.

emergency, pĭlĭkĭ'ă kŭhe'wă.

emotion, pihoĭhoĭ.

emperor, ĕmĕpĕ'lä.

emphasize, kälĕ'lĕ le'ŏ, hŏ'ŏmaŏpŏ'pŏ lĕ'ä.

emphatic, kŏ'ĭkŏ'ĭ.

employ, (use), lä'wĕlä'wĕ; (hire), hŏ'ŏlĭ'mä-lĭ'mä.

employer, hä'kŭ hä'nä.

employment, hä'nä, 'oĭhä'nä.

empty, hä'kähä'kä: to empty, nĭnĭ'nĭ, kiŏ'lä a'kŭ.

enable, 'āmä'nä.

enchant, (fascinate), hŏ'ŏhĭä'äĭ; (bewitch), hŏ'ŏkäläkŭpu'ä.

encore, hä'nä hoŭ.

encourage, hŏ'ŏlä'nä, paĭpaĭ i kä manä'ŏ.

encyclopedia, pu'kĕ hŏ'ĭ'kĕ poko'lĕ nŏ kēlä' mē kē'ĭä meä.

end, ho'pĕ, hopĕ'nä; (as of rope), pi'kŏ; (of house), kä'lä; (of a board), wēläŭ: to end, hŏ'ŏpäŭ.

endless, päŭ 'o'lĕ, mäŭ lŏ'ä.

endorse, (approve), 'äpo'nŏ; (as a note), kakäŭ kākŏ'ŏ.

endure, (last), mäŭ; (bear), hŏ'ŏmanawanu'ĭ, ähŏnu'ĭ.

enemy, ĕnĕ'mĭ.

energy, 'ĕlĕ'ŭ, mĭ'kĭmi'kĭ.

enforce, hŏ'ŏnĕ'ĕ ĭkäĭkä, hŏ'ŏŭnäŭnä.

engage, (promise), 'ōle'lŏ pa'ä; (hire), hŏ'ŏ-lĭ'mälĭ'mä; (employ), pa'ä i kä hä'nä; (in battle), hō'ū'kä käŭä; (betroth), hŏ'ŏpäläŭ.

engine, ĕnĭkĭ'nĭ, mĭkĭ'nĭ.

engineer, wĭlĭkĭ'.

England, English, Pĕlĕka'nĕ, Enĕla'nĭ.

engrave, kä'häkä'hä.

enjoy, hŏĭhŏĭ, lĕ'ălĕ'ă.

enlarge, hŏ'ŏmāhŭ'ăhŭ'ă, hŏ'ŏnu'ĭ; (as a picture), hŏ'ŏlĕ'lĕ.

enlist, kŏ'mŏ; (as sympathy), hō'a'lă.

enormous, nu'ĭ he'wăhe'wă, wĕ'lĭwĕ'lĭ kā nu'ĭ.

enough, la'wă.

enter, kŏ'mo, hŏ'ŏkŏ'mŏ; enter an action, hŏ'ŏpĭ'ĭ.

entertain, (receive), hŏ'ŏkĭ'pă; (divert), hŏ'ŏlĕ'ălĕ'ă.

enthusiasm, ŏhŏhĭ'ă.

entire, holŏ'ŏkoă.

entitle, hŏ'ŏkūleā'nă.

entrance, pu'kă kŏ'mŏ: to entrance, hŏ'ŏhŏĭhŏĭ, hŏ'ŏhĭä'äĭ.

envelop, wăhĭ', hŏ'ŏpŭ'nĭ.

envelope, wăhĭ' lĕ'kă.

envy, lĭ'lĭ.

epidemic, mă'ĭ ähŭlăŭ.

Episcopalian, Hŏ'ŏmā'nă Piho'pă.

equal, (similar), lĭ'kĕ; (tied), pă'ĭ a pă'ĭ.

equation, kăŭlĭ'kĕ.

equator, pŏ'äĭ waĕnă.

erase, holoĭ.

eraser, meă holoĭ.

erect, kū pololeĭ: to erect, kūku'lŭ.

err, error, (sin), he'wă; (mistake), kuhĭhe'wă; (wander), lălăŭ; (in grammar), pāhe'măhe'mă.

errand, hŏ'ŏŭnăŭnă ă'nă.

eruption, (volcanic), hū kā pĕ'lĕ; (skin), pŭ'ŭpŭ'ŭ, hŭ'ĕhŭ'ĕ.

escape, palĕkă'nă: to escape, pake'lĕ.

escort, (formal), hŭăkă'ĭ hŏ'ŏhă'nŏhă'nŏ: to escort, he'lĕ pū.

especial. manǎ'ǒ nu'ǐ ǐ'ǒ.

especially, 'oǐaǐ ho'ǐ.

essay, kǔmǔmanǎ'ǒ i hǎkǔǐ'ǎ: to essay, hǒa'o.

essence, (extract), wǎǐ hō'ǎ'ǎ'lǎ; (character), ǐ'ǒ.

establish, (settle), hǒ'ǒno'hǒno'hǒ; (set up), hǒ'ǒkǎhǔ'ǎ; (as laws), hǒ'ǒkǔpǎ'ǎ.

establishment, ha'lě 'oǐhǎ'nǎ.

estate, (realty), wǎǐwǎǐ pa'ǎ; (rank), kūlǎ'nǎ; (deceased's), hǒ'ǒǐlǐ'nǎ; (chief's), (ke) ahǔpuǎ'ǎ.

esteem, māhǎ'lǒ nu'ǐ.

estimate, kǒ'hǒ, manǎ'ǒ, kǎǔpǎǒnǎ.

eternal, mǎǔ lǒ'ǎ.

eternity, (ke) āǒ pǎǔ 'o'lě.

Europe, Eulo'pǎ.

evade, 'ǎ'lǒ.

even, (smooth), lǎǔmǎnǐ'ǎ; (equal), pǎ'ǐ a pǎ'ǐ; (balanced), kǎǔlǐ'kě: even so, pēlǎ' ǐ'ǒ nō.

evening, (ke) ǎ'hǐǎ'hǐ.

event, hǎ'na nu'ǐ, meǎ hi'kǐ mǎǐ.

ever, (at any time), kekǎ'hǐ wǎ; (always), mǎǔ.

everlasting, mǎǔ lǒ'ǎ.

every, a pǎǔ: everybody, everything, kēlǎ' meǎ kě'ǐǎ meǎ: everywhere, mā nǎ wǎ'hǐ a pǎǔ.

evidence, 'ōle'lǒ hō'ǐ'kě.

evident, maopǒ'pǒ lě'ǎ, akǎ'ka.

evil, (bad), 'ǐ'nǒ; (sinful), he'wǎ; (disastrous), pō'ǐ'nǒ.

evolution, meǎ i kǔ'pǔ no'nǎ ǐ'hǒ.

exact, lǐ'kě lǒ'ǎ, kūpo'nǒ: to exact, kǒǐ.

exacting, pa'ǎkikǐ', 'o'olě'ǎ.

exactly, pēlā' ĭ'ŏ.

exaggerate, hŏ'ŏnu'ĭ; (boast), hă'ānu'ĭ.

examine, (handle), mi'līmi'lĭ; (interrogate), ninaninaŭ; (at school), hŏ'ĭ'kĕ ku'lă.

example, kŭmŭhŏ'ŏhālĭ'kă.

exceed, 'oĭ, pākĕ'lă.

exceedingly, lō'ă.

excellent, măĭkă'ĭ 'oĭ, kĭlŏhă'nă.

except, (omitting), kŏĕ: (to omit), hŏ'ŏkoĕ.

exceptional, pŏ'ŏke'lă.

excess, kăŭlĕ'lĕ; (dissipation), ŭ'hăŭ'hă.

exchange, hŭ'ĭ kŭkā kălĕ'pă: to exchange, pānă'ĭ, kŭă'pŏ.

excite, hŏ'ŏlă'lĕlă'lĕ; (arouse), hŏ'ĕŭ'ĕŭ.

excitement, pihoĭhoĭ; (tumult), ulŭao'ă.

exclaim, hŏ'o'hŏ.

exclude, pă'nĭ a'kŭ.

exclusive, (excepting), he'lŭ 'o'lĕ ĭ'ă; (reserved), no'hŏ kă'āwa'lĕ, lăŭnă 'o'lĕ.

excursion, hŭăkă'ĭ māka'ĭka'ĭ.

excuse, (regret), mi'hĭ; (pretext), 'ōle'lŏ hŏ-'ă'lŏ'ă'lŏ: (to pardon), kă'lă; (exempt), hŏ'ŏkŭ'ŭ.

execute, (perform), hŏ'ŏkō'; (kill), hŏ'ŏmă'kĕ.

exempt, hŏ'ŏkŭ'ŭĭ'ă: to exempt, hŏ'ŏkŭ'ŭ.

exercise, hŏ'ŏikăĭkă kĭ'nŏ; (lesson), hāăwi'nă hŏ'ŏmă'āmă'ă: (to use), hŏ'ŏhă'nă.

exhaust, (empty), hŏ'ŏpăŭ; (tire out), mālu'-hĭlu'hĭ, păŭpăŭa'hŏ.

exhibit, exhibition, hŏ'ĭ'kĕ, hŏ'ĭ'kĕ'ĭ'kĕ.

exile, wăĭlă'nă, kue'wă: to exile, kĭpă'kŭ.

exist, (live), o'lă.

existence, o'lă ă'nă.

expand, (extend), hŏ'ŏnu'ĭ; (open up), moha'-lĭ.

expanse, (ke) āke′ă.

expansion, hŏ′ake′ă ă′nă.

expect, (await), kăkă′lĭ; (hope), mană′ŏlă′nă.

expel, kĭpă′kŭ, hŏ′ŏkŭ′kĕ.

expend, hŏ′ŏlĭ′lŏ.

expense, lĭ′lŏ.

expensive, pipĭ′ĭ.

experience, ′ĭ′kĕ.

experiment, hŏa′o.

expert, ăkămăĭ, ′ăĭlŏ′lŏ.

expire, (breathe), hă′nŭ; (die), mă′kĕ; (end), pău.

explain, wĕ′hĕwĕ′hĕ, hŏ′ăkă′kă.

explode, păhŭ′, pŏhă′.

explore, ′ĭ′mĭ lŏ′ă, hŭ′lĭ.

export, hŏ′ŏĭ′lĭ wăĭwăĭ i nă ′ăĭnă ′ĕ.

expose, hŏ′ĭ′kĕ āke′ă, waĭhŏ wa′lĕ.

exposition, hŏ′ĭ′kĕ′ĭ′kĕ.

express, (company), hu′ĭ hă′lĭ ŭka′nă; (messenger), ′ĕlĕ′lĕ: (to state), hă′ĭ, hŏ′ăkă′kă; (signify), hŏ′ĭ′kĕ.

expression, (phrase), ′ŏle′lŏ; (face), ′ă′nŏ.

exquisite, ′ăŭlĭ′ĭ, nă′nĭ, măĭkă′ĭ lŏ′ă.

extend, (expand), hŏ′akeă, hŏ′ŏpālă′hălă′hă; (stretch forth), kĭkŏ′ŏ; (prolong), hŏ′ŏlo-′ĭ′hĭ.

extensive, (wide), lăŭla′hă; (large scale), nu′ĭ.

extent, lăŭlă′.

extinct, mă′kĕ, pi′ŏ, na′lŏ.

extinguish, hŏ′ŏmă′ke, hŏ′ŏpi′ŏ; (as a fire), kinăĭ.

extra, hoŭ, ′oĭ a′ĕ; (surplus), kĕ′ŭ, kăŭlĕ′lĕ.

extract, (essence), wăĭ hŏ′ă′ă′lă meă ′ăĭ: to extract, unu′hĭ.

extraordinary, kupăĭăna′hă.

extreme, wēlăŭ, pale'nă: (utmost), 'oĭ lō'a
a'kŭ.

eye, mă'kă: eyeball, 'ono'hĭ; eyebrow, kŭ'ĕ-
mă'kă; eyelash, lĭ'hĭlĭ'hĭ; eyelid, kuăpo'ĭ
mă'kă.

F

fable, 'ōle'lŏ na'nĕ.

face, helĕhĕle'nă, mă'kă; (front), (ke) a'lŏ.

fact, 'o'ĭai'ŏ, meă i hŏ'ŏkōĭ'ă.

faction, mokuahă'nă.

factory, halĕ hă'nă.

faculty, (power), mă'nă; (of university), po'ĕ
kŭmŭă'ŏ.

fade, (wilt), măĕ, lo'hă; (as colors), hākĕăkĕă.

fail, (in class), ha'u'lĕ; (in business), pohō';
(in health), nāwa'lĭwa'lĭ; (disappoint), hŏ-
'ŏho'kă.

faint, (weak), nāwa'lĭwa'lĭ: to faint, ma'ū'lĕ.

fair, fĕă, hŏ'ĭ'kĕ'ĭ'kĕ: (fine), măĭkă'ĭ; (beautiful), nōheă; (blond), hākĕăkĕă; (equit-
able), kăŭlĭ'kĕ; (honest), hŏ'ŏpo'nŏ; (pass-
able), 'ă'nŏ măĭkă'ĭ.

fairy, kŭpu'ă.

faith, mană'ŏĭ'ŏ, păŭlĕ'lĕ.

faithful, kūpă'ă, 'o'ĭai'ŏ.

fall, (water-fall), wăĭlĕ'lĕ: (to drop), ha'u'lĕ;
fall over, hi'nă; fall and shatter, hio'lŏ.

false, wahăhĕ'ĕ, hŏ'ŏpŭ'nĭpŭ'nĭ.

fame, famous, kăŭlă'nă.

familiar, mă'ă, wălĕ'a, kămă'ăĭnă ĭ'ă.

family, 'oha'nă.

famine, wī.

fan, pe'a'hĭ; sports fan, meă maha'lŏ, meă lĕ-
'ălĕ'ă i kā pā'a'nĭ ă'nă.

fancy, mană‘ŏ u‘lŭ wa‘lĕ.

far, mamaŏ, lŏ‘i‘hĭ.

fare, (charge), u‘kŭ; (food), ‘ăĭ.

farewell, (ke) alo‘hă.

farm, ‘ăĭnă măhĭ‘ăĭ; to farm, măhĭ‘ăĭ.

farther, maŏ‘ a‘kŭ.

fashion, păĭki‘nĭ.

fashionable, hŏ‘ŏmahu‘ĭ‘ă.

fast, (tight), pa‘ă; (swift), mămă; (dissi-
    pated), ‘ŭhă‘ŭ‘hă: to fast, hŏ‘ŏkē‘ăĭ.

fasten, hŏ‘ŏpa‘ă; (nail up), kakĭ‘ă.

fat, kĕ‘lĕkĕ‘lĕ; (plump), mōmo‘nă: to be fat,
    mōmo‘nă.

fatal, mă‘kĕ.

fate, hopĕ‘nă.

father, makuăka‘nĕ: to father, hŏ‘ŏkă‘mă.

fathom, ănă‘nă: to fathom, ă‘nă i kă hoho‘nŭ.

fault, he‘wă; (blemish), kĭnă‘.

favor, lokomăĭkăĭ; to favor, mali‘ŭ, kōkŭ‘ă.

favorable, ‘o‘lŭ‘o‘lŭ, kūpo‘nŏ.

favorite, punăhe‘lĕ.

fear, makă‘ŭ, wĕ‘lĭwĕ‘lĭ: to fear, makă‘ŭ, hŏ‘-
    pŏhŏ‘pŏ.

fearful, hŏ‘pŏhŏ‘pŏ.

fearless, wiwo‘o‘lĕ.

feast, lū‘ăŭ; (banquet), ‘ăhă‘aĭnă; (dinner), pa-
    ‘ĭ‘nă: to feast, ‘ăĭ a ma‘o‘nă.

feather, hŭlŭmă‘nŭ.

feature, (lineament), helĕhĕle‘nă; (prominent
    part), meă ‘ă‘nŏ nu‘ĭ.

February, Pepĕlŭa‘lĭ.

federal, hŭ‘ĭ, feđera‘lă.

fee, u‘kŭ, ‘aŭhăŭ.

feeble, năwa‘lĭwa‘lĭ, pă‘lŭpă‘lŭ.

feed, ‘ăĭ: to feed, hănăĭ.

feel, hāhā; (like the blind), hāpă'pă; (sympa-
thize), ālo'hă lĭkĕ; (sense), 'ĭ'kĕ.

feelingly, me'nĕme'nĕ.

fellow, (companion), hoă, kokŏ'ŏlu'ă; That fellow! Kēlā' kă'ă'kă.

felt, lo'lĕ mānoănoă; felt hat, pāpa'lĕ kalĕpo'nĭ.

female, wăhi'nĕ: females, wā'hĭnĕ.

fence, pă: to fence with swords, kākāpă'hĭ.

ferns, pălăĭ, kŭ'pŭkŭ'pŭ.

ferry, mo'kŭ hă'lĭhă'lĭ.

fertile, hu'ă nu'ĭ; (as soil), mōmŏ'nă.

fertilize, kīpŭ'lŭ.

festival, (ke) ānăĭnă lĕ'ălĕ'ă.

fetch, kĭ'ĭ.

feud, hŏ'ŏmăŭha'lă, hăkăkā'.

fever, pĭ'wă, 'ŏwĕ'lăwĕ'lă.

few, kakă'ĭkă'hĭ; (scattering), kăwă'lăwă'lă.

fiber, ma'a'wĕ.

fiction, 'o'ĭai'ŏ 'o'lĕ; (novel), ka'aŏ hă'kŭ wa'lĕ
ĭ'ă.

fictitious, kă'păkā'pă, 'o'ĭai'ŏ 'o'lĕ.

field, (cultivated), kīhapăĭ; (open), ku'lă.

fierce, 'ahĭ'ŭ, haĕ.

fifteen, 'ŭmĭkūmamalĭ'mă: fifteenth, kā 'ŭmĭkūmamalĭ'mă.

fifty, kănălĭ'mă: fiftieth, kē kănălĭ'mă.

fig, pĭ'kŭ.

fight, hăkăkā'; (battle), kăŭă.

figure, hu'ă he'lŭ; (shape), kĭ'nŏ; (picture),
kĭ'ĭ; to figure, kakăŭ he'lŭ; (be prominent),
kăŭlă'nă.

file, (rasp), a'pŭa'pŭ; (row), lăla'nĭ; file of papers, pŭ'o'lŏ: to file, (as papers), hŏ'ŏkŏ'mŏ.

fill, hŏ'ŭpĭ'hă.

film, 'ĭ'lĭ la'hĭla'hĭ, 'ă'ămŏ'ŏ: films, kĭ'ĭ 'ŏ'nĭ'ŏ'nĭ

filth, filthy, pě'lăpě'lă, haŭmi'ă.

fin, (back), kuălă'; (side), pě'wăpě'wă; (tail),
hi'ŭ.

final, ho'pě lō'ă, pāni'nă.

finance, mălă'mă kālā.

financial, nō nā kālā.

find, lōa'a.

fine, u'kŭ hŏ'ōpăĭ: (small), măkălĭ'ĭ; (as dust),
'aě'aě; (comely), nă'nĭ, 'ăŭlĭ'ĭ.

finger, mănămănăli'mă.

finish, (polish), hŏ'ōhĭ'nŭhĭ'nŭ; (goal), pa'hŭ
hŏ'pŭ: to finish, hŏ'ōpăŭ po'nŏ, hŏ'ŏkō'.

fire, (ke) a'hĭ: to fire, (as a gun), kĭ; (kindle),
ho'ā'.

firearms, nā pū kĭ: fireworks, kăŏlě'lě.

firm, (business), hŭ'ĭ: (stable), năŭě 'o'lě, pa'ă;
(resolute), 'ŏnĭpă'ă, kūpă'ă.

first, mu'ă, măkămu'ă; (chief), pŏ'ŏke'lă; first-
born, măkăhĭa'pŏ.

fish, ĭ'ă: to fish, lăwăĭ'ă.

fish-hook, makăŭ.

fishnet, 'upe'nă.

fishpond, lŏ'kŏ ĭ'ă.

fist, pŭ'ŭpŭ'ŭli'mă.

fit, mă'ĭ hŭ'kĭ: (suitable), pilĭpo'nŏ: to fit, hŏ'ŏ-
kupo'nŏ; (as clothing), hŏ'ŏkūkū.

five, lĭ'mă, elĭ'mă, 'alĭ'mă: fifth, kā lĭ'mă.

fix, (trouble), pĭlĭkĭ'ă: to fix, (fasten), hŏ'ŏ-
pă'ă; (mend), kāpĭ'lĭ hoŭ.

flag, haě: to flag (signal), pe'a'hĭ.

flame, lă'pălapă a'hĭ, 'u'lă o kě a'hĭ.

flap, (as wings), kăpălŭ'lŭ; (as flag), kĭlě'pă-
lě'pă, wě'lŏ.

flash, 'ănă'pă.

flashlight, kūku'ĭ pa'ă lĭ'mă.

flat, pāla'hăla'hă, 'Ī'līwăī.

flatter, flattery, pĕ'lŏ, hŏ'ŏmă'līmă'lī.

flavor, 'o'nŏ: to flavor, hō'o'nŏ'o'nŏ.

flea, 'ŭkŭlĕ'lĕ.

flee, 'aŭhĕ'ĕ, măhu'kă.

fleece, hŭ'lŭ hi'pă: to fleece, 'apŭ'kă.

fleet, ulŭmo'kŭ, 'aŭmo'kŭ: (swift), māmā, hikĭ-
    wa'wĕ.

flesh, 'Ī'ŏ.

flexible, nă'pĕnă'pĕ, hŏ'lŭhŏ'lŭ.

flight, (as of birds), lĕ'lĕ ă'nă; (fleeing), hĕ'ĕ
    ă'nă; put to flight, hō'aŭhĕ'ĕ.

flighty, 'ōpu'lĕpu'lĕ.

flirt, hŏ'ŏhă'Ī, hŏ'ŏmahi'ĕ.

float, meă lă'na; net float, mo'ŭo: to float,
    lă'nă; float ashore, paĕ.

flock, (birds, people), 'aŭnă; (sheep), pū'ā'.

flood, wăĭkă'hĕ nu'Ī; The Flood, Kăĭ-a-kahină-
    lī'Ī.

floor, păpăhŭ'lŏ, păpăhŭ'hī.

flour, pala'oă, pala'oă mă'kă.

flow, kă'hĕ.

flower, pu'ă.

fluid, wăĭ, kēlā' mē kē' Īă 'ă'nŏ wăĭ: (not solid),
    hĕhĕ'ĕ.

flunk, pohŏ', ha'u'lĕ.

flute, 'o'hĕ kă'nĭ, 'o'hĕ pu'hĭ.

flutter, kăpălī'lī.

fly, na'lŏ: to fly, lĕ'lĕ, hŏ'ŏlĕ'lĕ; 'aŭhĕ'ĕ; (as
    clouds), kă'ălĕlĕ'wă; (speed), ho'lŏ māmā.

flying-fish, mālŏ'lŏ.

foam, hŭ'ăhŭ'ă; foaming sea, kăĭahŭ'lŭ.

fog, 'o'hŭ.

fold, (ke) 'o'pĭ, pe'lŭ; sheep-fold, pā hi'pă:

-fold, pa-, e g. pāhā', "4-fold:" to fold over, pe'lŭ; fold up, 'o'pĭ'o'pĭ.

foliage, lăŭ lā'ăŭ.

folk, po'ĕ, nā kā'năkă.

follow, hahăĭ, ukă'lĭ.

follower, meă ukă'lĭ; (disciple), haŭmā'nă.

folly, nā'ăŭpō, lăpŭwa'lĕ.

fond, pu'nĭ; (affectionate), ālo'hă.

fondle, mi'lĭmi'lĭ.

food, meă 'ăĭ: food for journey, (ke) ō.

fool, hūpō, kănă'kă punĭwa'lĕ: to fool, kŏlŏ'hĕ.

foolish, hūpō; (partly demented), olalăŭ.

foot, wăwaĕ; (measure), kăpúa'ĭ; (base), kŭ'mŭ: to foot a bill, hŏ'ŏkă'ă.

football, pōpō pĕ'kŭ.

for, i, nŏ, nă: (because), nŏ kā meă.

forbid, pā'pā'.

force, ĭkăĭkă, mă'nă. to force, (by urging), 'ŏnŏ'ŏnŏŭ; (physically), lĭmănu'ĭ; (ravish), pŭ'ĕ.

forecast, wānă'nă.

forehead, laĕ.

foreign, 'ē, haolĕ.

foreigner, haolĕ, kănă'kă 'ĕ.

foreman, lu'nă.

foremost, mu'ă lō'ă; (in competition), pŏ'ŏkĕ'lă.

foresee, wānă'nă, kĭ'lŏkĭ'lŏ.

forest, ulŭlā'ăŭ.

forever, măŭ lō'ă.

forfeit, u'kŭ hŏ'ŏpă'ĭ, lĭ'lŏ, hŏ'ŏnĕ'lĕ.

forge, kăpŭa'hĭ: to forge, (counterfeit), 'āpŭ'kă; (fashion), kŭ'ĭhaŏ; forge ahead, nĕ'ĕ ĭmu'ă.

forget, poĭnă, hŏ'ŏpoĭnă.

forgive, kă'lă.

forgiveness, kă'lă ă'nă.

fork, (ke) 'ō; (branch), mă'nă.

form, (image), kĭ'ĭ; (body), kĭ'nŏ; (shape), 'ă'nŏ: to form, (become), lĭ'lŏ; form a company, kūku'lŭ i hŭ'ĭ.

formal, mē nā lōină.

formation, hŏ'ŏkŭ'mŭ ă'nă; (military), lāla'nĭ ă'nă.

former, mu'ă.

formerly, māmu'ă.

forsake, hă'ălĕ'lĕ.

fort, pāpū, pā kăŭă.

forth, a'kŭ, ĭmu'ă.

forthwith, ānŏ'.

fortune, wăĭwăĭ nu'ĭ; good fortune, pŏmaĭka'ĭ; bad fortune, pŏ'ĭ'nŏ.

forty, kănāhā': fortieth, kē kănăhā'.

forward, (onward), ĭmu'ă: (impertinent), maha'ŏĭ.

foul, (in sports), he'wă, kūpo'nŏ 'o'lĕ: (filthy), pĕ'lăpĕ'lă, haŭmĭ'ă.

found, hŏ'ŏkŭ'mŭ.

foundation, kŭ'mŭ, kăhŭ'ă.

founder, meă hŏ'ŏkŭ'mŭ: (to sink), pĭho'lŏ, pălĕ'mŏ.

fountain, wăĭ pūă'ĭ, kĭ'ŏwăĭ.

four, hā, ehā', 'ahā': fourth, kă hā.

fourteen, 'ūmĭkūmamahā'; fourteenth, kă 'ūmĭkūmamahā'.

fowl, moă, mă'nŭ.

fox, ălŏpĕ'kă.

fraction, ha'pă, hākĭ'nă.

fragment, (part), 'āpă'nă; (crumb), hŭ'măhŭ'nă; (very small piece), lĭ'hĭ ĭ'kĭ.

fragrant, 'ă'ă'lă, 'ă'lă.

frame, meă hŏ'ŏpă'ă; framework, nă ĭ'wĭ: to
    frame, kāpĭ'lĭ, kūku'lŭ; frame up, hă'kŭ
    'ĕ'pă.

France, French, Păla'nĭ.

frank, hunăhunā' 'o'lĕ, 'o'ĭai'ŏ.

fraternal, hoăhānăŭ, 'ă'nŏ hoăhānăŭ.

fraud, 'apŭ'kă, 'ĕ'pă, hŏ'ŏpŭ'nĭpŭ'nĭ.

freckle, luluā'ĭ'nă.

free, (independent), kūoko'ă; (loose), hŏ'ŏho'-
    lŏ; (gratis), mănŭa'hĭ; (relaxed), năne'ă:
    to free, hŏ'ŏkŭ'ŭ.

freeze, (congeal), pa'ă i kĕ a'nŭ; (be be-
    numbed), 'ōpĭ'lĭ; freeze to death, mă'kĕ i kĕ
    a'nŭ.

freight, ukă'nă.

frequent, pĭ'nĕpĭ'nĕ: to frequent, he'lĕ măŭ.

fresh, (new), hoŭ; (raw), mă'kă; (as water),
    hŭ'ĭhŭ'ĭ.

fret, nĕ, hŏ'ŏha'lăha'lă.

Friday, Pō'alĭ'mă.

friend, hoalo'hă; (chum), hoăpi'lĭ; (very
    close), aĭka'nĕ; (home sharing), mă'kă-
    mă'kă.

friendly, hoălaŭnă.

frigate-bird, man-of-war hawk, i'wă.

fright, hikĭle'lĕ, pū'iwă: to frighten, hŏ'ŏwĕ'-
    lĭwĕ'lĭ.

fringe, kŭ'ŭwe'lŭ; (border), kă'ĕ.

frivolous, lĕ'ălĕ'ă no'ŏno'ŏ 'o'lĕ.

frog, pŏlo'kă, la'nă.

from, măĭ; măĭ . . . măĭ; măĭ . . . a'kŭ.

front, a'lŏ: in front, māmu'ă.

frost, hăŭ, kēhăŭ a'nŭ.

froth, hŭ'ă, hŭ'ăhŭ'ă.

frown, hŏ'ŏkŭ'ĕmä'kă: to frown, hŏ'ŏkŭ'ĕkŭ'e-
    mä'kă.

fruit, hu'ă; edible fruit, hŭä'ăĭ.

fry, pălăĭ.

fuel, nā meă 'a i kē a'hĭ.

fugitive, măhu'kă.

fulfill, hŏ'ŏkō'.

full, pĭ'hă; (satisfied), ma'o'nă.

fun, lĕ'ălĕ'ă.

function, 'oĭhă'nă: to function, hă'nă.

fund, waĭho'nă.

funeral, hŏ'ŏlĕ'wă.

funnel, (engine), pu'kă ŭa'hĭ; (liquid), kanŭ'-
    kŭ.

funny, mĕă 'ă'kă'ă'kă.

fur, hŭ'lŭ pă'lŭpă'lŭ.

furious, (angry), ĭnăĭnă; (tempestuous), pŭ-
    kikĭ'.

furlough, wā hŏ'ŏma'hă.

furnish, hŏ'ŏlă'kŏ.

furniture, la'kŏ.

further, (to help), kōkŭ'ă: (distance), maō'
    a'kŭ.

fury, ĭnăĭnă, hūhū' wĕ'lĭwĕ'lĭ.

future, kō mu'ă a'kŭ, kā wā maho'pĕ.

G

gain, pu'kă; (winnings), ĕŏ.

gale, maka'nĭ nu'ĭ.

gallon, kālä'nĭ.

gallows, 'āmă'nă.

gamble, pilĭwăĭwăĭ.

game, (play), pā'a'nĭ; wild game, meă hĭhĭ'ŭ.

gang, hŭ'ĭ.

gap, hă'kăhă'kă; gap in range, mawaĕ, wă'hĭ
   hă'ăhă'ă.

garage, hă'lĕ kă'ă.

garbage, 'ōpă'lă.

garden, mā'lă, kīhapăĭ.

garlic, 'ākă'ăkaĭ pūpū.

garment, lo'lĕ kŏ'mŏ, 'ă'ă'hŭ.

gas, ĕă māmā.

gasoline, kăkălĭ'nă, aĭleă.

gate, pu'kă pā; (turnstile), pu'kă ŭwăĭ.

gather, (assemble), hō'ākŏăkŏă, hō'u'lŭ'u'lŭ;
   (harvest), 'o'hĭ; (c o l l e c t), hō'ĭ'lĭ'ĭ'lĭ;
   (hoard), hō'a'hŭ.

gauge, (ke) ā'nă.

gay, lĕ'ălĕ'ă, hăŭ'o'lĭ.

gem, pōha'kŭ măkămăĕ.

general, ălĭhĭkăŭă, kĕnĕlă'lă: (common), lăŭla'hă.

generation, (production), hŏ'ŏhu'ă ă'nă; (unit),
   hanaŭnă.

genial, 'o'lŭ'o'lŭ, lăŭnă.

genitals, mă'ĭ.

genius, (ke) ăkămăĭ maolĭ.

gentle, (tame), la'kă; (quiet), māli'ĕ.

gentleman, kĕŏnĭmă'nă.

genuine, maolĭ, 'o'ĭai'ŏ.

geography, hō'ĭ'kĕ honu'ă.

germ, mŏ'lĕ; (bacteria), mū mă'ĭ.

German, Germany, Kĕlĕmani'ă.

gesture, ku'hĭ.

get, (obtain), lōa'a.

ghost, lă'pŭ.

giant, pilĭku'ă.

giddy, ponĭ'ŭnĭ'ŭ; (frivolous), haŭlă'nĭ, lĕ'ălĕ'ă.

gift, (present), maka'nă; (talent), 'ĭ'kĕ.

ginger, 'awapŭ'hĭ.

gipsy, 'oha'nă kue'wă.

girl, kăĭkămăhĭ'nĕ: (girls), kăĭkămā'hĭnĕ.

give, hăă'wĭ; (present), maka'nă; (alms), ma-
    nawăle'ă; give up, hăă'wĭ pi'ŏ, păŭa'hŏ.

glad, hăŭ'o'lĭ, 'o'lĭ'o'lĭ.

glance, ăla'wă, lĕ'hă.

glare, 'olĭ'nŏlĭ'nŏ: (to shine), hulĭ'lĭ; glare with
    anger, nănă hŭhŭ', hulĭ'lĭ kā mă'kă.

glass, (ke) a'nĭa'nĭ; (tumbler), kĭ'ă'hă.

glide, nĭaŭ.

glimpse, 'ĭ'kĕ li'hĭ.

glitter, hulă'lĭ, (ke) alo'hĭlo'hĭ.

globe, (sphere), kĭ'nŏ poĕpoĕ; The Globe, Kā
    Honu'ă.

gloomy,(dark), poŭ'lĭŭ'lĭ; (sullen), nŭnu'hă.

glorify, hŏ'ŏnă'nĭ.

glory, glorious, nă'nĭ.

glottal stop, 'ŭ'ĭ'nă.

glove, mĭkĭlĭ'mă.

glow, (as of fire), ĕ'năĕ'nă; (of face), 'u'lă'u'lă.

glue, kŏlŭ', pĭla'lĭ: to glue, hŏ'ŏpĭpĭ'lĭ.

gnaw, nă'lĭnă'lĭ, 'ă'kĭ'ă'kĭ.

go, he'lĕ; go afoot, he'lĕ wăwaĕ; (run), ho'lŏ;
    go in, kŏ'mŏ; go out, pu'kă ĭwa'hŏ.

goal, pahŭhŏ'pŭ.

goat, kăŏ.

goat-fishes, wĕ'kĕ, mōa'nŏ, kumŭ'.

goby, 'ô'o'pŭ, paŏ'ŏ, pănŏ'ŏ.

god, (ke) akŭ'ă; God, Kē Aku'ă, Iĕho'vă.

goggler, aku'lĕ.

gold, ku'lă.

golf, kolo'pă, kĭnĭpōpō hi'lĭ.

good, (upright), po'nŏ, măĭkă'ĭ; (flawless), kĭ-
    nă' 'o'lĕ; (correct), pololeĭ.

goodbye, good morning, (ke) alo′hă.

goose, nēnē.

gospel, ĕŭănĕli′ŏ.

gossip, holŏholŏ′ōle′lŏ.

gourd, hŭ′ĕ, ĭpŭ′ă′wă′ă′wă, pōhu′ĕ.

govern, hŏ′ŏmă′lŭ.

government, (ke) aŭpu′nĭ.

governor, kĭă′ăĭnă.

gown, holŏkū′, lo′lĕ.

grab, kā′ĭ′lĭ, ′ă′pŏ.

grace, (kindness), lŏkŏmăĭkă′ĭ; (beauty), nă′nĭ.

grade, kūlă′nă, pă′pă; road grade, moĕ ă′nă.

gradual, māli′ĕ.

graduate, (from university), pu′kă po′nŏ;
    (mark degrees), kă′hă i kā hanŭ′ŭ.

graft, (join), pakŭ′ĭ; (cheat), ′apŭ′kă, ′alŭ′nŭ.

grain, (seed), hu′ă; (minute particle), hŭ′nă.

grammar, pilĭ′ōle′lŏ, hō′ĭ′kĕ ′ōle′lŏ.

grand, kămăhă′ŏ.

grandchild, mŏ′ŏpu′nă: grandparent, ĸŭpu′nă,
    kūkū: grandparents, kū′pună.

grant, (assent), aĕ; (give), hāă′wĭ.

grape, huăwăĭnă.

grasp, hŏ′pŭ, ′ă′pŏ, lālaŭ.

grass, măŭ′ŭ, wĕ′ŭwĕ′ŭ.

grasshopper, ′ūhĭ′nĭ.

grate, o′lŏ, ′ănăĭ.

grateful, hŏ′ŏmaĭka′ĭ; (pleasing), ′o′lŭ′o′lŭ.

grave, lu′ă kūpāpa′ŭ; (mound), hē; graveyard,
    ĭlĭ′nă: (serious), kŭo′ŏ.

gravity, kăŭmă′hă, kŏ′ĭkŏ′ĭ.

gravy, kăĭ.

gray, ′ahĭ′năhĭ′nă, hi′năhi′nă.

graze, (eat grass), ′ăĭ măŭ′ŭ; (touch lightly),
    hŏ′ŏpā′ ĭ′kĭ.

grease, aĭlă.

greasy, kĕ′lĕkĕ′lĕ.

great, nu′ĭ, nunu′ĭ; (eminent), hă′nŏhă′nŏ, kŏ′ĭ-kŏ′ĭ.

Greece, Greek, Hĕlĕ′nĕ.

greed, greedy, ′alŭ′nŭ, ′anŭ′nŭ.

green, (light), ′omä′ŏmă′ŏ; (dark), u′ĭu′lĭ; (un-ripe), mă′kă.

greet, alo′hă a′kŭ: greeting, (ke) alo′hă.

grief, kănĭŭhū′.

grieve, ŭwē′, kăŭmă′hă.

grin, hŏ′ŏkēkē i kā ni′hŏ.

grind, (sharpen), hŏ′ŏkă′lă; grind sugar-cane, wĭ′lĭ kŏ; (oppress), hŏ′ŏkăŭmă′hă.

grindstone, hoa′nă, hoa′nă kă′ă.

grip, pa′ă a pa′ă, ′ă′pŏ.

grit, (sand), (ke) o′neo′nĕ; (pluck), mană′ŏ kūpă′ă.

groan, ′ŭhū, nā.

groove, huăĭ: to groove, hu′lĕ.

gross, (twelve dozen), ′ŭmĭkŭmamalu′ă kakĭ′-nĭ: (bulky), nunu′ĭ; (uncleanly), kāpŭ′lŭ.

ground, lĕ′pŏ, honu′ă: to run aground, ĭ′lĭ.

group, po′ĕ, pač, pŭ′ŭ; (herd, bundle), pŭ′ă′; (cluster), huhu′ĭ; (of islands), paĕmo′kŭ; (of houses), kaŭhă′lĕ.

grouper, hāpŭ′ŭpŭ′ŭ.

grove, ulŭlā′ăŭ.

grow, u′lŭ, māhu′ăhu′ă; (become), lĭ′lŏ.

growl, nunu′lŭ; (grumble), na′mŭna′mŭ, ′ohŭ′-mŭ; (snarl), hŏ′ŏkēkē.

grudge, hŏ′ŏmăŭha′lă.

guarantee, hŏ′ŏhi′kĭ nŏ kā po′nŏ o kekă′hĭ meă.

guard, kiă′ĭ.

guardian, kă′hŭ.

guess, kŏ′hŏ wa′lĕ.

guest, mĕă i hŏ′ŏkĭpăĭ′ă, mălĭhĭ′nĭ, hoă′ăĭ.

guide, alăkă′ĭ: guide-post, kĭ′ă ku′hĭku′hĭ.

guilty, he′wă, ′ahĕwăĭ′ă.

guitar, kīkā′.

gulf, kăĭku′ŏ′nŏ.

gum, pīla′lĭ.

gun, pū kĭ; (cannon), pūkŭnĭa′hĭ.

gut, nā′ăŭ.

gutter, hāwăĭ, ăŭwā′hă.

H

habit, hă′nă mă′ă.

habitual, mă′ă măŭ.

hail, hu′ă hēki′lĭ.

hair, (on human scalp), (ke) o′hŏ, lăŭŏ′hŏ;
    (human body), hŭ′lŭhŭ′lŭ; (on beasts), hŭ′-
    lŭ; (beard), ′ŭ′mĭ′ŭ′mĭ; (fuzz), hĕ′ŭ.

hairless, ′ōlo′hĕ; (bald), ′ohu′lĕ; (beardless),
    hĕ′ŭ ′o′lĕ.

hairy, hŭ′lŭhŭ′lŭ.

half, hapălu′ă.

hall, hŏ′lŏ; (entrance), lānaĭ; meeting hall,
    keĕ′nă hălăwăĭ; hall of justice, keĕ′nă hŏ′ŏ-
    kŏ′lŏkŏ′lŏ.

halt, (stop), kū; (hesitate), hăpăku′ĕ.

ham, ′uhā′ pua′a, pua′a ha′mĕ.

hammer, hāma′lĕ.

hamza, kĭ′kŏ ′ŭ′ĭ′nă.

hand, lĭ′mă: to hand, hōmăĭ.

handicap, kūwa′lŏ, kū′alŏ.

handkerchief, hăĭnăkā′.

handle, (ke) ′ăŭ; kă′nŏ: to handle, lă′wĕlă′wĕ;
    (feel), hāhā.

handsome, nŏhĕă, măĭkă′ĭ, u′ĭ.

hang, (on gallows), lī; hang self, kă'ă'wĕ; hang up, kăŭ ĭlu'nă; hang out to dry, kăŭlă'ĭ; (be hung on cross), kăŭlĭ'ă.

happen, lŏ'ŏhi'ă, kūlĭ'ă, ulĭ'ă.

happy, happiness, hăŭ'o'lĭ.

harbor, (ke) ă'wă, ă'wă kū mo'kŭ: to harbor, hŏ'ŏkĭ'pă.

hard, (firm), pa'ă, pa'ăkikĭ'; (severe), 'o'olĕ'ă.

hardly, (not quite), 'āpŭ'ĕpŭ'ĕ 'ă'nĕ'ă'nĕ; (severely), 'o'olĕ'ă.

hardware, nā mĕă pa'ă.

hardy, ūăŭ'ă.

harm, pō'ĭ'nŏ; to harm, hŏ'ŏpĭlĭkĭ'ă.

harmony, (accord), lōka'hĭ; (music), nă'hĕnă'hĕ o kā le'ŏ.

harsh, (in manner), nĭ'hă; (in voice), kă'lăkă'lă.

harvest, wă 'o'hĭ: to harvest, 'o'hĭ.

haste, 'āwīwī, hikīwa'wĕ: (walk fast), aŭaŭ.

hasty, pūpuahŭ'lŭ, māmā.

hat, pāpa'lĕ.

hatch, (of ship), pu'kă: to hatch, kĭ'kŏ kă hu'ă, hŏ'ŏkĭ'kŏ.

hate, ĭnăĭnă, nĭ'nĭ.

haul, (pull), hŭ'kĭ; (drag), kăŭwō'.

haunt, wă'hĭ mă'ă măŭ: to haunt, (as a ghost), lă'pŭ.

have, (own), no Hawaiian term, but expressed by placing subject in possessive case; as an auxiliary, 'u'ă.

Hawaiian, Hāwaĭ'ĭ; Hawaiian individual, kamă'ăĭnă o Hāwaĭ'ĭ, kănă'kă maoli.

hawk, ĭŏ.

hay, măŭ'u malo'ŭ.

hazard, (golf), kĕ'ăkĕ'ă, lu'ă kŭ'mŭ păpăo'nĕ.

he, ĭă, o'ĭă.

head, (ke) pŏ'ŏ: to head, alăkă'ĭ; head off, ālăĭ.

headache, nālŭ'lŭ.

headquarters, kĭkŏwaĕnă.

heal, hō'ō'lă, lāpāăŭ.

health, (ke) o'lă kĭ'nŏ; o'lă po'nŏ.

heap, (ke) ahu'ă, pŭ'ŭ, paĭlă: to heap, hō'a'hŭ.

hear, lo'hĕ.

heart, (organ), pŭ'ŭwăĭ; (figurative), nă'ăŭ.

heat, wĕ'lă; great heat, ĕ'năĕ'nă, hahă'nă: to
     heat, hă'nă a wĕ'lă.

heathen, pēka'nă.

heaven, la'nĭ, (ke) āŏu'lĭ, lĕ'wă.

heavy, kăŭmă'hă, kŏ'ĭkŏ'ĭ.

heed, hŏ'ŏlo'hĕ, mālă'mă.

heel, kŭ'ĕkŭ'ĕ wāwaĕ.

height, kĭ'ĕkĭ'ĕ; grand mountain height, kĭ'lă-
     kĭ'lă.

heir, hŏ'ŏĭlĭ'nă.

hell, kehĕ'nă; (pit of fire), luăa'hĭ.

hello, hĕ'lŏ, ālo'hă.

helm, hoĕu'lĭ.

helmet, măhĭo'lĕ.

help, kōkŭ'ă.

helpless, nāwa'lĭwa'lĭ.

hem, lĕ'pă, pe'lŭ: to hem, hŭ'mŭ wĭ'lĭ.

hen, moă wăhi'nĕ.

hence, măĭ nĕĭ a'kŭ; (therefore), nolăĭlă, nŏ lă
     meă: henceforth, măĭ kē'ĭă wā a'kŭ.

herb, lăŭ nahe'lĕ; (edible), lă'ăŭĭkĭ'ăĭ, lăŭ
     nahe'lĕ 'ăĭ i'ă.

herd, pū'ā': to herd, hŏ'ŏpū'ā', hō'ā.

here, 'eĭă, ma'anĕ'ĭ, nĕĭ.

hereafter, māho'pĕ a'kŭ.

hermit, kănă'kă no'hŏ me'hăme'hă.

hero, kănă′kă 'ă′′ă nu′ĭ i nā pĭlĭkĭ′ă; kănă′kă
    koă; wiwo‘o′lĕ.

heron, bittern, aŭkŭ′ŭ.

herring, makĭa′wă.

hesitate, (waver), kānălŭ′ă, kūlă′nălă′nă;
    (stammer), ‘u‘ŭ′.

hew, (shape), kalăĭ; (fell), kŭ′ă.

hibiscus, a′lŏa′lŏ; (flower), pua′lŏa′lŏ.

hide, (skin), ‘ĭ′lĭ: (to secrete), hūnā′; hide self,
    pĕ‘ĕ.

hideous, pūpu′kă.

high, kĭ‘ĕkĭ‘ĕ.

highway, (ke) alănŭ′ĭ aŭpu′nĭ.

hike, he′lĕ wāwaĕ i kā lō′ă.

hill, pŭ′ŭ; (of potatoes), pŭ‘ĕ.

hinder, kō ho′pĕ: to hinder, kĕ‘ăkĕ′ă, hŏ‘ŏhā-
    kālĭ′ă.

hinge, ‘ă′mĭ.

hint, (remind), hŏ‘ŏhe′lĕ ‘ōle′lŏ; (for gain),
    hŏ‘ŏmaŏĕ.

hip, kĭkă′lă, păpăko′lĕ.

hire, (wages), u′kŭ hŏ‘ŏlĭ′mălĭ′mă: to hire,
    hŏ‘ŏlĭ′mălĭ′mă.

history, mŏ‘ole′lŏ.

historian, kūăŭhăŭ.

hit, (slap), pă‘ĭ; (punch), kŭ‘ĭ; (pommel), pa-
    lŭ′kŭ; (whip), hahaŭ: to be hit, pā, kū.

hitch, hikĭ‘ĭ; hitch along, nĕ‘ĕ.

hither, ĭă′ nĕ‘ĭ, i kĕ′ĭă wă′hĭ.

hive, pa′hŭ me′lĭ.

hoarse, leŏhā′; very hoarse, hanŏpi′lŏ.

hobby, hă′nă i mă′kĕmă′kĕ nu′ĭ ĭ′ă.

hoe, hō.

hog, pua‘a.

hoist, hŭ′kĭ ĭlu′nă.

hold, (grip), pa'ă; (claim), kŭleă'nă; (of ship), pu'kă: to hold, hŏ'ŏpă'ă, mālă'mă.

hole, pu'kă; (pit), lu'ă; (cave), (ke) ă'nă; (tear), năhaĕ.

holiday, lā nu'ĭ, kulāĭ'ă.

hollow, (depression), pŏ'hŏ, ho'nŏ: (in face), hŏ'mă; (empty), hă'kăhă'kă; hollow tree, pūhă', pūhŏ'.

holy, hĕmŏlĕ'lĕ, hŏ'ă'nŏ.

home, hŏ'mĕ, ha'lĕ, kaŭhă'lĕ.

homely, mūkŏ'kĭ.

honest, hŏ'ŏpo'nŏ.

honey, wăĭ me'lĭ, hŏ'nĕ.

honey-bee, nalŏme'lĭ.

honeycomb, waĭho'nă me'lĭ.

honor, 'ă'nŏ hŏ'ŏpo'nŏ: to honor, hŏ'ŏhă'nŏhă'-nŏ.

honorable, hă'nŏhă'nŏ.

hoof, māĭ'aŏ holŏhŏlo'nă, maĭ'ŭ'ŭ.

hook, loŭ, kīloŭ: fishhook, makăŭ.

hoop, (ke) a'pŏ.

hop, lelĕ'lĕ.

hope, mană'ŏlă'nă.

horizon, 'ălĭhĭla'nĭ, hālāwăĭ.

horizontal, 'ĭlĭwăĭ.

horn, (animal), kĭ'wĭ, hăŏ; (trumpet), pū pu'-hĭ.

horrible, wĕ'lĭwĕ'lĭ kā 'ĭ'nŏ.

horse, li'ŏ.

hose, (stockings), kakĭ'nĭ; water hose, 'ĭlĭwăĭ.

hospitable, mă'kămă'kă nu'ĭ, hŏ'ŏkĭ'pă.

hospital, haŭkăpi'lă, halĕmă'ĭ.

host, (crowd), pū'ă'lĭ; party-host, mă'kămă'-kă; inn-host, hă'kŭ ha'lĕ.

hostile, ĕnĕ'mĭ; (unfriendly), lŏkŏ'ĭ'nŏ.

hot, wĕ'lă; (feverish), 'ōwĕ'lăwĕ'lă; (close), ĭkĭĭ'kĭ.

hotel, hokĕ'lĕ; (inn), ha'lĕ hŏ'ŏkĭ'pă.

hour, ho'lă.

house, ha'lĕ; long house, halăŭ.

household, 'ohu'ă.

how, (?), peheă? (the way that), kē 'ă'nŏ e ... ăĭ.

however, akā' nă'ĕ, akā' ho'ĭ.

howl, kuwŏ'.

hub, pukŭ'ĭ.

huddle, pū'ŭ'lŭ'ŭ'lŭ, pukŭ'ĭ.

hug, pūlĭ'kĭ, a'pŏ: hug a shore, ho'lŏ pi'lĭ 'ăĭnă.

huge, nu'ĭ he'wăhe'wă.

hulk, mo'kŭ pōpŏ'pŏ.

hull, (of vessel), kĭ'nŏ o kā mo'kŭ.

hum, hămŭ'mŭ, hū: humming-top, hū.

human, kănă'kă, 'ă'nŏ kănă'kă.

humane, lokomāĭkă'ĭ.

humanity, kā'năkă.

humble, hă'ăhă'ă, ăkăhaĭ.

humid, kăwăŭ', ma'ū'; humid and hot, ĭkĭĭ'kĭ.

humiliate, hŏ'ŏhĭ'lăhĭ'lă.

humility, hă'ăhă'ă.

humor, (wit), hŏ'ōmăkē'ăkă: to humor, aĕ i kā mă'kĕmă'kĕ.

hunch, (premonition), halĭ'ă.

hunchback, kuăpŭ'ŭ.

hundred, hane'lĭ: hundredth, kā hane'lĭ.

hunger, pōlo'lĭ.

hunt, (chase), hahăĭ holŏhŏlo'nĭ · (search), 'ĭ'mĭ.

hurricane, maka'nĭ pūkikĭ', maka'nĭ nu'ĭ.

hurry, (haste), 'āwīwī, lǎ'lělǎ'lě; (urge), hǒ-
  'ǒkǐkǐ'nǎ.
hurt, 'ě'hǎ: to hurt, hō'ě'hǎ.
husband, ka'ně; ka'ně ma'lě.
hush, hamǎǔ; hush, as a child, hǒ'ǒnǎ'; (be
  quiet!), kǔ'lǐkǔ'lǐ!
hut, pūpǔ'pǔ ha'lě, kāmǎ'lǎ.
hymn, hīme'nǐ.
hypocrite, hǒ'ǒkǎmǎ'nǐ.

I, aǔ, wǎǔ.
ice, hǎǔ.
ice-cream, hǎǔkalǐ'mǎ, aǐkalǐ'mǎ.
idea, manǎ'ǒ.
ideal, ā'nǎ hǒ'ǒkō' po'nǒ.
identify, hō'ō'lǎ 'ǐkěmǎ'kǎ.
identity, 'ō'lǎ nō.
idiot, lōlō, hūpō.
idle, no'hǒ wa'lě; (at ease), nǎneǎ.
idol, (ke) akǔ'ǎ kǐ'ǐ.
if, ǐnǎ'.
ignorant, nǎ'ǎǔpō, 'ǐ'kě 'o'lě.
ignore, nānā 'o'lě.
ill, mǎ'ǐ, 'ōmǎ'ǐmǎ'ǐ.
illegal, kū 'o'lě i kē kānǎwǎǐ.
illegitimate, māwa'hǒ o kē kānǎwǎǐ, mǎnǔ-
  a'hǐ.
illustrate, (with pictures), hǒ'ǒnǎ'nǐ mē nǎ kǐ'ǐ;
  (exemplify), hǒ'ǒhālǐ'kělǐ'kě manǎ'ǒ.
image, (statue), kǐ'ǐ kalǎǐǐ'ǎ; (reflection), (ke)
  a'kǎ; (likeness), lǐ'kě.
imagine, manǎ'ǒ kǒ'hǒ wa'lě.
imitate, hǒ'ǒmahǔ'ǐ, hǒ'ǒma'ǎǔe'.
imitation, hǒ'ǒhālǐ'kě.

immediate, kŏ′kĕ: immediately, ānō′, hākalĭ′ă ‘o′lĕ.

immense, nu′ĭ pale′nă ‘o′lĕ, hi′kĭ ‘o′lĕ kē ănăĭ′ă.

immoral, he′wă haŭmi′ă, kūpo′nŏ ‘o′lĕ.

immortal, o′lă măŭ, mă′kĕ ‘o′lĕ.

impatient, păŭa′hŏ wa′lĕ, āhŏnu′ĭ ‘o′lĕ.

imperfect, kīnā′, he′măhe′mă.

impiety, ‘ăĭā′, hŏ′ŏmalŏ′kă.

implement, meă hŏ′ŏhă′nă.

implore, noĭ hă′ăhă′ă.

imply, kăŏnă.

import, (meaning), kăŏnă: to import, hŏ‘ŏkŏ′-mŏ ukă′nă i kā ‘aina: imports, ukă′nă hŏ-‘ŏkŏmŏĭ′ă.

importance, ‘ă′nŏ nu′ĭ.

impose, (lay on), kăŭ; (deceive), ‘ĕ′pă, hă′nă ‘āpĭ′kĭ.

impossible, hi′kĭ ‘o′lĕ.

impression, (mental), kū i kā mană′ŏ; (printing), pă‘ĭ ă′nă.

imprison, hŏ‘ŏpă′ăhaŏ.

improper, kūpo′nŏ ‘o′lĕ, kŏ′hŭ ‘o′lĕ.

improve, holŏmu′ă, hŏ‘oĭ a‘ĕ kā măĭkă‘ĭ.

impudent, hŏ‘ŏkă′nŏ, maha‘ŏĭ.

impulse, mană‘ŏ u′lŭ wa′lĕ.

in, i, mă, mālo‘kŏ, ĭlo′kŏ.

inability, hi′kĭ ‘o′lĕ.

inaugurate, hŏ‘ŏkŭ′mŭ.

incentive, kŭ′mŭ hŏ‘ŏlă′lĕlă′lĕ.

inch, inĭ′hă.

incident, meă e pi′lĭ ă′nă, meă hi′kĭ wa′lĕ măĭ.

incline, lă′pă: to incline, (lean), hĭŏ′; (be disposed), no‘ŏno‘ŏ a‘ĕ.

inclose, (surround), hŏ‘ŏpŭ′nĭ; (put in), hŏ-‘ŏkŏ′mŏ.

include, hŏ'ŏhŭ'ĭ pū; (inclose), hŏ'ŏkŏ'mŏ pū.

income, nā lōa'a.

inconsistent, kūlĭ'kĕ 'o'lĕ.

inconvenience, meă hŏ'ŏpĭlĭkĭ'ă.

incorrect, kuhĭhe'wă, pololeĭ 'o'lĕ.

increase, hŏ'ŏmāhŭ'ăhŭ'ă, hŏ'ŏnu'ĭ a'ĕ.

incur, lŏ'ŏhi'ă.

indeed, pēlā' ĭ'ŏ, pēlā' nŏ.

indefinite, maopŏ'pŏ 'o'lĕ.

independent, kūoko'ă.

index, pă'pă ku'hĭku'hĭ.

India, Inĭ'ă.

indicate, ku'hĭku'hĭ, hŏ'ĭ'ke.

indifference, pălă'kă, nānā 'o'lĕ.

indignant, u'kĭu'kĭ, hūhū'.

individual, meă, meă hŏ'ŏkă'hĭ; (single), pā-
    ka'hĭ.

induce, hŏ'ŏkō'nŏkō'nŏ.

indulge, hŏ'ŏ'lŭ'ŏ'lŭ, hŏ'ŏkō' wa'lĕ i kā mă'kĕ-
    mă'kĕ.

industry, (diligence), hŏ'ŏikăĭkă, hă'nă măŭ;
    (branch of work or trade), 'oĭhă'nă hănă-
    li'mă.

inevitable, hi'kĭ 'o'le kē 'ă'lŏ.

inexperienced, hāwăwă'.

infant, pēpē.

infantry, pū'ă'lĭ koă he'lĕ wăwaĕ.

infection, mă'ĭ lĕ'lĕ, 'ĕ'hă 'a'ăĭ.

inferior, hă'ăhă'ă ĭ'hŏ.

infirm, nāwa'lĭwa'lĭ, pă'lŭpă lŭ.

inflame, ho'ā'.

inflammation, ūpĕ'hŭpĕ'hŭ.

inflate, hŏ'ŏpĭ'hă i kā maka'nĭ.

inflation, hŏ'ŏnu'ĭ ĭ'ă.

inflict, kăŭ a'kŭ, hŏ'ŏĭ'lĭ mālu'nă.

infliction, hŏ‘ŏpā‘ĭ.

influence, mă'nă hŏ‘ŏhŭ'lĭ.

influenza, falū'.

inform, (tell), hă'ĭ; (instruct), hŏ‘ŏna‘ăŭaŏ a'kŭ.

informal, lăŭnă ‘o'lŭ‘o'lŭ.

information, lōa‘a măĭ kā hŏ‘ĭ'kĕ, ‘ĭ'kĕ; (news), nŭhoŭ.

inhabit, no'hŏ.

inhabitants, po‘ĕ no'hŏ.

inheritance, hŏ‘ŏĭlĭ'nă.

initial, mu'ă: initial letter, hu'ă mu'ă.

initiate, hŏ‘ŏkŭ'mŭ.

initiation, kŏ'mŏ mu'ă ă'nă.

injunction, ‘ōle'lŏ pāpā, ‘ōle'lŏ ā'ŏ.

injure, hŏ‘ĕ'hă, hŏ‘ŏpo'ĭ'nŏ.

injury, ‘ĕ'hă, pŏ'ĭ'nŏ.

injustice, hă'nă pa‘e'wă‘e'wă, pololeĭ ‘o'le.

ink, inĭ'kă.

inland, māu'kă, ĭu'kă.

inn, ha'lĕ hŏ‘ŏkĭ'pă.

innocent, ha'lă ‘o'lĕ.

innumerable, le'hŭle'hŭ.

inquire, (ask), ninaŭ; (seek), ‘ĭ'mĭ.

insane, pūpu'lĕ.

insect, hŏlōhŏlo'nă lĭ'ĭlĭ'ĭ, mū; (no generic term).

insert, hŏ‘ŏkŏ'mŏ.

inside, ĭlo'kŏ, mālo'kŏ.

insinuate, hŏ‘ŏkŏ'mŏ; (imply), ‘ōle'lŏ mă‘ăleă.

insipid, hŭkăkăĭ, manana'lŏ.

insist, kŏĭ ĭkăĭkă.

inspect, nānā i ‘ĭ'kĕ pŏ'nŏ.

inspire, (inhale), hă'nŭ; (infuse), hŏ‘ŏŭ'lŭ; to be inspired, u'lŭ.

install, hŏʻŏkŏ'mŏ.

installment, māhe'lĕ, u'kŭ lĭʻĭlĭ'ĭ.

instance, meă hŏʻŏhālĭ'kĕ; for instance, e lă'ă mē kē'ĭă.

instant, mănā'wă poko'lĕ lŏ'ă: instantly, ănŏ', ʻĕmŏʻŏlĕ.

instead, mā kă'hĭ o kekă'hĭ meă.

instinct, noʻŏnoʻŏ u'lŭ wa'lĕ, ʻoŭlĭ kŭ'mŭ.

institute, hŏʻŏkŭ'mŭ, hŏʻŏmā'kă.

institution, meă i hŏʻŏkŭmŭĭ'ă.

instruct, ā'ŏ, hŏʻŏnā'ăŭaŏ.

instrument, meă paʻăha'nă; (musical), meă hŏʻŏkă'nĭ.

insult, hōʻĭ'nŏ wa'lĕ.

insure, ĭnĭku'ă, pānă'ĭ kālā.

integrity, ʻă'nŏ hŏʻŏpo'nŏ.

intellect, noʻŏnoʻŏ.

intelligence, nā'ăŭaŏ, ʻĭ'kĕ.

intend, intention, mană'ŏ e hŏʻŏkŏĭ'ă.

intercede, ŭwaŏ.

intercourse, lāŭnă ă'nă.

interest, (payment), u'kŭ panĕ'ĕ; (stake), kŭleă'nă: to interest, hōʻa'lă i kā mană'ŏ.

interesting, năne'ă, hŏʻŏnănĕ'ă.

interfere, kŏ'mŏ mawaĕnă, ʻăkĕʻăkĕ'ă.

interior, internal, kūlo'kŏ.

intermediate, māwaĕnă.

international, māwaĕnă o nā aŭpu'nĭ.

interpret, unu'hĭ, māhe'lĕ ʻōle'lŏ, hōʻĭ'kĕ ʻă'nŏ.

interrupt, (conversation), kăhămă'hă; (work), hŏʻŏpĭlĭkĭ'ă wa'lĕ.

interval, wā, kōwā' māwaĕnă.

intervene, kŏ'mŏ māwaĕnă.

interview, kūkă'ĭ kămă'ĭlĭ'ŏ, ninaninaŭ.

intestines, nā'ăŭ.

intimate, pi'lĭ lō'a: to intimate, hō'ĭ'kĕ, hŏ-
'ŏhe'lĕ 'ōle'lŏ.

into, ĭlo'kŏ.

intoxicate, intoxication, 'o'nă.

introduce, (bring in), hŏ'ŏkŏ'mŏ, hŏ'ŏlă'hă
mu'ă; (acquaint), hŏ'ŏlaŭnă.

intrude, kŏ'mŏ wa'lĕ, kŏ'mŏ he'wă.

invade, kŏ'mŏ kăŭă.

invalid, meă nāwa'lĭwa'lĭ, meă 'ōmă'ĭmă'ĭ:
(not valid), mă'nă 'o'lĕ, wăĭwăĭ 'o'lĕ.

invent, 'ĭ'mĭ i nă meă i 'oĭ a'ĕ; no'ŏno'ŏ a
hă'nă.

invention, hă'nă hoŭ.

invest, hŏ'ŏmoĕ kālā, hŏ'ŏpŭ'kăpŭ'kă; (surround), hŏ'ŏpŭ'nĭ; (in office), hŏ'ŏno'hŏ
'oĭhă'nă.

investigate, noĭ'ĭ, ninanĭnaŭ.

invisible, 'ĭ'kĕ mă'kă 'o'lĕ ĭ'ă.

invite, invitation, kō'nŏ.

involve, (entangle), hĭhĭ'ă; (implicate), hŏ-
'ahe'wă.

Ireland, Eire, Ilĕla'nĭ.

iron, hăŏ; flat-iron, ăĭă'nă.

irrigate, hŏ'ŏkă'hĕ.

irritable, hūhū' kŏ'kĕ.

irritate, (vex), hò'ŏnaŭ'kĭŭ'kĭ; (as a wound),
hŏ'ŏpĕ'hŭ.

irritation, u'kĭu'kĭ, hŏ'ŏpĕ'hŭ ă'nă.

island, mokupu'nĭ, mo'kŭ.

issue, (progeny), ke'ĭkĭ ponŏĭ'; (result), hopĕ'nă: (to emerge), pu'kă; (publish), hŏ'ŏ-
pu'kă.

isthmus, pū'ă'lĭ.

it, ĭă, o'ĭă: itself, ĭă meă ĭ'hŏ.

Italy, Ikalĭ'ă.

itch, kakī'ŏ, mě'ĕaŭ: to itch, mane'ŏ.

item, itā'mŭ.

ivory, păla'oă, nihŏpăla'ŏă.

J

jail, halĕpă'ăhaŏ.

jam, (conserve), kě'lě; (difficulty), kūpĭlĭkī'ĭ
ă'nă: (to crush), hŏ'ŏpē'pē'; (to crowd),
hŏ'ŏkē'.

janitor, kănă'kă mălă'mă ha'lě.

January, Ianŭa'lĭ.

Japan, Iapa'nă. Japanese, Kěpănĭ'.

jar, (container), ĭ'pŭ; (shock), nāuĕuĕ: (to
clash), hŏ'ŏkŭ'ĭ.

jaw, (ke) ā: to jaw, hŏ'ŏpă'ăpă'ă.

jealous, lĭ'lĭ.

Jehovah, Iĕho'vă.

jerk, hō'ănŭ'ŭ.

Jesus, Ie'sū.

Jew, Jewish, Iukaĭŏ.

jewel, pōha'kŭ măkămăĕ, mŏ'mĭ.

job, (work), hă'nă; (contract), u'kŭ păŭ.

join, (assemble), hŭ'ĭ; (connect), hŏ'ŏkŭ'ĭ.

joint, hŏ'ŏku'ĭ'nă; (of limb), 'ă'mĭ; (of cane),
pu'nă, po'nă.

joke, hŏ'ŏmăkě'ă'kă.

jolly, hoĭhoĭ.

journal, mŏ'ole'lŏ kakăŭ.

journey, kă'ăhě'lě.

joy, hăŭ'o'lĭ, 'o'li'o'lĭ.

judge, lu'nă nănă; (legal), lunăkānāwăĭ: to
judge, hŏ'ŏkŏ'lŏkŏ'lŏ, hŏ'ŏho'lŏ i kā po'nŏ.

juice, wăĭ.

July, Iulaĭ.

jump, lě'lě, lēheĭ, lēkeĭ; (hop, frisk), lelě'lě.

June. Iu'ně.

junior, (second of name), opī'ŏ; (younger), opī'ŏ ī'hŏ.

jury. kiu'lě.

just, (impartial), kăŭlī'kě; (upright), hŏ'ŏpo'nŏ: (barely), 'ănĕ'ănĕ.

justice, kăŭlī'kě.

justify, hŏ'apo'nŏ.

K

keel, ĭwĭkă'ě'lě.

keen, (sharp), 'oĭ; (clever), ăkămăĭ, no'ĕaŭ.

keep, (preserve), mălă'mă; keep on, hŏ'ŏmăŭ; (restrain), kao'hī.

kerosene, aĭlă ma'hŭ, aĭlă honu'ă.

kettle, ī'pŭ hăŏ.

key, door-key, kī; (in music), le'ŏ kŭ'mŭ.

kick, pě'kŭ.

kid, kăŏ ke'ĭkĭ.

kidnap, kă'ĭ'lĭ kănă'kă.

kidney, pŭ'ŭpă'ă.

kill, pēpe'hĭ, pēpe'hĭ a mă'kě, hŏ'ŏmă'kě.

kind, (sort), (ke) 'ā'nŏ: (gentle), lokomăĭkă'Ľ

kindle, ho'ā', kŭ'nī.

kindling. pŭ'lŭpŭ'lŭ, ho'āā'.

king. mōī', ălĭ'ĭ.

kingdom, (ke) aŭpu'nĭ ălĭ'ĭ.

kiss, ho'nĭ.

kitchen, lŭ'mĭ kū'kě.

kite, lŭ'pě.

knapsack, 'ě'kě hăă'wě.

knee, ku'lĭ.

kneel, kūkŭ'lĭ.

knife, pă'hĭ.

knit, kă.

knob, pōhe'ŏhe'ŏ.

knock, (on door), kīkēkē; (on head), kīko'nǐ;
(punch), kǔ'ǐ; knock down, kūlǎ'ǐ: knocked-
out, pǎŭ kā 'ǐ'kě.

knot, hipǔ'ǔ; to knot, hikǐ'ǐ, nakǐ'ǐ, mukǐ'ǐ.

know, 'ǐ'kě.

knowledge, 'ǐ'kě, nā'ǎŭaŏ.

knuckle, pǔ'ǔpǔ'ǔli'mǎ.

Korea, Korean, Kōleǎ.

L

labor, (work), hǎ'nǎ, hǎnǎli'mǎ; (toil), lu'hǐ;
(travail), nǎ'hǔnǎ'hǔ.

lace, lǐ'hǐlǐ'hǐ; shoe-lace, li kamǎ'ǎ: to lace, li.

lack, ne'lě, he'mǎhę'mǎ.

lad, ke'ǐkǐ, keǐkǐka'ně.

ladder, (ke) alǎpǐ'ǐ; step-ladder, (ke) alǎhǎ'kǎ.

lady, le'kě, wǎhi'ně mǎǐkǎ'ǐ.

lake, mōanǎwǎǐ, lŏkŏwǎǐ.

lamb, hi'pǎ ke'ǐkǐ; (biblical), keǐkǐhi'pǎ.

lame, 'ō'ŏ'pǎ.

lamp, kūku'ǐ, ǐ'pǔ kūku'ǐ.

land, 'ǎǐnǎ: to land, paě, lě'lě ǐu'kǎ.

landlord, (innkeeper), hǎ'kǔ halěkǐ'pǎ; (landowner), hǎkǔ'ǎǐnǎ.

landscape, hǐ'ŏhǐ'ŏ'nǎ 'ǎǐnǎ.

lane, (ke) alǎnǔ'ǐ, alǎnǔ'ǐ 'olŏlǐ'.

language, 'ōle'lŏ; (foreign), nǎ'mǔ.

lantern, kūku'ǐ he'lě pō.

lap, 'uhā: to lap up, pǎ'lǔ.

large, nu'ǐ, nunu'ǐ; (extensive), āke'ǎ.

lash, kǎǔlǎ hi'lǐ: (to whip), 'ǔhaǔ; (to tie),
hǎǔho'ǎ: lashings. (of canoe), 'ǎhǎ lǎ'nǎ-
lǎ'nǎ.

lasso, kǎǔlǎ'ǐ'lǐ: to lasso, hŏ'ŏhěǐ.

last, ho′pĕ lō′ă: to last, măŭ.

late, (tardy), lo′hĭ, lōlo′hĭ, ho′pĕ; (recent), ĭ′hŏ
    nĕĭ.

latitude, lākĭkū′.

latter, ho′pĕ a‘ĕ, ho′pĕ ĭ′hŏ.

laugh, laughter, ‘ăkă‘ăkă.

launch, (boat) wă‘ăpā′ ma′hŭ: to launch, hŏ‘ŏ-
    lā′nă.

lava, lua‘ĭpĕ′lĕ; sheet lava, pahoĕhoĕ; clinker
    lava, (ke) ‘ă′ă′; (pumice), pōha′kŭ ŏa′hĭ,
    ‘ă′nă.

lavatory, wă′hĭ holoĭ; (latrine), wă′hĭ hŏ‘ŏpăŭ-
    pilikĭ′ă.

law, kānāwăĭ.

lawn, pāmăŭ‘ŭ.

lawyer, lō′ĭŏ.

lay, waĭhŏ; (as eggs), hănaŭ; (as bricks), hŏ-
    ‘ŏmoĕ.

layer, kūlă′nă.

lazy, molowā′, pălaŭalĕ′lŏ.

lead, (metal), kepăŭ: to lead, leader, (ke) ălă-
    kă′ĭ.

leaf, lăŭ; cane-leaf, lā‘ō; ti-leaf, lā‘ĭ.

league, kŭ‘ĭka′hĭ; (three miles), ĕko′lŭ mi′lĕ.

leak, (roof), kŭ′lŭ; (ship), li′ŭ.

lean, (thin), wīwī, ‘olă′lă: to lean over, hiŏ; to
    lean upon, hilĭnă‘ĭ.

leap, lēheĭ, lĕ′lĕ.

learn, ā‘ŏ, ‘ĭmĭ nā‘ăŭăŏ.

learning, nā‘ăŭăŏ.

lease, hŏ‘ŏlĭ′mălĭ′mă.

least, ‘u‘u′kŭ lō′ă, meă ĭ′kĭ.

leather, ‘ĭlĭ, ‘ĭlĭ hŏ‘ŏlŭ‘ŭĭ′ă.

leave, (let alone), waĭhŏ; (depart), hă‘ălĕ′lĕ;
    (will), hŏ‘ŏĭ′lĭ.

lecture, hă'ĭa'ŏ, hă'ĭ'ōle'lŏ.

ledge, niăŏ, (ke) 'ānŭ'ŭ.

lee, 'ăŏ'ăŏ māla'lŏ.

leeward, māla'lŏ.

left, he'mă.

leg, wāwaĕ.

legend, ka'aŏ.

leggings, lĭki'nĭ, pa'lĕ wāwaĕ.

legion, lēkeŏ'nă, le'hŭle'hŭ.

legislature, 'ăhă'ōle'lŏ, 'ăhă'ōle'lŏ kăŭkānāwăĭ.

legitimate. (legal), kū i kē kānāwăĭ; (admissi-
    ble), 'āponŏĭ'ă.

leisure. lua'nă, năne'ă.

lemon, lĕ'mĭ.

lemonade, wăĭ lĕ'mĭ.

lend, hăă'wĭ lĭ'lŏ 'o'lĕ.

length, lō'ĭ'hĭ, lō'ă.

leper, lēpĕ'lă.

leprosy, mă'ĭ pākē, mă'ĭ lēpĕ'lă, mă'ĭ hŏ'ŏkă'ă-
    wa'lĕ.

less, e'mĭ ĭ'hŏ.

lesson, hăăwi'nă, 'ōlelŏă'ŏ.

lest, o, i 'o'lĕ.

let, (permit), aĕ; (lease), hŏ'ŏlĭ'mălĭ'mă; (with
    imperative), e, i, o, ĭnă'.

letter, (missive), lĕ'kă; (character), hu'ă pă'-
    lăpă'lă.

level, 'ĭlĭwăĭ.

lever, ŭ'nĕ, lōhăĭ.

liability, kū.

liable, kū: to be liable, i'lĭ.

liar, meă wahăhĕ'ĕ, pe'lŏ.

liberal, manawăle'ă.

liberate, hŏ'ŏkŭ'ŭ.

liberty, (freedom), kūoko'ă; (release), hŏ'ŏkŭ'ŭ ä'nă; (permission), aĕ.

library, waĭho'nă pu'kĕ.

license, laĭkĭ'nĭ.

lick, pä'lŭ.

lid, (ke) po'ĭ, (ke) pă'nĭ: eyelid, po'ĭ mä'kă.

lie, (falsify), hŏ'ŏpŭ'nĭpŭ'nĭ, wahähĕ'ĕ, pe'lŏ; (recline), moĕ; lie off and on, kālĕ'wă; lie to, pŏhŏlu'ă.

lieutenant, lŭkāne'lă.

life, (ke) o'lă.

lift, häpăĭ.

light, mală'mă, mālă'mălă'mă; daylight, ăŏ: (not heavy), māmā; (slight), ĭ'kĭ; light-minded, pu'nĭ lĕ'ălĕ'ă: to light, (kindle), ho'ă, kŭ'nĭ; (illuminate), hŏ'ŏmălă'mălă'mă.

lighthouse, ha'lĕ ĭpŭkŭkŭ'ĭ.

lightning, üwi'lă.

like, lĭ'kĕ, (ke) 'a'nŏ: to like, (be fond of), pu'nĭ; (wish), mä'kĕmä'kĕ: (so), pē; like this, pēneĭ; like that, pē'ĭă.

likely, (probably), pa'hă; (suitable), kŭpo'nŏ.

likeness, kŏ'hŭ lĭ'kĕ; (photograph), kĭ'ĭ.

likewise, nŏhŏ'ĭ, pēlā' hŏ'ĭ.

lily, lĭlĭ'ă.

limb, lălă.

lime, (calcium), pu'nă; (fruit), hu'ă lĕ'mĭ.

limit, pale'nă: to limit, kăŭpale'nă.

limp, 'o'i.

limpet, 'opi'hĭ.

line, (rope), kăŭlă; fish-line, (ke) a'hŏ; (row), lăla'nĭ; line drawn, kă'hă; (Equator), Pō-'ăĭwăĕnă-honu'ă.

linen, lĭlĭ'nă.

link, meă hŏ'ŏkŭ'ĭ; (of chain), păŭkŭ' kăŭlă hăŏ: to link, hŏ'ŏhŭ'ĭ, hŏ'ŏkŭ'ĭ pŭ.

lion, liō'nă.

lip, lĕ'hĕlĕ'hĕ; (edge), kă'ĕ.

liquid, wăĭ, hĕhĕ'ĕ.

liquor, wăĭ 'o'nă.

list, păpăhĕ'lŭ, pă'pă hō'ĭ'kĕ: to list, kakăŭ
ĭnŏă.

listen, hŏ'ŏlo'hĕ.

literally, pĭ'lĭ lō'ă i kā huă'ōle'lŏ.

literary, hŭ'lĭ pu'kĕ.

literature, nā pă'lăpă'lă.

litter, 'ōpă'lă; (stretcher), mănĕ'lĕ: to litter,
hŏ'ŏmokākĭ'.

little, lĭ'ĭlĭ'ĭ, ĭ'kĭ, 'u'u'kŭ.

live, (exist), o'lă; (dwell), no'hŏ.

livelihood, 'oĭhă'na.

lively, 'ĕle'ŭ.

liver, (ke) a'kĕ.

lizard, mŏ'ŏ.

load, hăă'wĕ; ukă'nă: to load, (as freight),
hŏ'ŏū'kă; (as a gun), hŏ'ŏpĭ'hă.

loaf, (bread), 'o'mŏ'o'mŏ pala'oă, pōpō pala'ŏă:
to loaf, hŏ'ŏnăneă, hŏ'ŏhalămănă'wă.

loan, meă i hăăwĭĭ'ă nō kā mănā'wă; (money
borrowed), kālā hō'ăĭ'ē'.

loathe, hŏ'ŏpăĭlŭ'ă.

lobby, hă'nă hŏ'ŏpāĭpăĭ: to lobby, păĭpăĭ.

lobster, (crayfish), u'lă, u'lă papă'pă.

local, kūlo'kŏ.

locality, kăŭwă'hĭ.

locate, (place), hŏ'ŏno'hŏ; (find), lōa'a.

location, wă'hĭ, kăhu'ă.

lock, (of door), la'kă; (as of hair), 'ōwĭ'lĭ: to
lock, kĭ: lock-up, halĕpă'ăhaŏ, halĕwăĭ.

lodge, (secret order), hŭ'ĭ malū': to lodge, no'-
hŏ ĭ'kĭ; (as a complaint), waĭhŏ.

lodgings, wǎ′hǐ no′hǒ.

log, pǎŭkū′ kǔmŭlā′ǎŭ.

loiter, mǐlǐ′ǎ′pǎ, lōlo′hǐ, kǎkǎ′lǐ.

London, Lakǎ′nǎ.

lone, lonely, me′hǎme′hǎ.

long, lō′ǎ, lōlō′ǎ; lō′ǐ′hǐ: to long for, 'Ǐ′Ǐ′nǐ.

longitude, lōnikū′.

look, nānā; look for, 'Ǐ′mǐ, hǔ′lǐ; look out
   for, mǎkǎa′lǎ, hāki′lǒ.

looking-glass, (ke) a′nǐa′nǐ nānā, a′nǐa′nǐ ki-
   lǒ′hǐ.

lookout, (place), wǎ′hǐ kiǎ′ǐ, wǎ′hǐ nānā;
   (structure), 'ālǒ′ǒ.

loop, kīpǔ′kǎ.

loose, (slack), 'ǎ′lǔ′ǎ′lǔ; (free), he′mǒ; (prodigal), 'u′hǎ'u′hǎ.

lord, hǎ′kǔ.

lose, (financially), pohō′; (as a race), ha'u′lě;
   (be lost), nalǒwa′lě, lǐ′lǒ.

lot, (quantity), nu′ǐ; (share), māhe′lě; house-
   lot, pā ha′lě; (destiny), hāāwi′nǎ.

lottery, pilǐwǎǐwǎǐ.

loud, kǎ′nǐ nu′ǐ; (voice), nu′ǐ kā le′ǒ.

loud-speaker, hǒ′ǒnu′ǐ le′ǒ.

louse, 'ǔ′kǔ; head-louse, 'ǔ′kǔ pǒ′ǒ.

love, (ke) alo′hǎ; to make love, hǒ′ǒǐ′pǒǐ′pǒ;
   (hold dear), hǒ′ǒālo′hǎlo′hǎ.

lovely, nǒhěǎ, onao′na.

lover, ǐ′pǒ.

low, (not high), hǎ′ǎhǎ′ǎ; (cheap), mǎkěpo′nǒ,
   e′mǐ; (meek), ākǎhaǐ; (feeble), pǎ′lǔpǎ′lǔ;
   (vulgar), pě′lǎpě′lǎ.

lower, (below), māla′lǒ ǐ′hǒ: (let down), kǔ′ǔ,
   hō′ǎlǔ′ǎlǔ.

lowland, honu′ǎ, ku′lǎ.

loyal, loyalty, kūpă'ă.

lubricate, hŏ'ŏpāhĕ'ĕ.

luck, lucky, lă'kĭ, pŏmaïka'ĭ.

luggage, ukă'nă, ukă'nă pilĭkĭ'nŏ.

lull, (to soothe), hŏ'ŏnā'; (abate), māli'ĕ;
    (calm), ho'omāli'ĕli'ĕ.

lumber, pă'pă lā'ăŭ.

lump, pŭ'ŭ.

lumpy, pŭ'ŭpŭ'ŭ, hă'kŭhă'kŭ.

lunatic, pūpu'lĕ.

lunch, 'ăĭnă āwakĕă, pa'ĭnă āwakĕă.

lung, (ke) akĕmāmā.

lure, hŏ'ŏwălĕwă'lĕ, hŏ'ŏhālu'ă.

lurk, hŏ'ŏmākākĭ'ŭ, pĕ'ĕ.

lust, măkăle'hŏ, kŭ'kŏ.

luxury, la'kŏ lo'ă.

M

machine, mīkĭ'nĭ.

mackerel, mackerel scad, 'ope'lŭ.

mad, pūpu'lĕ, hehe'nă; (angry), hūhū' lŏ'ă;
    (infatuated), hŏ'ŏhĭ'hĭ 'ĭ'nŏ.

magazine, (periodical), pu'kĕ he'lŭhe'lŭ; pow-
    der-magazine, waĭho'nă păŭkă.

maggot, ĭ'lŏ.

magic, hŏ'ŏkă'lă kupu'ă; (sorcery), 'ană'ănă'.

magistrate, lu'nă kānāwăĭ.

magnet, magneto, mākēnĕ'kĭ.

magnificent, nă'nĭ lŏ'ă.

magnify, hŏ'ŏnu'ĭ, hŏ'ŏmāhŭ'ăhŭ'ă; (exalt),
    hŏ'ŏnă'nĭ, hŏ'ŏlĕ'ă.

maid, (servant), kăŭwāwăhi'nĕ; (girl), wă-
    hi'nĕ opĭ'ŏ.

mail, 'ĕ'kĕ lĕ'kă.

main, (ke) 'ă'nŏ nu'ĭ.

mainland, **'ăĭnă makuʻă.**

maintain, (support), **hŏʻŏlăʻkŏ**; (affirm), **hŏ-ʻōʻĭă**; (continue), **hŏʻŏmăŭ.**

majesty, **ʻĬʻhĭʻĬʻhĭ, mōĭʻ.**

major, (officer), **mekĭʻă**; (greater), **haʻpă nuʻĬ.**

make, (do), **hăʻnă**; (build), **kūkuʻlŭ**; (compel), **kŏĭ**; (earn), **lōăʻă**; make known, **hŏʻŏlăʻhă**; make good (a promise), **hŏʻŏkōʻ**; make good (a loss), **hoʻĭhoʻĭ**; make light of, **manăʻŏ ʻoʻlĕ**; make much of, **manăʻŏ nuʻĭ**; make out (understand), **hŏʻŏmaŏpŏʻpŏ, akăʻka**; make out (accomplish), **kō**; make over, **hŏʻŏlĭʻlŏ**; make up (reconcile), **hŏ-ʻŏlăŭlĕʻă**; make-up (adorn), **peʻnă, hŏʻŏu-ʻĭuʻĭ**; make water (leak), **liʻŭ**; (urinate), **mĭʻmĭ.**

male, **kaʻnĕ**; (breeder), **kĕʻă.**

malice, **manăʻŏ ʻĬʻnŏ, ʻŏpūkoʻpĕkoʻpĕ.**

man, **kănăʻkă, kaʻnĕ**; mankind, men, **kăʻnăkă.**

manage, **hŏʻŏpoʻnŏpoʻnŏ.**

manager, **lūʻnă hŏʻŏpoʻnŏpoʻnŏ**; (plantation), **haʻkŭ.**

mango, **manăkōʻ.**

manifest, (of ship), **pĕʻpă hōʻĬʻkĕ ukăʻnă**: (evident), **moakăʻkă, akăkalĕʻă**: to manifest, **hōʻĬʻkĕ.**

manner, (ke) **ʻăʻnŏ**: manners, **ʻăʻnŏ lăŭnă.**

manual, (book), **puʻkĕ laʻwĕ lĭʻmă**: (of the hands), **lĭʻmă.**

manufacture, **hăʻnă.**

manuscript, **păʻlăpăʻlă.**

many, **leʻhŭleʻhŭ, nuʻĭ waʻlĕ.**

map, **păʻlăpăʻlă ʻăĭnă.**

mar, **hŏʻŏkĭnăʻ.**

marble, pōha'kŭ māpǎ'lǎ: marbles, kǐ'nǐkǐ'nǐ, māpǎ'lǎ.

march, (month), Mala'kǐ: to march, kǎ'ǐ, paǐkaŭ.

margin, kǎ'ĕ, lǐ'hǐ; stock margin, kōwā'.

marine, (soldier), koǎ manŭwā'; (navy), nǎ mo'kŭ: (of the sea), o kē kǎǐ.

mariner, lui'nǎ.

mark, kǎ'hǎ, hō'ǎǐlō'nǎ: (distinction), kǎŭlǎ'nǎ.

market, mākĕ'kĕ, 'oǐhǎ'nǎ kālĕ'pǎ.

Marquesas Islands, Nŭ'ŭhi'wǎ.

marry, ma'lĕ, hō'ǎŏ.

marshal, ǐlamŭ'kŭ, ǎlǐhǐkǎŭǎ nu'ǐ, (ke) alǎkǎ'ǐ.

marvelous, kupǎiǎna'hǎ.

mascot, meǎ hŏ'ŏla'kǐ.

mask, pŏ'ŏkǐ'ǐ, uhǐmǎ'kǎ.

mass, (bulk), nunu'ǐ; (people), le'hŭle'hŭ; (at church), me'kǎ.

massacre, lŭ'kŭ.

massage, lo'mǐlo'mǐ, lo'mǐ.

mast, kǐ'ǎ.

master, (lord), hǎ'kŭ; (teacher), kŭ'mŭ: (to overcome), lǎnǎki'lǎ, hŏ'ŏpi'ŏ.

mat, moĕnǎ.

match, (lucifer), kūkaĕpĕ'lĕ; (similarity), lǐ'kĕ; (contest), hŏ'ŏkūkū: to match, hŏ-'ŏhālǐ'kĕlǐ'kĕ, kŏ'hŭ.

mate, (companion), hoǎ, kokŏ'ŏlu'ǎ; first mate of ship, mālǎmǎmo'kŭ; second mate, hŭlǐpǎ'hŭ.

material, meǎ.

matter, meǎ; (pus), pǎlǎhēhē'; (difficulty), pilikǐǎ, hǐhǐ'ǎ.

mature, o'o, pǎ'lǎ, maku'ǎ.

may, (month), Mei: (permissive), aĕĭ'ă, hi'kĭ
nō; (potential), māli'ă, pa'hă.

maybe, pēlā' pa'hă, aĕ pa'hă.

mayor, me'ĭă.

meal, pa'ĭnă; (ground grain), hu'ă hŏ'aĕ'aĕ.

mean, (stingy), pī; (harsh), uahō'ă; (middle),
ĭwăĕnăkŏ'nŭ: (signify), mană'ŏ: means,
wāĭwăĭ.

meantime, i'ă wa nō, i'ă mănā'wă.

measure, (ke) ā'nă.

meat, (flesh), 'i'o.

mechanic, mechanical, hă'nă lĭ'mă.

medal, mekă'lă.

meddle, (with hands), lālă'mă; (in affairs),
hōkăĭ.

mediate, ŭwaŏ.

medical, lāpăăŭ.

medicine, lā'ăŭ.

medium, (means), kŭ'mŭ; (middle), meă mawaĕnă; (spiritualistic), hă'kă.

meek, ākăhaĭ.

meet, meeting, hālāwăĭ.

melody, le'ŏ me'lĕ.

melon, ĭ'pŭ; water-melon, ĭpŭ'ăĭmă'kă, ĭpŭ-
ha'ŏlĕ; musk-melon, ĭpŭ'ă'lă.

melt, hŏ'ŏhehĕ'ĕ.

member, hoă, lālā.

memorial, meă hŏ'ŏmănă'ŏ; (petition), pă'lăpă'lă hŏ'ŏpĭ'ĭ.

memorize, hŏ'ŏpă'ănā'ăŭ.

memory, hŏ'ŏmănă'ŏ.

mend, hă'nă hoŭ, kāpĭ'lĭ; (cloth), paho'nŏho'nŏ; mend in health, o'lă hoŭ.

mental, o kā no'ŏno'ŏ, o kā nā'ăŭ.

mention, hă'ĭ, hō'ĭ'kĕ.

merchandise, wăĭwăĭ kălĕ'pă.

merchant, kălĕ'pă.

mercury, wăĭ kălā, meă ā'nă wĕ'lă.

mercy, lokomāĭkă'ĭ, (ke) ālo'hă.

mere, merely, wa'lĕ nŏ.

merit, hu'ă o kā hă'nă: to merit, po'nŏ kĕ lōa'a.

merry, 'ŏ'lĭ'ŏ'lĭ, lĕ'ălĕ'ă.

mess, (company), po'ĕ 'ăĭ pū; (individual), măhe'lĕ 'ăĭ; (disorder), hōkăĭ: (to dirty), hōkă'ĕ.

message, 'ōle'lŏ hŏ'ŏunăĭ'ă.

messenger, 'ĕlĕ'lĕ.

metal, mĕka'lă, hāŏ.

meteor, hōkūlĕ'lĕ, kŏ'lĭ.

method, hŏ'ŏno'hŏno'hŏ mikĭoĭ.

methodical, 'ă'nŏ mikĭoĭ.

Methodist, Mekoki'kŏ.

Mexico, Mēki'kŏ.

midday, (ke) āwakĕă.

middle, waĕnăko'nŭ.

midnight, (ke) aŭmoĕ.

might, mă'nă, ĭkăĭkă.

mild, (gentle), ākăhaĭ; (of voice), nă'hĕnă'hĕ.

mile, mi'lĕ.

military, 'oĭhă'nă koă.

milk, wăĭū'.

milk-fish, a'wă.

mill, wĭ'lĭ; sugar-mill, wĭlĭkō'.

million, mĭlĭo'nă: millionth, kā mĭlĭo'nă.

mimic, hŏ'ŏpi'lĭ, hŏ'ŏmahŭ'ĭ.

mind, no'ŏno'ŏ, nă'ăŭ; (will, thought), mană'ŏ: (to heed), hŏ'ŏlŏ'hĕ, malĭ'ŭ; (care for), mălă'mă.

mine, (excavation), lu'ă 'ĕlĭĭ'ă, (ke) ā'nă
'ĕlĭĭ'ă; (submerged), pōkā' păhū' kăĭ: (belonging to me), ko'ŭ, na'ŭ, etc.

mineral, mĭnela'lă.

minister, (pastor), kăhŭnăpŭ'lĕ; minister of
state, kuhi'nă aŭpu'nĭ; (ambassador), kuhi'nă 'ĕlĕ'lĕ.

minor, 'u'u'kŭ ĭ'hŏ.

minority, ha'pă 'ŭ'kŭ.

minute, (60 seconds), minu'kĕ: (very small),
'u'u'kŭ lō'ă, măkălĭ'ĭ: minutes, mō'ole'lŏ
hālāwăĭ.

miracle, hănămă'nă.

mirror, (ke) a'nĭa'nĭ nānā, a'nĭa'nĭ kilo'hĭ.

miscellaneous, kĕlā' mē kĕ'ĭă.

mischief, hă'nă 'ă'pă, kŏlŏ'hĕ, 'ăpĭ'kĭ.

mischievous, 'ĕŭ.

miser, punĭkālă, pī.

miserable, (u n h a p p y), lŭ'ŭlŭ'ŭ, hă'ălŏ'ŭ;
(worthless), lăpŭwa'lĕ.

misfortune, pō'ĭ'nŏ, pōpilĭki'ă.

miss, (maid), wăhi'nĕ ma'lĕ 'olĕ: to miss,
ha'lă, halăhĭ'.

mission, mikĭo'nă.

missionary, mikane'lĕ, mīkĭōnā'lĭ.

mist, (fog), 'o'hŭ; (fine rain), noĕ.

mistake, kuhĭhe'wă, lălăŭ.

Mister, Mr., Mĭ'kă, Mī.

mistress, (Mrs.), wăhi'nĕ ma'lĕ; kept mistress,
wăhi'nĕ mănŭa'hĭ.

mix, (blend), kāwĭ'lĭ; (mingle), hŏ'ōhŭ'ĭ, hŭ'ĭ
pū.

mob, le'hŭle'hŭ, ulŭao'ă, po'ĕ hŏ'ŏhaŭnaĕlĕ.

mock, hŏ'ōmāe'wăe'wă, he'nĕhe'nĕ.

mode, (manner), (ke) 'ă'nŏ; (fashion), 'ă'nŏ
   măŭ.

model, (ke) ā'nă hŏ'ŏhālĭ'kĕ: to model, hă'nă
   i lĭ'kĕ.

moderate, pāki'kŏ: to moderate, hŏ'e'mĭ.

modern, nō kē̦'ĭă wā.

modest, ākăhaĭ, hă'ăhă'ă.

moist, moisture, kăwăŭ', ma'ū'.

molasses, mălăkĕ'kĕ.

mold, (mildew), punăhe'lŭ; (soil), lĕ'pŏ mōmo'nă; (form), (ke) ā'nă: (to make), hă'-
   nă; (decay), pōpŏ'pŏ.

moment, keko'nă, wā poko'lĕ lō'ă; (importance), (ke) 'ă'nŏ nu'ĭ.

Monday, Pō'akă'hĭ, Monĕke'.

money, kālā, mo'nĭ.

mongoose, mănăku'kĕ.

monkey, kĕ'kŏ.

monstrous, (fearful), wĕ'lĭwĕ'lĭ; (great), nu'ĭ.

month, (lunar), māhi'nă; (calendar), mală'mă.

monument, kĭ'ă hŏ'ŏmană'ŏ.

mood, (ke) 'ă'nŏ.

moon, māhi'nă.

Moorish Idol, (fish), kĭ'hĭkĭ'hĭ.

moral, po'nŏ, hŏ'ŏpo'nŏ.

more, nu'ĭ a'ĕ, hoŭ: to be more, 'oĭ.

moreover, ho'ĭ, nŏho'ĭ, 'e'ĭă ho'ĭ.

Mormon, Molĕmo'nă.

morning, kakăhĭă'kă.

mortal, (human being), kănă'kă: (fatal), mă'kĕ.

mortar, (cement), pu'nă hă'mŏ; (utensil), ĭ'pŭ
   kŭ'ĭ; (ordnance), pū kī pōkāpăhū'.

mortgage, mōla'kĭ.

mosquito, māki'kă.

moss, lĭ'mŭ.

most, nu'ĭ lō'ă, hapănu'ĭ.

moth, pūlĕlĕhu'ă, oka'ĭ; clothesmoth, mū.

mother, makuăhi'nĕ; mother-in-law, maku'ă hŭnoăĭ wăhi'nĕ.

motion, 'o'nĭ, nĕ'ĕnĕ'ĕ ă'nă; make a motioı. in meeting, noĭ; second a motion, kōkŭ'ă.

motive, kŭ'mŭ i hă'nă ăĭ.

motor, mă'nă e nĕ'ĕ ăĭ; (machine), mīkĭ'nĭ.

motorcycle, mokokăĭkă'lă.

mound, (ke) ahu'ă, pŭ'ŭ.

mount, (as a picture), hŏ'ŏkŏ'mŏ; (as a horse), 'ĕ'ĕ; mount guard, hŏ'ŏno'hŏ i kiă'ĭ.

mountain, măŭnă, kuăhĭ'wĭ.

mourn, mourning, kănĭkăŭ, kănĭŭhū', kūma-ke'nă.

mouse, 'ĭo'lĕ lĭ'ĭlĭ'ĭ.

mouth, wa'hă; mouth of river, snout, etc., nŭ'kŭ.

mouthpiece, wahă'ŏle'lŏ.

move, 'o'nĭ, nĕ'ĕ, hŏ'ŏnĕ'ĕ; move an adjourn-ment, mană'ŏ e hŏ'ŏpănĕ'ĕ.

moving-pictures, kĭ'ĭ 'ŏ'nĭ'ŏ'nĭ.

much, nu'ĭ, nu'ĭ lō'ă, nu'ĭ wa'lĕ.

mucus, wă'lĕwă'lĕ, hūpē.

mud, kĕ'lĕkĕ'lĕ, ūkĕ'lĕ.

mud-hen, (coot), 'alaĕ.

mule, hŏ'kĭ.

mullet, 'ă'mă'ă'mă, 'ănăĕ.

multiply, hŏ'ŏnu'ĭ, hŏ'ŏmāhŭ'ăhŭ'ă.

multitude, le'hŭle'hŭ.

murder, pēpe'hĭ kănă'kă.

muscle, olonā', 'ĭ'ŏ.

museum, ha'lĕ hō'ĭ'kĕ'ĭ'kĕ.

music, (vocal), me′lĕ; (instrumental), pi′lă hŏ-
   ‘ŏkă′nĭ.

musician, (performer), meă hŏ‘ŏkă′nĭ pi′lă;
   (composer), meă hä′kŭ me′lĕ.

mussel, nahăwe′lĕ, pio‘ĕo‘ĕ.

must, po′nŏ.

muster, hŏ‘äko′äko‘ă; muster cattle, hŏ‘ŏhu′lĭ
   pĭ′pĭ.

mute, mūmu′lĕ, le′ŏ ‘o′lĕ.

mutiny, kĭ′pĭ.

mutter, na′mŭna′mŭ, ‘ohu′mŭ.

mutton, ‘ĭ‘ŏ hi′pă.

mutual, lĭ′kĕ, kăŭlĭ′kĕ.

muzzle, wa′hă; (snout), nŭ′kŭ; (cover), pū-
   nŭ′kŭ.

my, a‘ŭ, o‘ŭ, etc.

mynah, pĭhă‘ĕkĕ′lŏ.

myself, ŏwăŭ nŏ, no‘ŭ ĭ′hŏ, etc.

mystery, pāha‘ŏha‘ŏ, meă pohĭhi′hĭ.

N

nail, ku′ĭ, kakĭ′ă; human nail, mĭkĭ‘ăŏ, māĭ‘aŏ.

naked, kōhă′nă, ‘olo′hĕlo′hĕ.

name, ĭnŏă: to name, kă′pă.

namely, ‘ŏ′ĭă ho‘ĭ.

nap, kŭlŭĭhĭămoĕ, hō‘o′lŭ‘o′lŭ.

napkin, kāwe′lĕ; table napkin, kāwe′lĕ păpă-
   ‘āĭnă.

narrow, ‘olŏlĭ′, haĭkĭ.

narrows, kōwă.

nasty, (dirty), pe′lăpĕ′lă, haŭka‘ĕ; (mean),
   ‘ĭ′nŏ.

nation, lāhu′ĭ, (ke) aŭpu′nĭ.

national, nō kē aŭpu′nĭ.

nationality, lāhu′ĭ.

native, maolĭ: a native, kŭ'pă, kămă'ăĭnă: native land, (ke) o'nĕ hānaŭ.

natural, maolĭ; (unassuming), ākăhaĭ.

nature, (personified), Naku'ră; (character), (ke) 'ă'nŏ maolĭ.

naughty, kŏlŏ'hĕ, 'āpĭ'kĭ.

nautilus, 'āŭwă'ălălu'ă.

naval, 'oĭhă'nă mo'kŭ.

navel, pi'kŏ, pi'kŏ 'ōpū'.

navigate, hŏ'ŏho'lŏ mo'kŭ, hŏ'ŏkĕ'lĕ.

navy, ulŭmokŭkăŭă; (fleet), ulŭmo'kŭ.

near, kokŏ'kĕ.

nearly, 'ă'nĕ'ă'nĕ.

neat, mikĭoĭ, ma'ĕma'ĕ; (dainty), 'ăŭlĭ'ĭ.

necessary, kūpo'nŏ: to be necessary, e po'nŏ ăĭ.

necessity, kā meă e po'nŏ ăĭ; (want), ne'lĕ.

neck, 'ă'ĭ.

necklace, neck-tie, lĕĭ'ă'ĭ.

need, ne'lĕ.

needle, kŭ'ĭ, kŭĭkŏ'lŏ, kŭ'ĭ hŭ'mŭhŭ'mŭ.

negative (denial), hŏ'ŏ'lĕ; photographic negative, (ke) a'nĭa'nĭ pă'ĭkĭ'ĭ; a'nĭa'nĭ a'kă kĭ'ĭ.

neglect, hŏ'ŏhe'măhe'mă; waĭhŏ wa'lĕ.

negligent, pălă'kă, hŏ'ŏhe'măhe'mă.

negro, pă'ĕlĕ, ni'kă, neke'lŏ.

neighbor, hoălaŭnă, hoăno'hŏ.

neighborhood, kă'hĭ kokŏ'kĕ.

neither, 'ă'ŏ'lĕ kĕlă', 'ă'ŏ'lĕ kĕ'ĭă; 'ă'ŏ'lĕ ho'ĭ.

nephew, ke'ĭkĭ.

nerve, (ke) a'ălŏ'lŏ; man of nerve, pŭko'năko'nă.

nervous, pihoĭhoĭ wa'lŏ.

nest, pūnă'nă.

net, (fish), 'upe'nă; (small-meshed), năĕ;
    (mosquito), pākū; (netted bag), kōkō: (to
    gain), pu'kă.

neutral, kā'oko'ă.

never, 'ā'ŏ'lĕ lŏ'ă.

nevertheless, akā' ho'ĭ.

new, hoŭ.

news, nūhoŭ.

newspaper, nūpe'pă.

New York, Nū Io'kă.

New Zealand, Nūkila'nĭ.

next, kekă'hĭ a'ĕ, māho'pĕ măĭ.

nibble, nă'lĭnă'lĭ.

nice, măĭkă'ĭ, 'ăŭlĭ'ĭ.

nickel, (money), hapău'mĭ, ĕlĭ'mă kēnĕ'kă.

nickname, ĭnŏă kă'păkă'pă.

niece, kăĭkămăhĭ'nĕ.

night, pō.

nightmare, moĕ'ĭ'nŏ.

nine, ĭ'wă, eĭ'wă, 'aĭ'wă: ninth, kă ĭ'wă.

nineteen, 'ŭmĭkūmamaĭ'wă: nineteenth, kā
    'ŭmĭkūmamaĭ'wă.

ninety, kănăĭ'wă: ninetieth, kē kănăĭ'wă.

no, 'ā'ŏ'lĕ, 'ā'ŏ'hĕ, 'o'lĕ.

noble, kăŭkăŭălĭ'ĭ, hă'nŏhă'nŏ.

nobody, 'ā'ŏ'hĕ meă, meă 'ŏ'lĕ.

nod, (as signal), kunŏŭ; (drowsily), kĭ'mŏ.

noise, hănăkŭ'lĭ, kă'nĭ; (soft rustle), ne'hĕ;
    (rustle, rattle), nakĕ'kĕ; (sharp creak),
    'ŭ'ĭ'nă; (crackle of thunder, rattle), nakŭ'-
    lŭ; (hum, rumble), hămŭ'mŭ; (roar of
    waters, of thunder), hălŭ'lŭ; (roar of surf),
    pă'ĕpū'; (roar of animal), 'ŭwō'; (sound
    of rhythmic beat), ko'ĕ'lĕ; (gabble), wălă-
    'ăŭ, hăŭwălă'ăŭ: to noise about, hŏ'ŏlă'hă.

none, ʻāʻōʻlĕ hŏʻōkăʻhĭ, ʻāʻōʻhĕ.

nonsense, ʻōleʻlŏ lăpŭwaʻlĕ.

noon, (ke) āwakĕă.

nor, ʻāʻōʻlĕ hoʻĭ.

normal, meă măŭ, kūlĭʻkĕ mē nā luʻlă; normal school, kuʻlă āʻŏ kŭʻmŭ.

north, ʻākaŭ; northeast, hĭkiʻnă ʻākaŭ; north-west, kŏmŏhăʻnă ʻākaŭ.

nose, ĭʻhŭ.

not, ʻāʻōʻlĕ, ʻōʻlĕ.

notary, luʻnă hōʻōʻĭă păʻlăpăʻlă.

note, (letter), lĕʻkă pokoʻlĕ; (explanatory), ʻōleʻlŏ wĕʻhĕwĕʻhĕ; (memo.), ʻōleʻlŏ hŏʻōma-năʻŏ; (promissory), păʻlăpăʻlă kīkŏʻŏ, piʻlă hōʻăĭʻē.

nothing, ʻāʻōʻhĕ nō, meă ʻōʻlĕ.

notice, ʻĭʻkĕ; public notice, ʻōleʻlŏ hŏʻōlăʻhă: to notice, ʻĭʻkĕ.

noticeable, maopŏʻpŏ lĕʻă.

notify, kūkăʻlă, hōʻĭʻkĕ.

notion, manăʻŏ uʻlŭ waʻlĕ.

notwithstanding, akā' năʻŏ, ʻāʻōʻlŏ năʻŏ.

novel, hoŭ; (romance), kaʻaŏ.

novelty, (ke) ʻăʻnŏ hoŭ, meă hoŭ.

November, Nowĕmaʻpă.

now, ānō'.

nucleus, kŭʻmŭ, kĭkŏwaĕnă.

nude, kōhăʻnă, kăʻpă ʻōʻlĕ.

nudist, meă heʻlŏ waʻlĕ.

nuisance, meă hŏʻŏpĭlĭkĭʻă waʻlĕ.

number, heluʻnă: (to count), heʻlŭ.

numerous, leʻhŭleʻhŭ.

nurse, kăʻhŭ măʻĭ; nursemaid, meă mālăʻmă; (to suckle), hānăĭ.

nut, kukuʻĭ, kukuʻĭ haŏlĕ.

O

O, oh, (exclamation), ăŭwē'; (vocative), ē.

oar, hoĕ.

oath, hŏ'ŏhĭ'kĭ.

obey, hŏ'ŏlo'hĕ.

object, meă; (purpose), mană'ŏ pa'ă: (to oppose), kū'ē.

objection, kŭ'mŭ kū'ē.

objective, mĕă i kăŭlo'nă ĭ'ă.

obligation, (debt), 'ăĭ'ē; (duty), po'nŏ.

oblige, (compel), kŏĭ; (gratify), 'o'lŭ'o'lŭ;
(assist), kōkŭ'ă.

obscure, (of sight), pōwe'hĭwe'hĭ; (vague), pohĭhi'hĭ, maopŏ'pŏ 'ŏ'lĕ; (humble), hă'ăhă'ă.

observe, (see), 'ĭ'kĕ; (watch), hăkăpo'nŏ, hāki'lŏ.

obstinate, pă'ăkĭ'kĭ.

obstruct, obstruction, kĕ'ăkĕ'ă, ălăĭ.

obtain, lōa'a.

obvious, maopŏ'pŏ lĕ'ă, moakă'kă.

occasion, wă; (cause), kŭ'mŭ.

occasionally, i kă'hĭ wă.

occidental, kŏmŏhă'nă.

occupation, hă'nă, 'oĭha'nă.

occupy, (as a house), kŏ'mŏ, no'hŏ; occupy
oneself, hă'nă, hŏ'ŏpă'ă po'nŏ.

occur, (happen), lŏ'ŏhĭ'ă; (come to mind),
a'lă măĭ.

occurrence, ulĭ'ă.

ocean, mōa'nă.

o'clock, ho'lă.

October, Okako'pă.

octopus, (locally, "squid"), hĕ'ĕ.

odd, (unlike), lĭ'kĕ 'ŏ'lĕ; (eccentric), 'ă'nŏ'ē;
(uneven), kăŭpa'e'wă.

odds, 'oĭ, kŏĕnă, kĕ'ŭ.

odor, (fragrance), 'ă'lă; (stink), pĭlaŭ.

of, kā, kō, ă, ō.

off, a'kŭ: be off, he'lĕ pēlā'.

offend, (violate), kū'ē; (anger), hŏ'ŏnaŭ'kĭŭ'kĭ.

offense, hă'nă he'wă.

offer, (give), hăă'wĭ; offer food, kăŭ 'ăĭ; offer sacrifice, kăŭmă'hă, hăĭ.

offering, hăăwi'nă, mohaĭ.

office, 'oĭhă'nă, keĕ'nă 'oĭhă'nă.

officer, lu'nă.

official, mē kē kăŭo'hă, mă'nă 'oĭhă'nă.

officious, lālă'mă.

often, pĭ'nĕpĭ'nĕ.

oil, aĭlă, hi'nŭ; (coconut), mănŏ'Ĭ: to oil, kahĭ'nŭ.

ointment, meă po'nĭ, hi'nŭ.

O.K., O.K.

old, (ancient, aged), kăhi'kŏ; (worn-out), 'apŭ'lŭ: old man, 'ĕlĕmăkŭ'lĕ; old woman, luăhi'nĕ.

omit, (neglect), waĭhŏ wa'lĕ; (exclude), pă'lĕ.

on, (onward), ĭmŭ'ă: (upon), mālu'nă, ĭlu'nă; (at or with), mă, i.

once, i kekă'hĭ wā, 'akă'hĭ; at once, ānŏ', kŏ'kĕ.

one, ka'hĭ, 'akă'hĭ, hŏ'ŏkă'hĭ, kekă'hĭ.

onion, 'ākă'ăkăĭ.

only, wa'lĕ nŏ.

open, hamă'mă: to open, wĕ'hĕ, he'mŏ; (unfold), moha'lă.

opening, pu'kă; (in woods), kĭpŭ'kă.

opera, kĕă'kă me'lĕ.

operate, (work), hă'nă; operate surgically, 'o'kĭ, kă'hă.

opinion, mană'ŏ.

opportunity, wā kŭpo'nŏ.

oppose, kū'ē, kĕ'ăkĕ'ă.

opposite, (facing), mā kē a'lŏ, mā kēlā' 'ăŏ'ăŏ;
   (contrary), kū'ē.

oppress, hŏ'ŏkuăpă'ă.

oppression, hŏ'ŏkăŭmă'hă.

or, pa'hă, i 'ŏ'lĕ.

orange, ală'nĭ.

orator, kănă'kă hă'ĭ'ŏle'lŏ.

orchard, kīhapăĭ, u'lŭ huă'ăĭ.

orchestra, po'ĕ hŏ'ŏkă'nĭ pi'lă.

order, (a command), kăŭo'hă; (arrangement),
   hŏ'ŏno'hŏno'hŏ po'nŏ; (rank), kūlă'nă;
   (fraternity), pă'pă; (check), pi'lă kīkŏ'ŏ
   kālā: to order, kăŭo'hă, kēnă'.

ordinance, lu'lă, kănăwăĭ.

ordinary, mă'ă măŭ.

organ, okă'nă; (of body), pa'ăha'nă.

organization, hŭ'ĭ.

organize, hŏ'ŏkŭ'mŭ.

oriental, hĭki'nă.

origin, kŭ'mŭ, măkămu'ă.

original, mu'ă lŏ'ă, kĭ'nŏ hoŭ.

originate, hŏ'ŏkŭ'mŭ, hŏ'ŏmă'kă.

ornament, kāhi'kŏ: to ornament, hŏ'ŏnă'nĭ.

other, 'ē, 'ē ă'ĕ: the other, kekă'hĭ meă 'ē, kā
   lu'ă, hē meă 'ē ă'ĕ.

otherwise, i 'ŏ'lĕ ĭă.

ought, po'nŏ.

our, kō kā'ŭă, kō măkŏŭ, (see pp. 19-20)

out, outward, ĭwă'hŏ, māwă'hŏ: (directive),
   a'kŭ: outside, kowă'hŏ.

outbreak, (volcanic), hū, păhū'; (on skin),
   pŭ'ŭpŭ'ŭ; (insurrection), kĭ'pĭ,. hăŭnaĕlĕ.

outfit, nā la'kŏ: to outfit, hŏ'ŏlă'kŏ.

outing, pi'kĭni'kĭ, māka'ĭka'ĭ.

outline, kă'hă ŏwă'hŏ; (of discourse), ĭ'wĭ hă'ĭa'ŏ.

outrigger of canoe, 'ĭa'kŏ; (float), (ke) a'mă.

outstanding, (due), kă'ă 'ŏ'lĕ; (prominent), kĭ'ĕkĭ'ĕ.

oven, (modern), (ke) 'o'mă; ground oven, ĭ'mŭ, ŭ'mŭ.

over, mālu'nă; (across), maŏ' ă'ĕ; (excess), 'oĭ.

overcome, lănăki'lă, hŏ'ŏpi'ŏ; to be overcome, pi'ŏ.

overlook, (see over), nānā mālu'nă; (oversee), kiă'ĭ, hŏ'ŏpo'nŏpo'nŏ; (miss), ha'lă; (neglect), pălă'kă; (condone), waĭhŏ.

overseer, lu'nă.

owe, 'ăĭ'ē'.

owl, pūĕ'ŏ.

own, (self), ponŏ'ĭ': to own, lōa'a; (admit), aĕ.

owner, o'nă, meă nŏ'nă.

oyster, pĭ'pĭ, 'ōlĕ'pĕ.

P

pacific, mali'nŏ, lă'ĭ: Pacific Ocean, Mōa'nă Pakĭpi'kă.

pack, (knapsack), hăă'wĕ: to pack, (trunk), hăhaŏ, hō'ō', hăŏ; (to load), hŏ'ŏkăŭ, hŏ-'ōĭ'lĭ.

package, (bundle), pū'o'lŏ, pū'ā', (ke) 'o'pĕ; (box), pa'hŭ.

paddle, hoĕ: (to play), e pā'a'nĭ ilo'kŏ o kē kăĭ.

page, (of book), 'ăŏ'ăŏ; (boy), keĭkĭ lă'wĕlă'wĕ.

pageant, hŏʻïʻkĕʻïʻkĕ.

pail, pākĕʻkĕ.

pain, ʻĕʻhă; (pang), ʻumïʻï; (ache), hŭʻï; mental), ʻĕʻhăʻĕʻhă: (to hurt), hŏʻĕʻhă.

paint, peʻnă: to paint, (as the face), peʻnă, nŏŭnŏŭneă; (to daub), hāpaʻlă.

painter, (artisan), meă hăʻmŏ peʻnă; (artist), meă peʻnă kïʻï; (rope), kăŭlă wăʻăpāʻ.

pair, paʻă, kăŭluʻă: to pair, kăŭluʻă, pāluʻă.

pajamas, loʻlĕ moĕ.

pal, hoʻă, hoăpiʻlï.

palace, haʻlĕ ălïʻï.

pale, haïkeă, hakeă, nanănăkeă.

palm, (tree), pāʻmă, loŭʻlŭ; (hand), pŏhŏliʻmă.

pamphlet, păʻlăpăʻlă păʻïïʻă.

pan, (ke) pā kïʻnï.

pancake, palaʻoă pălaï.

Panama, Pănămāʻ.

pandanus, haʻlă; (tree), pūhăʻlă; (leaf), lăŭhaʻlă.

pane, ʻāpăʻnă aʻnïaʻnï.

panic, makăʻŭ kŭheʻwă.

pant, năĕnăĕ, păŭpăŭaʻhŏ; (as a dog), ăʻhăăʻhă.

pants, loʻlĕ wāwaĕ.

papaya, mikăʻnă, heʻï, papăïă.

papaya-bird, ʻăïmikăʻnă.

paper, pĕʻpă; (writing), kălăʻnă; newspaper, nŭpĕʻpă; (essay), manăʻŏ i hăkŭïʻă.

par, lïʻkĕ.

parade, hŏʻŏkăʻhăkăʻhă; (military), païkaŭ: to parade, kăʻï.

paradise, parađaiso.

paragraph, păŭkŭʻ ʻōleʻlŏ.

parallel, moĕ lïʻkĕ.

paralysis, măʻï lōlō.

parcel, pū'o'lŏ lǐ'ǐlǐ'ǐ: (to divide), māhe'lĕ.

pardon, hŭǐkä'lä; (forgive), kä'lä.

pare, kŏ'lǐ.

parent, (Hawaiian), maku'ă; own parent, lū-
    ăŭ'ǐ; parent-in-law, hŭnoăǐ.

park, pā'kă, kīhăpăǐ hō'ŏlŭ'ŏlŭ: to park the
    car, kū.

parlor, lŭ'mǐ hŏ'ŏkǐ'pă, keĕ'nă.

parrot, mă'nŭ alo'hă, palo'kă.

parrot-fish, ŭ'hŭ.

parson, kăhŭnăpŭ'lĕ, kä'hŭ ekalĕsi'ă.

part, ha'pă, māhe'lĕ, 'āpä'nă, păŭkū'.

partial, (biased), 'ĕ'wä'ĕ'wă; (fond of), pu'nǐ.

particle, hŭ'nă.

particular, (precise), mikǐoǐ; (careful), ākă-
    hĕ'lĕ.

partner, ho'ă, hoăhă'nă.

partnership, hŭ'ǐ 'oǐhă'nă.

party, (person), meă; (group), po'ĕ, hŭ'ǐ; (din-
    ner), 'ăhă'ǐnă; (social), hō'ŏlăŭlĕ'ă; (fac-
    tion), 'ăŏ'ăŏ.

pass, (defile), a'lă 'olŏlǐ'; free pass, pă'lă-
    pă'lă kŏ'mŏ wa'lĕ; (thrust), hoŭ: to pass,
    mā'a'lŏ; (as a bill), hŏ'ŏho'lŏ; (as hand),
    ā'nǐ.

passenger, 'ohu'ă.

passion, (anger), hūhū' 'ǐ'nŏ; (lust), kŭ'kŏ.

passport, pă'lăpă'lă aĕ.

password, 'ōle'lŏ kiă'ǐ, 'ōle'lo hūnā'.

past, ha'lă: the past, māmu'ă, wā i ha'lă.

paste, meă hŏ'ŏpǐpǐ'lǐ.

pastor, kăhŭnăpŭ'lĕ, kä'hŭ ekalĕsi'ă.

pasture, pā holŏhŏlo'nă, ku'lă holŏhŏlo'nă.

pat, (apt), makăŭkăŭ: to pat, pă'ǐpă'ǐ māli'ĕ.

patch, (taro), lŏʻĭ: to patch, paho'nŏho'nŏ,
 pŏ'hŏ.

path, (ke) a'lă, kuămŏ'ŏ.

patience, (ke) āhŏnu'ĭ, hŏʻŏmanawanu'ĭ.

patient, (invalid), meă mă'ĭ.

patriotic, ālo'hă ʻăĭnă, măkĕʻĕ aŭpu'nĭ.

patrol, kiă'ĭ kăʻăhĕ'lĕ.

patronage, hŏʻŏpōmaĭkaʻĭ ă'nă.

pattern, (ke) ā'nă, kŭ'mŭ hŏʻŏhālĭ'kĕ.

pause, ma'hă ĭ'kĭ.

pave, pavement, kīpă'pă, kīpaĕpaĕ.

paw, wāwaĕ: to paw ground, he'lŭ; (to handle), hāpă'pă.

pawn, pānă'ĭ wăĭwăĭ, kūʻăĭ nō kā mănā'wă.

pay, u'kŭ, hŏʻŏkă'ă; (profit), pu'kă.

pea, pī.

peace, malŭhi'ă, kŭʻĭka'hĭ.

peacock, pikă'kĕ.

peanut, pinē'kĭ.

pear, peă.

pearl, mŏ'mĭ.

pebble, ʻĭ'lĭʻĭ'lĭ.

peck, kĭ'kŏ, paŏ; peck repeatedly, paŏpaŏ.

peculiar, (one's own), ponŏĭ'; (odd), ʻănŏ'ē.

pedal, he'hĭ.

peddle, peddler, kālĕ'wă, piĕ'lĕ, maʻăŭʻăŭwā'.

pedigree, mŏʻŏkūăŭhăŭ.

peel, paʻă'ā, ʻĭ'lĭ: to peel, ĭ'hĭ, ho'lĕho'lĕ.

peep, ki'eĭ, hālō; (sound), pi'ŏpi'ŏ, ʻĭ'ŏʻĭ'ŏ.

peer, (associate), ho'ă; (noble), ălĭ'ĭ: to peer,
 nānā.

peevish, ʻa'ă'kă, hūhū' wa'lĕ.

peg, pĭ'nĕ lā'ăŭ; (surveyor's), pa'hŭ: to peg,
 māki'ă.

pen, pĕ'nĭ, pĕnĭki'lă; (yard), pā.

penalty, hŏ'ŏpā'ī.

penance, hŏ'ŏpă'ī hŭīkă'lă.

pencil, pĕnĭka'lă.

peninsula, 'ănĕmŏ'kŭ.

penny, pĕ'nĭ, kēnĕ'kă.

pension, u'kŭ hŏ'ŏmäŭ.

people, kā'năkă, po'ĕ: to people, hŏ'ŏŭ'lŭ lā-hŭ'ī.

pepper, (plant, pod), nioī; (ground), lū pĕ'pă.

perceive, (see), 'ī'kĕ; (understand), hŏ'ŏmaŏpŏ'pŏ.

percentage, pākēnĕ'kă.

perch, kăŭ.

perfect, hemŏlĕ'lĕ, kīnā' 'ŏ'lĕ: to perfect, hŏ-'ŏkō' po'nŏ.

perform, hă'nă, hŏ'ŏkō'.

performance, hă'nă.

perfume, (natural), mōa'nĭ, (ke) 'ā'lă, 'a'ā'lă; (bottled), lukĭ'nĭ, wăī'ā'lă: to perfume, hŏ'ŏpē'.

perhaps, pa'hă, mălī'ă pa'hă, īnā' pa'hă.

period, (time), wā, mana'wă; (punctuation), kĭ'kŏ, kĭkŏkă'hĭ.

perjury, hŏ'ŏhī'kĭ wahăhĕ'ĕ.

permanent, măŭ, pa'ă.

permit, permission, aĕ: written permit, pă'lăpă'lă aĕ.

perpendicular, kūpo'nŏ, kūpololeī.

perplex, hŏ'ŏpĭlĭhu'ă, hŏ'ŏhŭīkaŭ.

perplexity, pĭ'ō'ō', hŭīkăŭ.

persecute, hŏ'ŏma'ăŭ, hō'ī'nŏ.

persist, hŏ'ŏmăŭ, hŏ'ŏkupă'ă.

person, kănă'kă, meă.

personable, 'upă'lŭ, onao'na.

personage, meă hă'nŏhă'nŏ.

personal, pilīkĭ'nŏ.

personality, kūlă'nă; (remark), 'ōle'lŏ pilikĭ'nŏ.

personally, ĭ'hŏ.

personnel, po'ĕ.

persuade, kŏĭ.

perverse, kekĕ'ĕ, 'o'ole'ă.

pervert, hŏ'ŏkăhŭ'lĭ.

pest, meă 'ĭ'nŏ.

pestilence, ahulaŭ.

pet, (favorite), punăhe'lĕ; (anger), nu'hă; to pet, mi'līmi'lĭ.

petition, pă'lăpă'lă hŏŏ'pĭ'ĭ: to petition, noĭ, hŏ'ŏpĭ'ĭ, pu'lĕ.

petrel, ŭă'ŭ, ŭwă'ŭ.

pheasant, kŏlŏhă'lă.

Philippines, Filipino, Pilĭpĭ'nŏ.

phone, kĕlĕpo'nă.

phonograph, pahŭ'ōle'lŏ.

photograph, kĭ'ĭ: to photograph, pă'ĭkĭ'ĭ.

phrase, māmă'lă 'ōle'lŏ.

physic, lă'ăŭ.

physical, kĭ'nŏ.

physician, kăŭkă lăpăăŭ.

piano, piă'nŏ.

pick, pŏ'ŏke'lă; pickax, kĭpĭkŭ'ă: to pick, kŏ'hŏ, waĕ; (as fruit), 'o'hĭ; (as a lock), wĕ'hĕ; (as ground), pă 'ĕ'lĭ.

picket, (guard), kiă'ĭ; (paling), lă'ăŭ pă.

pickles, hu'ă hŏ'ŏmĭkŏĭ'ă.

picnic, pikĭni'kĭ.

picture, kĭ'ĭ.

pie, păĭ.

piece, 'ăpă'nă, hāki'nă, păŭkŭ'; (bolt, as of cloth), āpă'.

pier, ŭwa′pŏ, ŭa′pŏ.

pierce, ‘ō, hoŭ.

piety, (religious), hăĭpu′lĕ; (filial), (ke) ālo′hă.

pig, pua‘a.

pigeon, nūnū, mănŭkū′.

pile, (beam), poŭ lōi′hĭ; (heap), paĭlă, (ke) ahu′ă; (nap of cloth), ohŭ′lŭhŭ′lŭ: to pile, hō‘a′hŭ.

pill, huăă′lĕ.

pillar, kĭ′ă, poŭ.

pillow, ulu′nă.

pilot, (ke) paĭla′kă, (ke) alăka‘ĭ.

pin, kŭ′ĭ pĭ′nĕ, māki′ă.

pinch, ‘ĭnĭ′kĭ; (squeeze), ‘umĭ′kĭ; (be narrowed), hŏ‘ŏmĭ′ŏmĭ′ŏ; (steal), ‘ăĭhu′ĕ; (arrest), hŏ′pŭ.

pine, lă‘ăŭ paĭnă: to pine, li‘ă.

pineapple, halăkahĭ′kĭ.

pink, ‘ākă′lă.

pint, paĭnă.

pioneer, paĭŏnĭ′ă.

pipe, păĭpŭ, ‘o′hĕ; waterpipe, pĭŭ′lă wăĭ; tobacco pipe, ĭ′pŭ pă′kă.

pirate, pōwă′, pōwă′ mo′kŭ.

pistol, pūpă′năpă′nă.

pit, lu′ă.

pitch, kă, kepăŭ hă′mŏ; (slope), lă′pă: to pitch, (throw), nŏŭ; (as a tune), pua′nă; (as a tent), kūku′lŭ.

pitcher, (jug), pi′kă; (ball), meă nŏŭ.

pity, (ke) alo′hă me′nĕme′nĕ.

place, wă′hĭ, kă′hĭ: to place, waĭhŏ, kăŭ; (establish), hŏ‘ŏno′hŏ.

plague, mă‘ĭ ahulaŭ; (nuisance), meă hŏ‘ŏpĭlĭkĭ′ă.

plain, (flat land), 'ăĭnă păla'hăla'hă, 'ăĭnă pāpū: (evident), akā'kă, maopŏ'pŏ; (homely),
nūkŏ'kĭ.

plait, ulă'nă, hī'lŏ.

plan, păpăhă'nă: to plan, hŏ'ōlālā.

plane, (even), lăŭmănĭ'ă; (tool), kŏ'ĭkă'hĭ;
airplane, mokŭlĕ'lĕ.

planet, hōkūhĕ'lĕ, hōkū'aĕ'ă.

plank, pă'pă māno'ăno'ă.

plant, (growth), meă u'lŭ, meă kă'nŭ; indus-
trial plant, nā meă 'oĭhă'nă: to plant, kă'nŭ.

plantation, mahină'āĭ, kīhapăĭ; (sugar), mă-
hĭkō'.

planter, kănă'kă măhĭ'āĭ.

plaster, (lime), pu'nă; (sticking), meă hŏ'ŏ-
pĭpĭ'lĭ.

plate, (ke) pā.

platform, (paved), paĕpaĕ; (rostrum), 'āwăĭ;
(political), păpăhă'nă.

play, pā'a'nĭ, lĕ'ălĕ'ă; (drama), hă'nă kĕă'kă:
to play music, hŏ'ŏkă'nĭ; (cards), hahaŭ;
(gamble), pi'lĭ.

pleasant, 'o'lŭ'o'lŭ, māli'ĕ.

please, (politeness in request), 'olŭ'olŭ; to
please, hō'ŏ'lŭ'ŏ'lŭ.

pleasure, lĕ'ălĕ'ă, 'ŏ'lĭ'ŏ'lĭ.

pledge, wăĭwăĭ pănă'ĭ: (to plight), hŏ'ŏhĭ'kĭ.

plenty, la'wă po'nŏ, hē nu'ĭ.

pliers, 'ūpā' hŏ'ŏpa'ă.

plot, (of story), kŭmŭmană'ŏ; (ground), 'āpă'-
nă: to plot, kĭ'pĭ malū'.

plover, kōlĕă.

plow, pălăŭ, 'ŏ'ŏpălăŭ.

pluck, 'ă'ă, koă: to pluck, (as fruit), 'o'hĭ; (as
a fowl), u'nŭu'nŭ; pluck out, ūhu'kĭ.

plug, (stopper), 'ŭmo'kī; (tobacco), pēpě'ě-
pa'kă.

plunder, wăïwăï hāŏ: to plunder, hāŏ, pōwā'.

plunge, (dive into water), lŭ'ŭ; (fall headlong),
kï'mŏ; (dip), hō'ŭ'.

P.M., (afternoon), 'aŭï'nălā; (evening), (ke)
ă'hĭă'hĭ; (night), pō.

pneumonia, nūmōnĭ'ă.

pocket, pākě'kě.

poet, hă'kŭ me'lě.

poetry, nă me'lě.

point, (tip), wēlăŭ, pi'kŏ; (subject), kŭmŭmană'ŏ; (cape), laě; (dot), kï'kŏ: to point,
kŭ'hĭku'hĭ.

poison, lā'ăŭ mă'kě.

pole, lā'ăŭ lō'ĭ'hĭ; (flag), pa'hŭ haě, kĭ'ă haě;
(telephone), poŭ; (fish), mŏkŏĭ; (axial extremity), wēlăŭ.

Pole Star, Hōkūpă'ă, Kiopă'ă.

police, policeman, māka'ĭ.

policy, mană'ŏ hŏ'ŏkŏ', păpăhă'nă; (insurance),
pă'lăpă'lă pānă'ĭ.

polish, hi'nŭhi'nŭ; (elegance), hŏ'ŏhi'ehi'e: to
polish, 'ānăĭ, hŏ'ŏhi'nŭhi'nŭ.

polite, wăïpăhē'.

politic, no'ěaŭ.

politics, kalăï'ăïnă.

poll, pŏ'ŏ; (tax), 'aŭhăŭ kï'nŏ; (voting), wă'hĭ
kŏ'hŏ pālo'kă.

pomp, hŏ'ŏkă'hăkă'hă.

pond, lŏ'kŏ; fishpond, lŏ'kŏ ĭ'ă.

pool, (freshwater), kï'ŏwăĭ; tidal pool, kāhě'kă.

poor, (needy), 'ĭlĭhŭ'ně, ne'lě; (lean), 'olă'lă,
wīwī; (ill), 'onawa'lĭwa'lĭ; (quality), ĭ'nŏ-
'ĭ'nŏ.

pop, pŏhā'; (soda water), wăĭ mōmo'nă.

pope, po'pĕ.

poppy, puăka'lă.

popular, kăŭlă'nă, hilĭnă'ĭĭ'ă.

population, lāhu'ĭ, kā'năkă.

porch, lānaĭ.

pork, 'ĭ'ŏ pua'ă.

porpoise, năĭ'ă.

port, (ke) ă'wă kūmo'kŭ; port side, 'ăŏ'ăŏ
    he'mă.

porter, (carrier), kănă'kă ha'lĭ ukă'nă; (door-
    man), kiă'ĭ pu'kă.

portion, māhe'lĕ, hāăwi'nă.

Porto Rico, Pŏkŏlĭ'kŏ.

portrait, kĭ'ĭ, kĭ'ĭ helĕhĕle'nă.

Portuguese, Pukikĭ'.

Portuguese man-of-war, pŏ'ĭmalaŭ.

position, wă'hĭ; (rank), kūlă'nă; (office), 'oĭ-
    hă'nă.

positive, maopŏ'pŏ, hō'ō'ĭai'ŏ ă'nă.

possess, lōa'a.

possession, lōa'a ă'nă; (colony), panălā'ăŭ.

possible, hĭ'kĭ.

possibly, pa'hă.

post, poŭ; (military), pāpū: to post, (mail),
    hŏ'ŏkŏ'mŏ lĕ'kă; (as sentry), hŏ'ŏno'hŏ.

postage, pŏ'ŏlĕ'kă.

poster, pă'lăpă'lă hŏ'ŏlă'hă.

postman, la'wĕ lĕ'kă.

postoffice, ha'lĕ lĕ'kă.

postpone, hŏ'ŏpanĕ'ĕ.

postscript, 'ŏle'lŏ pakŭ'ĭ.

pot, ĭ'pŭ; (earthenware crock), kĕlĕmani'ă.

potato, (sweet), 'ŭwa'lă, 'ŭwa'lă maolĭ; (Irish),
    'ŭwalăkăhĭ'kĭ.

poultry, moă, mă′nŭ la′kă.

pound, paonă; (cattle), pā aŭpu′nĭ: to pound, kŭ′ĭ.

pour, nīnĭ′nĭ, hŏ′ŏkă′hĕ.

poverty, ne′lĕ, hŭ′nĕ.

powder, păŭkă: to powder, hŏ′aĕ′aĕ.

power, mă′nă.

practicable, hĭ′kĭ.

practice, practical, hă′nă măŭ, lă′wĕlă′wĕ măŭ: to practice, hŏ′ŏmă′ămă′ă.

praise, māhā′lŏ: to praise, hŏ′ŏnă′nĭ, hŏ′ŏmaĭ-ka′ĭ.

pray, prayer, pu′lĕ, noĭ.

preach, hă′ĭ′ōle′lŏ.

preacher, hă′ĭ′ōle′lŏ, kăhŭnăpŭ′lĕ.

precede, he′lĕ māmu′ă.

precedent, (ke) ā′nă hŏ′ŏhālĭ′kĕ.

precinct, ′āpă′nă, māhe′lĕ.

precious, măkămăĕ, hĭ′wăhĭ′wă.

precipice, pa′lĭ.

prefer, ma′kĕma′kĕ; be preferable, a′hŏ.

pregnant, hāpăĭ.

prejudice, mană′ŏ kŭ′ē′.

premium, (insurance), u′kŭ īnĭkŭ′ă; (gift), ma-ka′nă ′āpo′nŏ, mănŭa′hĭ; (over-price), u′kŭ māhu′ăhu′ă.

prepare, hŏ′ŏmākăŭkăŭ.

presence, (ke) a′lŏ; presence of mind, makăŭ-kăŭ.

present, (gift), maka′nă; the present, ănŏ′: (here), ′e′ĭă: to present, hāă′wĭ, hō′ĭ′kĕ.

presently, kokŏ′kĕ.

preserve, (jam), kĕ′lĕ: to preserve, mălă′mă o ′ĭ′nŏ′ĭ′nŏ.

preside, hŏ′ŏmă′lŭ.

president, pĕlĕkike'nă.

press, (machine), mīkǐ'nǐ kāŏ'mǐ; (printing),
pǎ'ǐ pǎ'lǎpǎ'lǎ; The Press, nă nūpĕ'pǎ: to
press, kāŏ'mī; (to crowd), hŏ'ŏkĕ'; (with
iron), ǎǐǎ'nǎ, pākī.

presume, maha'ŏǐ; (suppose), manǎ'ŏ wa'lĕ.

pretend, pretense, hŏ'ŏkǎmǎ'nǐ.

pretty, u'ǐ, mǎǐkǎ'ǐ, nŏhĕǎ: pretty good, mǎǐkǎ'ǐ ǐ'kǐ; pretty bad, 'ǐ'nŏ nō.

prevail, (conquer), lǎnǎki'lǎ; (be prevalent),
lǎ'hǎ: prevailing wind, maka'nǐ mǎŭ.

prevent, pa'lĕ, kĕ'ǎkĕ'ǎ.

previous, mu'ǎ, māmu'ǎ a'ĕ.

price, kŭmŭkū'ǎǐ.

prick, meǎ 'o'oǐ, kūkū': to prick, hoŭ, 'ŏ.

prickly pear, pānǐ'nǐ, pāpǐ'pǐ.

pride, hǎ'ǎhe'ŏ, hŏ'ŏkǐ'ĕkǐ'ĕ.

priest, kǎhŭnǎpŭ'lĕ.

primary, mu'ǎ, kŭ'mŭ mu'ǎ; (election). kŏ'hŏ
mu'ǎ.

prime, (chief), mu'ǎ, nu'ǐ; (excellent), pŏ-
'ŏke'lǎ.

primitive, (original), mǎkǎmu'ǎ; (ancient),
kǎhǐ'kŏ.

prince, ke'ǐkǐ ǎlǐ'ǐ; (crown), hŏ'ŏǐlǐ'nǎ mŏǐ'.

princess, kǎmālǐ'ǐ, kǎǐkǎmǎhǐ'nĕ ǎlǐ'ǐ.

principal, nu'ǐ, mu'ǎ: (capital sum), kŭmŭ-
pǎ'ǎ; (head), (ke) pŏ'ŏ.

principle, lōinǎ, mŏ'lĕ.

print, (cloth), lo'lĕ kǎlǎkoǎ; (picture), kǐ'ǐ;
footprint, kǎpŭa'ǐ, mehe'ŭ: to print, pǎ'ǐ.

printer, kǎnǎ'kǎ pǎ'ǐ.

prior, māmu'ǎ a'ĕ.

prison, ha'lĕ pa'ǎhaŏ.

prisoner, pa'ǎhaŏ.

private, (soldier), **koă maolĭ**: (personal), po-
   nŏ'ĭ', **kūoko'ă**; (alone), **me'hăme'hă**; (secret), **malū'**.
privilege, **kūleă'nă**; (advantage), **pōmaĭka'ĭ**.
prize, **u'kŭ**, **maka'nă**: to prize, **mană'ŏ nu'ĭ**.
prize-fight, **pĕlēpĕlē'**, **mō'kŏmō'kŏ**.
probable, **'o'ĭai'ŏ pa'hă**.
problem, **nănĕhă'ĭ**, **mană'ŏhă'ĭ**.
proceed, **he'lĕ mu'ă**; proceed from, **pu'kă măĭ**.
process, **hă'nă**.
procession, **kă'ĭ**, **hŭăkă'ĭ he'lĕ**.
proclaim, **kūkă'lă**; (publish), **hŏ'ōlă'hă**.
produce, **nā hu'ă**: to produce, **hō'ĭ'kĕ**; (yield),
   hŏ'ōhu'ă.
profess, **hō'ō'ĭă**; (pretend), **hŏ'ōkămă'nĭ**.
profession, **'oĭhă'nă**.
professor, **pelopĕ'kă**.
profit, **pu'kă**, **pōmaĭka'ĭ**.
program, **kuhĭkuhĭ'nă**.
progress, **holŏmu'ă**: to progress, **nĕ'ĕ ĭmŭ'ă**.
prohibit, **pa'pa'**, **hŏ'ōkă'pŭ**.
prohibition, **hŏ'ō'lĕ wăĭ'ō'nă**.
project, **păpăhă'nă**: to project, **hō'oĭ**; (throw),
   nŏŭ.
prominent, **'oĭ**, **kĭ'ĕkĭ'ĕ**; (eminent), **kŏ'ĭkŏ'ĭ**.
promise, **'ōle'lŏ pa'ă**, **hŏ'ōhi'kĭ**.
promote, (in rank), **hŏ'ōkĭ'ĕkĭ'ĕ**; (initiate),
   hŏ'ōkŭ'mŭ.
prompt, **makăŭkăŭ**, **'ĕlĕ'ŭ**.
pronounce, **pua'nă**.
proof, **'ōle'lŏ hō'ō'ĭă**; (printer's), **pă'ĭ mu'ă**.
propaganda, **hŏ'ōlă'hă mană'ŏ**.
proper, **kūpo'nŏ**.
property, (real), **wăĭwăĭ pa'ă**; (personal),
   wăĭwăĭ lĕ'wă.

prophecy, prophesy, wānă'nă.

prophet, kāŭlă.

proportion, hŏ'ŏkăŭlĭ'kĕ.

propose, (propound), hă'ĭ mană'ŏ; (nominate), kŏ'hŏ ĭnŏ'ă; (marriage), noĭ e malĕ.

proposition, mană'ŏhă'ĭ.

proprietor, hă'kŭ, o'nă.

prose, 'ōle'lŏ mă'ămăŭ.

prosecute, (arraign), hŏ'ŏpĭ'ĭ; (carry on), hŏ-'ŏmăŭ.

prospect, (scene), nanăĭnă; (expectation), meă kăkălĭĭ'ă: to prospect, 'ĭ'mĭ lō'ă.

prosper, prosperity, kŭ'o'nŏ'o'nŏ.

prostitute, wăhi'nĕ hŏ'ŏkă'măkă'mă: (to debase), hŏ'ŏhă'ăhă'ă.

protect, hŏ'ŏmă'lŭ, mălă'mă.

protest, 'ōle'lŏ kŭ'ĕ': to protest, hŏ'ŏha'lăha'-lă, hŏ'ŏ'lĕ.

Protestant, Hō'ō'lĕ Po'pĕ.

proud, hŏ'ŏkă'nŏ, hă'ăhe'ŏ.

prove, hŏ'ŏ'ĭai'ŏ.

proverb, 'ōle'lŏ no'ĕaŭ.

provide, hŏ'ŏlă'kŏ, lōlĭ'ĭ.

providence, mălă'mă ă'nă.

province, panălā'ăŭ; (sphere), kŭleă'nă, măhe'lĕ o kā 'oĭhă'nă.

provisions, meă 'ăĭ.

provoke, hŏ'ŏnaŭ'kĭŭ'kĭ; (incite), hŏ'ŏlă'lĕ.

prudent, (cautious), ākăhĕ'lĕ; (wise), no'ĕaŭ.

pry, (spy), hŏ'ŏmākăkĭ'ŭ; (lever), ŭ'nĕ, 'ohĭ'kĭ.

public, lāhu'ĭ, le'hŭle'hŭ: (open), ākeă.

publicity, lăŭla'hă.

publish, (announce), hŏ'ŏlă'hă, kūkă'lă; (issue), hŏ'ŏpŭ'kă.

puff, (of wind), pūahi'ŏ: to puff, pŭ'hĭ.

pull, (backing), kōkŭ'ā: to pull, hŭ'kĭ; pull up, ūhu'kĭ; (row), hoĕ.

pulley, (block), pala'ka; (wheel), pokākā'ā.

pulse, pä'nă.

pump, paŭmă; (quiz), niĕnie'lĕ.

pumpkin, pălā'ăĭ, ĭ'pŭ pū.

punch, (with fist), kŭ'ĭ; (poke), hoŭ: metal punch, hāŏ hoŭ pu'kă.

punish, punishment, hŏ'ŏpă'ĭ.

punk, (for mosquitoes), păŭkă māki'kă.

pupil, haŭmā'nă; (of eye), 'ono'hĭ.

purchase, kū'āĭ māĭ.

pure, purity, ma'ĕma'ĕ.

purple, po'nĭ.

purpose, mană'ŏ pa'ă.

purse, 'ĕ'kĕ kālā, 'ă'ă mo'nĭ.

pursue, pursuit, hahăĭ, a'lŭă'lŭ: (occupation), 'oĭhă'nă.

push, pa'hŭ.

put, (place), waĭhŏ, kăŭ; (in golf), hĭ'lĭ.

puzzle, pohĭhi'hĭ: to puzzle, ho'opōhĭhi'hĭ.

pyramid, pu'o'ă.

Q

quail, ma'nŭ kăpălŭ'lŭ.

quake, earthquake, (ke) ola'ĭ, nāŭĕŭĕ: (to tremble), hă'ălŭ'lŭ.

qualification, mākăŭkăŭ.

qualify, hŏ'ŏkupo'nŏ, hŏ'ŏmākăŭkăŭ.

quality, 'ă'nŏ; (rank), kūlă'nă kĭ'ĕkĭ'ĕ.

quantity, nu'ĭ, kŭani'kĕ.

quarantine, hŏ'ŏmă'lŭ.

quarrel, hŏ'ŏpă'āpă'ă, hăkăka', pa'ĭŏ.

quart, kŭă'tă.

quarter, (a fourth), hapăhā'; (mercy), (ke)
   āhŏnu'ï: quarters, kăŭwă'hĭ.

quartet, le'ŏ me'lĕ pāhā'.

queen, mōīwăhi'nĕ, ălĭ'ĭwăhi'nĕ.

queer, 'ănŏĕ'.

question, ninaŭ, niĕ'lĕ, u'ĭ; (doubt), kānălŭ'ă;
   (subject of discussion), kŭ'mŭ pa'ĭŏ.

questionnaire, pă'lăpă'lă ninaninaŭ.

quick, wĭ'kĭwĭ'kĭ, hikĭwa'wĕ; (hasty), 'āwīwī;
   (nimble), māmā; quick-minded, 'a'ă'pŏ.

quicksand, (ke) o'nĕ pohŏ'.

quiet, māli'ĕ, nā, ma'lŭ, malŭhi'ă.

quilt, kă'pă 'āpă'nă, kīheĭ.

quisling, kūmakaĭă.

quit, (leave), hă'ălĕ'lĕ: Quit! 'uŏ'kĭ!

quite, (wholly), a păŭ; (very), lo'ă.

quiver, (as wings), kăpălĭ'lĭ; (as lips), hă-
   'ŭkĕ'kĕ.

quota, māhe'lĕ kănlĭ'kĕ.

quotation, 'ōle'lĕ i unuhĭĭ'ă; (market), pă'pă
   hō'ĭkĕ kŭmŭkū'ăĭ.

R

rabbit, 'ĭŏ'lĕ lăpā'kĭ.

race, hĕĭhĕĭ; footrace, kūki'nĭ; (breed), **ma'-
   mŏ**; human race, lāhu'ĭ kănă'kă.

radius, kăhăhănăĭ.

raffle, 'ĭ'mĭ lōa'a.

raft, lă'nă, meă hŏ'ōlă'nă.

rag, wĕ'lŭ.

rage, hūhŭ' nu'ĭ, ĭnăĭnă; (of sea or mob), kū-
   pĭkĭpĭkĭ'ō'.

raid, (incursion), pāka'hă; police raid, hŏ'pŭ-
   hŏ'pŭ.

rail, kaŏ'lă; to rail, kūa'mŭa'mŭ: railroad, (ke)
   alăhaŏ.

rain, u'ă.

rainbow, (ke) ānu'ĕnu'ĕ.

raise, (lift), hăpăĭ; (rouse), hō'a'lă; (grow),
   hŏ'ŏŭ'lŭ; (increase), hŏ'ŏmāhu'ăhu'ă; (bring
   up), hănăĭ.

rake, ko'pĕ, hăŏmă'nămă'nă: to rake, hāpu'kŭ,
   hăŏ.

rally, (stir up), hō'ĕ'ŭ'ĕ'ŭ; (combine), a'lŭ.

ram, hi'pă ka'nĕ: to ram, hoŭ, pa'hŭ.

ranch, wa'hĭ hānăĭ hŏlŏhŏlo'nă.

range, (row), lāla'nĭ; (extent), (ke) ākeă;
   (power), hi'kĭ.

rank, (grade), kūlă'nă, pă'pă; (row), lāla'nĭ:
   (foul-smelling), hăŭnă; rank growth, u'lŭ
   nu'ĭ, hĭ'hĭ.

ransom, ŭ'kŭ pănă'ĭ: to ransom, pānă'Ĭ.

rap, kīkē', kīkēkē'; (to hit), kiko'nĭ.

rapid, hikĭwa'wĕ, kĭkĭ'.

rare, (underdone), mo'ă i'ki; (scarce), kakăi-
   ka'hĭ; (choice), mi'lĭmi'lĭ.

rash, 'a'ă nă'ăŭpō.

raspberry, 'ākă'lă.

rat, 'ĭŏ'lĕ.

rate, (ke) 'ă'nŏ; (price), kŭmŭkū'ăĭ: to rate,
   hŏ'ŏkūlă'nă.

rather, (by preference), ā'hŏ; (somewhat), ĭ'kĭ.

rating, kūlă'nă.

ration, māhe'lĕ 'ăĭ.

rattle, nakĕ'kĕ.

ravage, lŭ'kŭ, hŏ'ŏnĕ'ŏnĕ'ŏ, hăŏwa'lĕ.

rave, kămă'ĭlĭ'ŏ pūpu'lĕ, wălă'ăŭ mĕ kā hŭhū';
   (go into raptures), ŏhŏhi'ă; (talk irration-
   ally), 'ŏlĕ'ŏlĕ'.

ravish, (rape), pŭ'ĕ; (enrapture), hŏĭhŏĭ.

raw, (uncooked), mă'kă; (of meat), kŏ'lĕkŏ'lĕ;
    (cold and damp), kŏ'ĕkŏ'ĕ; raw materials,
    nā meă mă'kă, nā la'kŏ maolĭ.

rayon, hapăkĭli'kă.

razor, pă'hĭ 'ŭ'mĭ'ŭ'mĭ.

reach, (stretch), kīkŏ'ŏ lālaŭ; (extend), hŏ-
    ho'lă.

read, he'lŭhe'lŭ.

ready, makăŭkăŭ, lōlĭ'ĭ.

real, 'o'ĭai'ŏ, maolĭ.

realize, (achieve), kō; (get), lōa'a; (appre-
    hend), hŏ'ŏmaŏpŏ'pŏ; (gain), pu'kă.

rear, ho'pĕ; (of army), hŭnăpa'a: (to foster),
    hănăĭ; (raise), hōa'lă; (build), kūku'lŭ.

reason, (faculty), no'ŏno'ŏ kănă'kă; (motive),
    kŭ'mŭ: to reason, no'ŏno'ŏ pū.

reasonable, kūpo'nŏ, kū i kā no'ŏno'ŏ.

rebel, kĭ'pĭ.

rebellion, kĭ'pĭ aŭpu'nĭ.

recall, (bring back), ho'ĭho'ĭ măĭ; (remember),
    hŏ'ŏmană'ŏ.

recede, recession, ho'ĭ ĭho'pĕ, e'mĭ.

receipt, (payment), likĭ'kĭ, pă'lăpă'lă hŏ'ŏkă'ă;
    (recipe), lu'lă wĕ'hĕwĕ'hĕ.

receive, lōa'a.

recent, ĭ'hŏ nĕĭ, hoŭ.

reception, (social), kĭ'pă ă'nă; (receiving), lō-
    a'a ă'nă.

recess, (nook), kū'o'nŏ; (vacation), hŏ'ŏma'hă.

reckon, (count), he'lŭ; (consider), ŏ'ŏno'ŏ.

recognize, recognition, 'ĭ'kĕ, hŏ'ŏmaŏpŏ'pŏ.

recommend, 'āpo'nŏ.

record, mŏ'ole'lŏ kakăŭ; (in sports), pŏ'ŏke'lă
    (phonograph), pā hŏ'ŏkă'nĭ.

recover, (regain), lōa‘a hoŭ; (in health), o‘lă
   hoŭ, konăkŏne‘ă; (cover again), u‘hĭ hoŭ.
recreation, pā‘a‘nĭ ă‘nă, hŏ‘ŏnănĕ‘ă ă‘nă.
recruit, koă hoŭ: (to recuperate), hŏ‘ŏĭkăĭkă
   hoŭ.
red, ‘u‘lă‘u‘lă.
reduce, (diminish), hō‘e‘mĭ; (conquer), hŏ‘ŏ-
   pĭ‘ŏ.
reef, pūko‘ă; bare reef, kūă‘ăŭ, kŏhŏ‘lă: to
   reef, lĭ.
reel, pokăkă‘ă wĭ‘lĭ: (to stagger), hĭkăkă.
refer, ku‘hĭku‘hĭ; (as to committee), waĭhŏ.
referee, meă ŭwaŏ.
reference, pi‘lĭ ă‘nă.
referendum, aĕ kūĭkăwă‘.
reflect, (consider), no‘ŏno‘ŏ; (as light), ‘ănă‘pă.
reflection, (image), (ke) a‘kă; (blot), kĭnă‘.
reform, hă‘nă hoŭ, hŏ‘ŏpo‘nŏ ă‘nă: (to reclaim),
   hŏ‘ŏhŭ‘lĭ hoŭ.
refrigerator, pa‘hŭ haŭ.
refuge, pŭ‘ŭhonu‘ă, wă‘hĭ palĕkă‘nă.
refund, (as over-payment), ho‘ĭho‘ĭ hoŭ; (to
   reimburse), pă‘nĭ hoŭ.
refuse, ‘ŏpă‘lă: to refuse, hō‘o‘lĕ.
regard, (attention), mali‘ŭ; (respect), māhă‘lŏ;
   (reference), ku‘hĭku‘hĭ ă‘nă: to regard, hŏ‘ŏ-
   lŏ‘hĕ.
regiment, pū‘ă‘lĭ koă.
region, wă‘hĭ, moku‘ăĭnă; (in compounds), ăŭ-,
   waŏ-.
register, pu‘kĕ hŏ‘ŏpa‘ă ĭnŏă: to register,
   (record), kakăŭ; (indicate), hŏ‘ĭ‘kĕ; (as
   letters), hŏ‘ŏpa‘ă.
regret, mĭ‘nămĭ‘nă, mi‘hĭ.
regular, kū i kā pololeĭ, wălĕă.

regulate, hŏ'ŏpo'nŏpo'nŏ.

regulation, lu'lă.

reign, no'hŏ ălĭ'ĭ ă'nă, (ke) aŭ.

rein, kăŭlăwă'hă.

rejoice, hăŭ'o'lĭ.

relate, (tell), hă'ĭ; (refer), pi'lĭ.

relation, (narrative), ka'aŏ; (kin), pi'lĭ kŏ'kŏ, 'oha'nă, pilĭka'nă.

release, hŏ'ŏkŭ'ŭ, wĕ'hĕ.

reliable, păŭlĕlĕĭ'ă, 'ŏ'iăi'ŏ.

relic, meă hŏ'ŏmană'ŏ, kŏĕnă nō kē kūpāpa'ŭ.

relief, (respite), ma'hă; (help), kōkŭ'ă; (substitute), (ke) pănĭhă'kăhă'kă, ho'pĕ.

relieve, hŏ'ŏma'hă.

religion, hŏ'ŏmă'nă.

religious, hăĭpu'lĕ, mană'ŏĭ'ŏ.

relish, meă mĭ'kŏmĭ'kŏꞏ to relish, 'o'nŏ.

rely, păŭlĕ'lĕ, hilĭnă'ĭ.

remain, (stay), no'hŏ; (be left), kŏĕ: remains, kŏĕnă.

remark, wă'hĭ 'ōle'lŏ: to remark, hă'ĭ.

remarkable, kămăhă'ŏ.

remedy, (physic), meă hōo'lă, lă'ăŭ lăpăăŭ; (redress), meă e po'nŏ ăĭ.

remember, hŏ'ŏmană'ŏ.

remind, hōa'lă mană'ŏ, paĭpaĭ.

remit, (as taxes), hŏ'ŏkŭ'ŭ; (transmit), hŏ-'ŏĭ'lĭ.

remittance, (money), kălā i hŏ'ŏĭlĭ'ĭ'ă.

remove, (take), la'wĕ ă'kŭ; (leave), he'lĕ ă'kŭ; (dismiss), hŏ'ŏpăŭ.

renew, hă'nă hoŭ; (note), hăă'wĭ hoŭ i pi'lă 'ăĭ'ē'.

renown, kăŭlă'nă.

rent, (fissure), mawaĕ; (tear), năhaĕhaĕ: to rent, hŏ'ŏlĭ'mălĭ'mă.

repair, 'ă'nŏ: to repair, hă'nă hoŭ, kāpĭ'lĭ.

repeal, hŏ'ŏpăŭ, hŏ'ŏno'ă.

repeat, hă'ĭ hoŭ, kūkă'ĭ'ole'lŏ.

repel, pa'lĕ, hŏ'ŏku'ĕ', kīpă'kŭ.

repent, mi'hĭ.

replace, ho'ĭho'ĭ; (supercede), pă'nĭ hoŭ.

reply, pa'nĕ; (rejoin), kīkē'.

report, lo'nŏ; formal report, hŏ'ĭ'kĕ; (noise), pŏhă'.

reporter, kakăŭ nūpĕ'pă.

represent, kū nŏ ha'ĭ, pă'nĭ; (show), hŏ'ĭ'kĕ.

representative, lu'nă măkă'ăĭnă'nă, ho'pĕ: (typical), kūli'kĕ.

republic, (ke) aŭpu'nĭ măkă'ăĭnă'nă.

Republican, Rĕpŭpălĭ'kă.

reputation, ĭnŏă.

request, noĭ.

require, kŏĭ, kăŭo'hă; (need), he'măhe'mă.

requisition, pă'lăpă'lă kŏĭ.

rescue, hŏ'ŏpake'lĕ.

research, noĭ'ĭ.

resemble, hŏ'ŏhălĭ'kĕ, kūlĭ'kĕ.

resent, u'kĭu'kĭ.

reserve, waĭho'nă, mălămăĭ'ă; (aloofness), hŏ-'ŏkă'nŏ, hŏ'ŏkă'ŏkŏ'ă: to reserve, hŏ-'ŏkŏĕ.

reservoir, lu'ă wăĭ, waĭho'nă wăĭ.

residence, wă'hĭ no'hŏ.

resign, waĭhŏ, hă'ălĕ'lĕ.

resist, pa'lĕ, ku'ĕ'.

resolute, kūpa'ă, 'ŏ'nĭ pa'ă.

resolution, (formality), 'ŏle'lŏ hŏ'ŏho'lŏ; (resolve), 'ŏ'nĭ pa'ă.

resolve, hŏʻŏhoʻlŏ, manäʻŏ.

resort, kăʻhĭ e heʻlĕ pĭʻnĕpĭʻnĕ äĭ: to resort, ʻäkŏʻäkŏʻä, heʻlĕ pĭʻnĕpĭʻnĕ; (for aid). ʻĭʻmĭ kōkŭʻä.

resources, wăĭwăĭ.

respect, māhäʻlŏ.

response, paʻnĕ.

responsible, kū; (important), kŏʻĭkŏʻĭ.

rest, maʻhä; (support), kŏʻŏ; (remainder), kŏĕnä: to rest, hŏʻŏmaʻhä.

restaurant, haʻlĕ ʻäĭnä.

restore, (return), hoʻihoʻĭ; (heal), hō̆ʻō̆ʻlä.

restrain, kaohĭ, kĕʻäkĕʻä.

restrict, käŭpălĕʻnä.

result, hopĕʻnä, huʻä i lōaʻa.

resume, hŏʻŏmäʻkä hoŭ.

retail, kūʻäĭ hŏʻŏpuʻkäpuʻkä.

retain, hŏʻŏpaʻä.

retainer, (fee), uʻkŭ hŏʻŏpaʻä lōʻĭŏ; (dependents), ʻohuʻä.

retire, (withdraw), heʻlĕ aʻkŭ; (as bonds), uʻkŭ.

retreat, wăʻhĭ malū', pŭʻŭhonuʻä: to retreat, ʻaŭhĕʻĕ.

return, (profit), puʻkä; (report), păʻpä hōʻĭ-kĕ: to return, hoʻĭ; (restore), hoʻihoʻĭ.

reveal, hōʻĭʻkĕ.

revenge, pänäʻĭ i kä ʻĭʻnŏ nō kä ʻĭʻnŏ; to seek revenge, hŏʻŏmäŭhaʻlä.

revenue, nä lōaʻa.

reverence, ʻĕʻĕhiʻä, hōʻäʻnŏ.

reverse, kekäʻhĭ ʻäŏʻäŏ äʻkŭ; (loss), pōʻĭʻnŏ: to reverse, hŏʻŏlŏʻlĭ aʻĕ.

review, nanäĭnä ĭhoʻpĕ: to review, hoʻĭ ĭhoʻpĕ; (as troops), mäkaʻĭkaʻĭ; (as a book), hŭʻlĭ.

revive, (recover), poha'lă; (revivify), hŏ'ŏ-
poha'lă; (as business), hō'a'lă hoŭ.

revolt, (to rebel), kĭ'pĭ; (disgust), hŏ'ŏpăĭlŭ'ă.

revolution, hō'äŭhŭ'lĭ ă'nă; (turning), ka'a
a'na.

revolve, kă'ă.

revolver, pūpă'năpă'nă.

reward, u'kŭ.

rheumatism, lūmakĭ'kă.

rib, ĭ'wĭ 'ăŏ'ăŏ; rib of ship, waĕ.

ribbon, līpĭ'nĕ.

rice, laĭkĭ.

rice-bird, 'äĭlaĭkĭ.

rich, wăĭwăĭ, la'kŏ.

rid, hŏ'ŏkă'äwa'lĕ a'kŭ.

riddle, nă'nĕ.

ride, kăŭ, hŏ'ŏho'lŏ.

ridge, (sharp), kuălă'pă; (broad), kuălŏ'nŏ.

ridicule, hŏ'ŏhĕ'nĕhĕ'nĕ.

ridiculous, hŏ'ŏmăkĕ'ă'kă.

rifle, pū; to rifle, pōwă'.

rigging, likĭ'nĭ.

right, (title), kūleă'nă: (proper), po'nŏ, kūpo'nŏ, pololeĭ; (dextral), 'äkaŭ: to right,
hŏ'ŏpo'nŏpo'nŏ, hŏ'ŏpololeĭ.

righteousness, po'nŏ.

rim, kă'ĕ, li'hĭ.

ring, (ke) a'pŏ; (finger), kŏ'mŏ; (group),
hŭ'ĭ; (boxing), wă'hĭ mō'kŏmō'kŏ: to ring,
kă'nĭ, hŏ'ŏkă'nĭ.

riot, hăŭnaĕlĕ.

rip, năhaĕ.

ripe, (mature), o'o; (mellow), pă'lă.

rise, (ascent), pĭ'ĭ'nă; (origin), kŭ'mŭ: (ascend), pĭ'ĭ; (arise), a'lă; (stand), kū;
(emerge), pu'kă.

risk, pĭlĭkĭ'ă: to risk, 'a'ă.

rival, hoăpaĭŏ: to rival, paĭŏ pū.

river, mulĭwăĭ; (stream), kăhăwăĭ.

roach, 'ĕlĕlū'.

road, (ke) a'lă, (ke) alănŭ'ĭ.

roar, (of animal), 'ŭwŏ'; (of surf), pă'ĕpŭ'.

roast, lo'kĕ, hō'ō' o'mă; (in ground), kālŭ'ă.

rob, robber, pōwă', hăŏ wa'lĕ.

rock, pōha'kŭ nunu'ĭ; sunken rock, pūko'ă:
to rock, (as a chair), paĭpaĭ; (as a ship),
kŭlă'nă, kū'ŏ'ĭ.

rod, lă'ăŭ; (staff), kŏ'ŏkŏ'ŏ; (fishing), mokŏĭ.

roll, 'ōwĭ'lĭ; (list), pă'pă ĭnŏ'ă; (bread), pala'oă lĭ'ĭlĭ'ĭ: to roll, kă'ă, hŏ'ŏkă'ă; (as a
stone), 'olŏkă'ă; roll over, kăkă'ă; roll up,
'ōwĭ'lĭ.

romance, (novel), ka'aŏ; (love affair), pi'lĭ
ālo'hă: to romance, hă'ănu'ĭ.

roof, kăŭpă'kŭ.

room, lŭ'mĭ, keĕ'nă; (space), wă'hĭ ākeă.

rooster, mo'ă ka'nĕ.

root, a'ă; taproot, mŏ'lĕ; (origin), kŭ'mŭ: to
take root, ko'lŏ kē a'ă; (as a hog), 'ĕ'kŭ;
root out, ūhu'kĭ.

rope, kăŭlă.

rose, lo'kĕ.

rot, pălăhō'; (nonsense), lăpŭwa'lĕ: to rot,
pŏ'pŏ.

rotten, pōpŏ'pŏ; (of eggs), aĕlŏ.

rough, kă'lăkă'lă; (as land), 'apŭ'ŭpŭ'ŭ, mă-
lu'ălu'ă; (as sea), kŭpĭkĭpĭkĭ'ō'; (uncivil),
ni'hă.

round, (cycle), pu'nĭ: (circular or globular),
poĕpoĕ: to make round, pōpō; to round
off, pōhŭ'kŭ; round-up. hōā', hŏ'ōhŭ'lĭ.

rout, 'aŭhĕ'ĕ: to rout, hō'āŭhĕ'ĕ; rout out,
hŏ'ōhū'.

route, (ke) alāhe'lĕ: to route, hŏ'ōmoĕ kē a'lā.

routine, hă'nă mă'āmăŭ.

row, (line), lāla'nĭ; (dispute), hŏ'ŏpa'ăpa'ă;
(riot), hăŭnaĕlĕ: to row boat, hoĕ.

rowboat, wă'āpā.

royal, ālĭ'ĭ.

rub, (lightly), kūăĭ; (heavily), 'ānăĭ; (back
and forth), kŭo'lŏ.

rubber, lahŏli'ŏ.

rubbish, (waste), 'ŏpă'lă; (nonsense), lăpŭwa'lĕ.

rudder, hoĕu'lĭ.

rude, (crude), hāwāwā', nā'ăŭpō; (impolite),
hŏ'ŏkă'nŏ, ni'hă.

rug, moĕnă pa'lĕ wāwaĕ.

ruin, (adversity), pŏ'ĭ'nŏ lŏ'ă; (destruction),
hio'lŏ ă'nă: to ruin, hŏ'ŏkăhŭ'lĭ.

rule, lōină, lu'lă: (to govern), hŏ'ŏmă'lŭ: to
rule a line, kă'hă lāla'nĭ.

ruler, (governor), (ke) pŏ'ŏ aŭpu'nĭ; (implement), lu'lă, kă'hă lāla'nĭ.

rumble, hămŭ'mŭ, kāmŭ'mŭ.

rumor, lo'nŏ wa'lĕ.

rump, kīkă'lă, ho'pĕ.

run, ho'lŏ; (flow), kă'hĕ.

runner, kūki'nĭ.

rural, kuă'ăină.

rush, (plant), nānă'kŭ, 'ākă'ăkaĭ; (hurry),
ho'lŏ nu'ĭ: to rush, 'āwīwĭ.

Russia, Lukĭ'ă.

Russian, Lukĭ'nĭ.

rust, kūkaĕhāŏ.

ruthless, lŏkŏ'ĭ'nŏ, me'nĕme'nĕ 'o'lĕ.

S

sabotage, hŏ'ŏpo'ĭ'nŏ malū'.

sack, 'ĕ'kĕ: to sack, pōwā'; (dismiss), kĭpă'kŭ.

sacred, (holy), hŏ'ā'nŏ; (consecrated), lă'ă.

sacrifice, (offering), mohăĭ; (loss), pohŏ': to
    sacrifice, hăĭ, mohăĭ, kăŭma'hă; (to lose),
    hŏ'ŏpohō'.

sad, kăŭmă'hă, lŭ'ŭlŭ'ŭ, 'ĕ'hă'ĕ'hă.

saddle, nohŏli'ŏ.

safe, palĕkă'nă, ma'lŭ: iron safe, pa'hŭ hăŏ.

safety, malŭhi'ă.

sail, pĕ'ă: to sail, ho'lŏ.

sailboat, wă'ăpā pĕ'ă.

sailor, lui'nă, kĕ'lă mo'kŭ.

saint, hăĭpu'lĕ.

sake, po'nŏ.

salad, (no Hawaiian term).

salary, u'kŭ kūmăŭ.

sale, kū'ăĭ lĭ'lŏ.

salesman, kănă'kă kū'ăĭ.

salmon, kămă'nŏ.

saloon, ha'lĕ ĭ'nŭ lă'mă.

salt, pa'ăkăĭ: (seasoned), mi'kŏ; (briny), li'ŭ:
    to salt, kōpĭ'.

salute, hŏ'ăĭlo'nă māhā'lŏ: to salute, hăă'wĭ
    māhā'lŏ.

salvation, (ke) o'lă, o'lă măŭ lŏ'ă.

same, lĭ'kĕ, hŏ'ŏkă'hĭ.

Samoa, Kāmoă.

sample, 'ă'nŏ hŏ'ŏhălĭ'kĕ, 'ă'nŏ lĭ'kĕ.

sanctuary, wǎ'hǐ hō'ā'nǒ; (asylum), pǔ'ǔhonu'ǎ.

sand, (ke) o'nĕ.

sandals, kāmǎ'ǎ, kāmǎ'ǎ hawĕ'lĕ.

sanderling, hunǎkǎǐ.

sandwich, 'ǎǐ māmā: to sandwich, hǒ'ǒkǒ'mǒ mawaĕnǎ o nā meǎ elu'ǎ.

sane, mǎǐka'ǐ kā no'ǒno'ǒ.

sanitarium, haǔkǎpi'lǎ.

sanitary, o'lǎ kǐ'nǒ.

sap, kǒ'hǔ, wǎǐ. sap-head, nā'ǎǔpǒ.

sarcasm, hǒ'ǒnā'ǎǐkǒ'lǎ.

sarcastic, kīkoǐ, hǒ'ǒhĕ'nĕhĕ'nĕ.

sash, kā'ĕǐ, a'pǒ, kūa'pǒ.

Satan, sata'nǎ, kǐǎ'pǒlǒ.

satin, kǐli'kǎ pahoĕhoĕ.

satisfaction, (ke) ā'nǎ o kā mǎ'kĕmǎ'kĕ, 'o'lǔo'lǔ o kā manǎ'ǒ.

satisfactory, 'āponǒǐ'ǎ, la'wǎ nǒ.

satisfy, (satiate), hǒ'ǒma'onǎ; (content), ma'hǎ; (prove), hǒ'ǒlǎ; (as of claim), hǒ'ǒkǎ'ǎ.

Saturday, Pǒ'ao'nǒ.

sauce, kǎǐ, mikǒ: to sauce, pākikĕ', hǒnĕkǒ'ǎ.

saucer, pā lǐ'ǐlǐ'ǐ.

sausage, nā'ǎǔ kā'kĕ.

savage, (barbarous), hihǐ'ǔ; (cruel), lǒkǒ'ǐ'nǒ; (uncivilized), hūpǒ.

save, (rescue), hǒ'ǒpākĕ'lĕ; (redeem), hǒ'ǒlǎ: (except), kǒĕ.

savings, lǒa'a hōǐ'lǐǐ'lǐ.

savior, meǎ hǒ'ǒpākĕ'lĕ ā'nǎ; The Savior, Kā Hǒ'ǒ'lǎ, Ie'sū Kri'sto.

saw, (ke) o'lǒ, pāhǐo'lǒ: to saw, o'lǒ.

say, 'ōle'lǒ, 'ǐ, hǎ'ǐ.

scale, (measure), (ke) ā'nă; (in music), pākō-
lī; fish-scale, una'hī: (to ascend), pǐ'ǐ; scale
fish, unăŭnă'hī.

scales, (balances), kăŭpăŏnă.

scalp, 'ǐlǐpŏ'ŏ.

scandal, hō'ǐ'nŏ, 'ōle'lŏ hŏ'ŏhaŭmi'ă.

scar, āli'nă, li'năli'nă.

scarce, kakă'ǐkă'hī.

scare, hŏ'ŏpuǐwă, hŏ'ŏmakă'ŭkă'ŭ.

scatter, (strew), lū, hŏ'ŏhelelĕǐ; (disperse),
hŏ'ŏpue'hŭ,

scene, nanāǐnă.

scent, (see "perfume"); (trail), mehe'ŭ: (to
track), hă'nŭhă'nŭ.

schedule, pă'pă hō'ǐ'kĕ; (of prices), pă'pă ku'-
hǐku'hī kŭmŭkū'ăǐ.

scheme, kŭmŭhă'nă: to scheme, hŏ'ŏno'hŏno'-
hŏ hă'nă.

scholar, (pupil), haumā'nă; (sage), kănă'kă
no'ĕaŭ.

school, ku'lă; school-teacher, kŭmŭku'lă.

science, (ke) ākĕăkămăǐ.

scissors, 'ūpā'.

scold, nŭ'kŭ.

scoop, kǐŏ'ĕ: (to beat competitor), kā'ǐlǐ mu'ă.

scorch, (as food), hŏ'ŏpapă'ă; (as clothes),
'ăni'ă.

score, (count), he'lŭ; (to scratch), kă'hăkă'hă.

scorn, hŏ'ŏwăhăwăha'.

scorpion, mŏ'ŏnihŏ'ă'wă, mŏ'ŏhuĕlŏ'ă'wă.

Scotland, Kekoki'ă.

scoundrel, kănă'kă 'ǐ'nŏ.

scout, kǐ'ŭ: boy or girl scouts, pūă'lǐ kămălǐ'ǐ.

scowl, hŏ'ŏkŭĕkŭĕmă'kă.

scramble, hŏ'pŭhŏ'pŭ.

scrap, hăki'nă, hu'nă; (fight), hăkăkă'.

scrape, hĭhĭ'ă, pĭlĭkĭ'ă: to scrape, kĕ'pă.

scratch, kă'hă: to scratch, wă'ŭwă'ŭ; (as a hen), he'lŭ; (as a cat), ŭwa'lŭ.

scream, ŭwā', ŭwē' nu'ĭ, ŭwa'lŏ.

screen, (sieve), kānă'nă; (partition), pākū; (moving-pictures), kĭ'ĭ 'ŏ'nĭ'ŏ'nĭ: to screen, pa'lĕ, hūnā'.

screw, kuĭnăŏ; (propellor), wĭ'lĭ kăkă'ă; corkscrew, wĭ'lĭ 'ŭmo'kĭ: to screw, wĭ'li.

Scriptures, Băĭba'lă, Pă'lăpă'lă Hemŏlĕ'lŏ.

scrub, (brushwood), nahe'lĕhe'lĕ; scrub-team, hu'ĭ holo'nă: to scrub, holoĭ.

sea, seawater, kăĭ.

seaman, lui'nă.

sea-sick, pŏlueă, lua'ĭ.

sea-urchin, wă'nă, 'ĭ'nă, hău'kĕu'kĕ, etc.

seaward, ĭkăĭ, mākăĭ.

seaweed, lĭ'mŭ.

seal, (mammal), 'ĭlĭ'ŏ ho'lŏ i Kăŭăŭă, ŭwa'lŏ; (die), kĭ'lă, hŏăllŏ'nă pa'ı: to seal, kı'lă.

seam, kŭ'ĭ'nă.

search, 'ĭ'mĭ, hŭ'lĭ.

search-light, mălă'mălă'mă kīkŏ'ŏ.

season, kăŭ; (of growth), lā'ăŭlŭ: out of season), lā'ăwe'lă: to season, (food), hŏ'ŏmĭ'kŏ; (as lumber), hŏ'ŏmalo'ŏ.

seat, no'hŏ: to seat, hŏ'ŏno'hŏ.

second, (in time), keko'nă; (backer), kŏkŭ'ă, ho'pĕ: (in order), kā lu'ă: (to support), kŏkŭ'ă.

secret, meă hu'nă, malŭ': to secrete, hūnā'.

secretary, kakăŭ'ōle'lŏ; secretary of state, kuhi'nă aŭpu'nĭ.

section, māhe'lĕ, hăki'nă.

secure, (tight), pa'ă; (protected), ma'lŭ: to se
  cure, lōa'a, hŏ'ŏpa'ă.

security, (safety), malŭhi'ă; (surety), wăïwăl
  hŏ'ŏpă'ă.

see, 'ï'kě, 'ïkěmă'kă; (look), nănă.

seed, (generally), 'ă'nŏ'ă'nŏ; (in pods), hu'ă.

seek, 'ï'mĭ, hŭ'lĭ.

seem, "it seems," mē hē meă lă, i kā nănă a'kŭ.

seize, (grasp), 'ă'pŏ; (arrest), hŏ'pŭ.

seldom, kakă'ïkă'hĭ.

select, mi'lĭmi'lĭ, pŏ'ŏke'lă: to select, waě,
  kŏ'hŏ.

self, ĭ'hŏ, ponŏ'ĭ.

selfish, pĭ, 'alŭ'nŭ, 'aŭ'ă.

sell, kū'ăï a'kŭ, kū'ăï lĭ'lŏ.

senate, kenā'kě.

senator, kenako'ă.

send, hŏ'ŏŭ'nă; send for, kēnă'; (as freight),
  hŏ'ŏï'lĭ.

senior, mu'ă, maku'ă.

sensation, (perception), hŏ'ŏmaŏpŏ'pŏ ă'nă.

sensational, hŏ'ŏpihŏïhŏï.

sense, 'ïkě; (meaning), 'ă'nŏ; (opinion), mană'ŏ: common sense, no'ŏno'ŏ maolĭ.

sensible, (cognizant), 'ï'kě; (reasonable), no'ŏ-
  no'ŏ.

sensitive, pihŏïhŏï kŏ'kě, kū'ï'ă wa'lě.

sentence, (clause), hōpună'ŏle'lŏ: to sentence,
  'ŏle'lŏ hŏ'ŏpă'ĭ.

sentiment, mană'ŏ, 'ŏle'lŏ pi'lĭ.

sentinel, sentry, ko'ă kiă'ĭ.

separate, kă'ăwa'lě, oko'ă: to separate, hŏ'ŏ-
  kă'ăwa'lě.

September, Kepakěma'pă.

sergeant, kakĭă'nă, lu'nă ko'ă.

series, pă'pă.

serious, (earnest), kūo'ŏ; (important), 'ă'nŏ kŏ'ĭkŏ'ĭ, 'ă'nŏ nu'ĭ.

sermon, hă'ĭa'ŏ.

servant, meă lă'wĕlă'wĕ, kăŭwā'.

serve, lă'wĕlă'wĕ, no'hŏ kăŭwā'.

service, lă'wĕlă'wĕ ă'nă; (duty), 'oĭhă'nă; (church), hālāwăĭ hăĭpu'lĕ.

session, no'hŏ ă'nă, hālāwăĭ.

set, (clique), hŭ'ĭ: (firm), pa'ă; (obstinate), pa'ăkikĭ', (immovable), 'ŏnĭpă'ă: to set, (place), kăŭ, hŏ'ŏno'hŏ, waĭhŏ; (as the sun), napŏ'ŏ.

settle, no'hŏ pa'ă; (sink), e'mĭ; (decide), hŏ'ŏ-ho'lŏ; (pay), hŏ'ŏkă'ă.

settlement, (village), kaŭhă'lĕ; (colony), pa-nālā'ăŭ.

seven, hĭkŭ, ehĭ'kŭ, 'ahĭ'kŭ: seventh, kă hĭ'kŭ.

seventeen, 'ŭmĭkŭmamahĭ'kŭ: seventeenth, kă 'umĭkŭmamahĭ'kŭ.

Seventh-Day Adventists, Hŏ'ŏmă'nă Pŏ'ao'nŏ.

seventy, kănăhĭ'kŭ: seventieth, kĕ kănăhĭ'ku.

several, măŭ, kekă'hĭ măŭ.

severe, (harsh), 'o'olĕ'ă; (violent), ĭkăĭkă; (as a storm), 'ĭ'nŏ.

sew, hŭ'mŭhŭ'mŭ.

sex, 'ă'nŏ ka'nĕ 'ă'nŏ wăhi'nĕ.

sextant, (ke) ā'nă hŭĭ'nă.

shade, ma'lŭ; eye-shade, u'hĭ mă'kă: to shade, hŏ'ŏmă'lŭmă'lŭ.

shadow, (ke) a'kă.

shaft, (column), kĭ'ă; mine-shaft, lu'ă 'ĕ'lĭ.

shake, lūlū', hŏ'ŏnaŭĕŭĕ; (as of earthquake), neĭ.

shallow, (shoal), păpă'ŭ; (as soil), hăpă'pă.

sham, hŏʻŏkămă'nĭ.

shame, hiʻlăhi'lă.

shape, hĭʻŏnă, 'ă'nŏ o kē kĭ'nŏ: to shape, hŏʻŏpo'nŏpo'nŏ; to shape a course, hŏʻŏpololeĭ.

shapely, 'ăŭlĭ'ĭ.

share, măhe'lĕ: to share, pŭʻŭnaŭĕ.

shark, (common), mănō'; man-eating shark,
nĭŭ'hĭ.

sharp, (in point), 'oĭ, wĭ'nĭwĭ'nĭ; (acid), 'ă'wă-
'ă'wă; (clever), ăkămăĭ; (in practice),
mă'ăle'ă.

shatter, wăwa'hĭ; shattered, nahahă'.

shave, (as beard), kă'hĭ; (whittle), kŏ'lĭ.

she, ĭă, o'ĭă.

shed, kămă'lă; to shed, pa'lĕ.

sheep, hi'pă.

sheet, (bed), u'hĭ pe'lă; (of paper), kălă'nă,
'ăpă'nă pĕ'pă.

shelf, kaŏ'lă, hăkăkăŭ.

shell, (as of crab), ĭ'wĭ; (projectile), pōkă'
păhŭ': to shell, (as beans), wĕ'hĕwĕ'hĕ.

shells, (most univalve mollusks), pūpū; of
bivalves: (clam), 'ŏlĕ'pĕ; (mussel), naha-
we'lĕ; (oyster), pĭ'pĭ.

shelter, wă'hĭ ma'lŭ, wă'hĭ lŭ'lŭ: to shelter,
hŏʻŏma'lŭma'lŭ.

shepherd, kahŭhi'pă.

sheriff, măka'ĭ nu'ĭ.

shield, pa'lĕ, pa'lĕ kăŭă.

shift, (share of work), măhe'lĕ hă'nă: to shift,
(change), hŏʻŏlŏ'lĭ; (as responsibility), ho-
ʻoĭ'lĭ.

shine, mălă'mălă'mă, alo'hĭ.

shingle, pilĭlă'ăŭ, pilĭha'lĕ: to shingle, kăpĭ'lĭ.

ship, mo'kŭ: to ship freight, hŏ'ŏĭ'lĭ ukā'nă
   hō'ŭ'ka: shipwreck, ĭlĭmo'kŭ.

shirt, pālu'lĕ.

shiver, hă'ŭkĕkĕ.

shoal, (shallows), pāpă'ŭ; shoal of fish, pū'ŭ'lĭ
   ĭ'ă.

shock, nāŭĕŭĕ: shock electrically, loă'ă i kā
   ŭwi'lă.

shocking, 'ĭlĭhĭ'ă, wĕ'lĭwĕ'lĭ.

shoe, kāmă'ă.

shoot, (young plant), 'ohā', pōhu'lĭ: to shoot,
   (as a gun), kĭ; (as an arrow), pa'nă;
   (sprout), kŭ'pŭ.

shop, (work), ha'lĕ 'oĭhă'nă; (store), ha'lĕ
   kŭ'ăi.

shore, kăhăkăĭ, kăpăkăĭ.

short, po'kŏ, poko'lĕ.

shortly, kokŏ'kĕ, 'ĕmŏ'ŏ'lĕ.

shot, (cannon), pōkă' pūkŭnĭă'hĭ; (bird), lū.

shoulder, pŏ'ŏhi'wĭ: (to carry), 'āŭă'mŏ, kăŭ-
   pŏ'ŏhĭ'wĭ; to shoulder off, hŏ'ŏkĕ'.

shout, hō'o'hŏ, ŭwā'.

shove, pa'hŭ, kŏ'ŏ maho'pĕ.

shovel, kopălă'.

show, hō'ĭ'kĕ: to show, hō'ĭ'kĕ'ĭ'kĕ; to show
   off, hŏ'ŏkă'hăkă'hă, hō'oĭŏ.

shower, (of rain), kūăŭă; sudden shower, naŭ
   lŭ; shower bath, 'ăŭ'ăŭ nĭnĭ'nĭ: (to rain
   u'ă, (to scatter), lū.

shrimp, 'ōpaĕ.

shrine, heĭaŭ, u'nŭ, ko'ă.

shrink, (contract), mĭmi'kĭ; (recoil), 'ĕ'ĕ'kĕ.

shrub, laălā'ăŭ.

shut, pă'nĭ.

shutter, 'olĕ'pĕlĕ'pĕ.

shy, (coy), hi'lăhi'lă; (timid), hŏ'pŏhŏ'pŏ, wi'-
   wo wa'lĕ.

shyster, 'apŭ'kă, ĕ'pă.

sick, (ill), mă'ĭ; (nauseated), pōlueă.

sickness, 'ŏmă'ĭmă'ĭ.

side, 'ăŏ'ăŏ; (of head), huăpŏ'ŏ: to side with,
   kōkŭ'ă.

siege, hŏ'ŏpŭ'nĭ kŭ'ĕ'.

sieve, sift, kănă'nă.

sight, 'ĭkĕmă'kă; (appearance), nanăĭnă: (to
   aim), lĕ'nă.

sign, hŏ'ăĭlŏ'nă; (omen), 'oŭlĭ: to sign, kakăŭ
   ĭnŏă.

signal, hŏ'ăĭlŏ'nă; (flag), haĕ hŏ'ăĭlŏ'nă: to
   signal, (nod) kunŏŭ; (by hand), pe'a'hĭ.

signature, ha'pă pūli'ma, ĭnŏă kakăŭĭ'ă.

silence, le'ŏ 'o'lĕ: to silence, hŏ'ŏpăŭ; (to hush),
   hamăŭ, hŏ'ŏmālĭ'ĕ.

silk, kĭli'kă.

silly, kŏ'hŭ 'o'lĕ, lăpŭwa'lĕ.

silver, kălă.

similar, 'ă'nŏ li'kĕ, lĭ'kĕ pū.

simple, (clear), maopŏ'pŏ, akă'ka; (natural),
   maolĭ; (i g n o r a n t), nă'ăŭpŏ; (feeble-
   minded), lŏlŏ.

sin, ha'lă, he'wă.

since, (ago), māmu'ă; (after), măho'pĕ măĭ;
   (because), nŏ kă meă; (while), 'oĭaĭ.

sincere, 'o'ĭai'ŏ, hŏ'ŏkămă'nĭ 'o'lĕ.

sing, hĭme'nĭ, me'lĕ.

single, hŏ'ŏkă'hĭ; (united), lŏka'hĭ; (unmar-
   ried), ma'lĕ 'o'lĕ: (to select), waĕ: (singly),
   pākă'hĭ.

sink, (kitchen), kă'hĭ holoĭ pā: to sink, pohŏ';
(in liquid), pălĕ'mŏ, piho'lŏ; (lessen),
hōe'mĭ.

sinner, lawĕha'lă, meă he'wă.

sip, mukīkī.

sir. No Hawaiian equivalent, but the following might serve: "Dear Sir," Alo'hă 'oĕ: (O
master), e kā hă'kŭ: (call for attention),
aŭhĕă 'oĕ, ĕĭă nĕĭ.

sister, hoăhānăŭ wăhi'nĕ; sister of brother,
kăĭkŭăhĭ'nĕ: o l d e r sister, kăĭkŭa'ă'nă;
younger sister, kăĭkăĭnă.

sit, no'hŏ.

site, kăhŭ'ă.

situation, (locality), kūlă'nă, kăŭwă'hĭ; (occupation), 'oĭhă'nă.

six, o'nŏ, eo'nŏ, 'ao'nŏ: sixth, kē o'nŏ.

sixteen, 'ŭmĭkūmamao'nŏ: sixteenth, kā 'ŭmĭkūmamao'nŏ.

sixty, kănăo'nŏ: sixtieth, kē kănăo'nŏ.

size, nu'ĭ.

skate, holŏhăŭ, he'lĕ păhĕ'ŏ.

skeleton, ĭ'wĭ kĭ'nŏ.

sketch, wă'hĭ kĭ'ĭ, wă'hĭ kăkăŭ: to sketch, kă'-
hăkă'hă.

skill, (ke) ăkămăĭ, no'ĕaŭ.

skillful, makăŭkăŭ.

skin, 'ĭ'lĭ, 'ă'lŭ'ă'lŭ; (rind), pa'ă'ă: to skin, lŏ'lĭ.

skip, (jump), lĕ'lĕlĕ'lĕ; (desert), hă'ălĕ'lĕ.

skirt, (dress), palĕko'kĭ; riding or hula skirt,
pă'ŭ'; (border), lĕ'pă, kă'pă: to skirt, kă'hă.

skull, ĭ'wĭ pŏ'ŏ, pūni'ŭ.

sky, (ke) āŏu'lĭ, la'nĭ, lĕ'wă.

slack, (loose), 'ä'lŭ'ä'lŭ; (negligent), pälä'kä:
   to slacken, hō'ä'lŭ'ä'lŭ; (to slow), hŏ'ŏkä-
   'ŭlŭ'ä.

slacker, meä pälä'kä.

slacks, lo'lĕ wäwaĕ.

slander, 'aläpä'hĭ, 'ä'kĭ'ä'kĭ.

slant, hiō', moĕ käpäkä'hĭ, pahĭ'ä.

slap, pä'ĭ.

slate, pä'pä pōha'kŭ; (candidates), pä'pä ĭnŏä.

slaughter, lŭ'kŭ, pēpe'hĭ wä'lĕ.

slave, käŭwä'; bond slave, käŭwä' kuäpa'ä.

sled, hōlu'ä.

sleep, hiämoĕ, moĕ.

sleepy, mäkähiamoĕ.

sleeve, lĭ'mä lo'lĕ.

slide, kähŭ'ä pähĕ'ĕ, kähŭ'ä hōlu'ä: to slide,
   pähĕ'ĕ; (as land), kä'ä; (to toboggan), hĕ'ŏ
   hōlu'ä.

slight, (slender), pūahĭ'lŏ, wĭwĭ; (trifling),
   meä ĭ'kĭ: (to snub), hŏ'ŏpäwĕ'ŏ, hŏ'ŏho'kä.

slime, a'wĕa'wĕ, wä'lĕwä'lĕ; (mucus), wä'lĕ.

sling, mä'ä; to sling, (as a hammock), hŏho'lä.

slip, (oversight), kuhĭhe'wä; (garment), mŭ'ŭ-
   mŭ'ŭ; (twig), lälä 'opĭ'ŏpĭ'ŏ: to slip, pähĕ'-
   mŏ; (in walking), paki'kä; slip away, mä-
   hu'kä; slip off, wĕ'hĕ.

slippers, kämä'ä hä'ähä'ä, pa'lĕ wäwaĕ.

slippery, pähĕ'ĕhĕ'ĕ, paki'kä.

slogan, 'ōle'lŏ hō'ĕ'ŭ'ĕ'ŭ.

slope, lä'pä: to slope, hiō'.

slow, (not quick), lo'hĭ; (dilatory), häkälĭ'ä.

sly, mä'äleä.

small, lĭ'ĭlĭ'ĭ, 'u'u'kŭ, ĭ'kĭ.

small-pox, hepĕ'lä.

Smart, äkämäĭ, 'ĕlĕ'ŭ, mi'kĭ; to smart, wälänĭ'ä.

smash, wāwa'hĭ; (with implement), kĭpō; (into), hŏ'ŏkŭ'ĭ.

smear, hāpa'lă.

smell, (sense), ho'nĭ; sweet smell, 'a'ă'lă; bad smell, pīlăŭ, hŏho'nŏ: to smell, ho'nĭ; (to snuff), hă'nŭhă'nŭ.

smile, mĭnŏ'a'kă.

smith, (ke) 'āmă'lă.

smoke, ŭwa'hĭ, ŭa'hĭ: to smoke, (as tobacco), pu'hĭ; (as hams), hŏ'ŏpīpī; to ascend as smoke, pūnŏ'hŭ.

smooth, (glossy), pāhĕ'ĕ, lăŭmănĭ'ă; (calm), mali'nŏ: to smooth, hă'nă ā mani'ă; (to regulate), hŏ'ŏpo'nŏpo'nŏ.

smother, pa'ă kā hă'nŭ, 'u'mĭ.

snail, kămălo'lĭ, pūpū kŏ'lŏ, pūpū kănĭ'oĕ.

snake, nahĕ'kă, mŏ'ŏ.

snap, (as fingers), pă'nă; (as teeth), kĕ'pă; (as gun), kănăpī'; (as whip), 'ŭ'ĭ'nă; (in speech), kĕ'ŭ; (as rope), pa'ĭ'nă; (as stick), uhă'kĭ.

snapper, u'lăŭ'lă, 'ŏpă'kăpă'kă.

snatch, kā'ĭ'lĭ.

sneak, ni'hĭ, kŏ'lŏ pĕ'ĕ.

sneer, he'nĕhe'nĕ, lŏĭlŏĭ.

sneeze, ki'hĕ, ki'hă.

snipe, wandering tattler, ulĭ'lĭ.

snore, nŏno', nono'lŏ.

snort, hă'ŭ, hŏhō'.

snout, nŭ'kŭ.

snow, hăŭ.

snuff, (tobacco), pă'kă 'aĕ'aĕ: to snuff, hă'ŭ, hă'nŭ; (as a dog), hă'nŭhă'nŭ.

so, (thus, likewise), pe, pēneĭ; (very), lŏ'ă; (therefore), nolăĭlă; "so it is," pēlă' nŏ.

soak, (to steep), hŏ'u', hŏ'ŏmăŭ'; (imbibe), 'o'mŏ.

soap, kŏ'pă.

sober, (serious), kŭo'ŏ; (not drunk), 'o'nă 'o'lĕ.

social, lăŭnă.

society, lăŭnă ă'nă; (company), hŭ'ĭ.

socket, kŭ'mŭ; socket of eye, măkălu'ă.

socks, kakĭ'nĭ.

soda, ko'kă; soda-pop, wăĭ mōmo'nă.

soft, pă'lŭpă'lŭ, wă'lĭ; (as poi), hĕhĕ'ĕ.

softly, măli'ĕ.

soil, lĕ'pŏ.

soldier, koă.

sole, (fish), păkĭ'ĭ; (of foot), kăpŭa'ĭ, po'lĭ wăwaĕ: (only), hŏ'ŏkă'hĭ wa'lĕ nō.

solemn, (grave), kŏ'ĭkŏ'ĭ; (sacred), 'ĕ'ĕhi'ă, hŏ'ă'nŏ.

solicit, (request), noĭ; (entice), pŭ'ĕ.

solid, pa'ă.

solitary, (alone), me'hăme'hă; (desolate), nĕ-ŏnĕ'ŏ.

solution, (dissolving), hŏ'ŏhĕhĕ'ĕ ă'nă; (explanation), wĕ'hĕwĕ'hĕ ă'nă.

some, (number), măŭ, kekă'hĭ; (quantity), kăŭwă'hĭ.

sometime, i kekă'hĭ wā.

somewhat, ĭ'kĭ.

somewhere, mā kăŭwă'hĭ, mā kekă'hĭ wă'hĭ.

son, keĭkĭka'nĕ.

son-in-law, hŭnonăka'nĕ.

song, hĭme'nĕ, me'lĕ.

soon, kŏ'kĕ, kokŏ'kĕ, hikĭwa'wĕ.

soot, pă'ŭ.

soothe, hŏ'ŏmălĭ'ĕlĭ'ĕ, hŏ'ŏnā'.

sorcery, 'ană'ănā', hŏ'ŏpī'ŏpī'ŏ.

sore, 'ē'hă.

sorrow, 'ē'hă'ē'hă, lŭ'ŭlŭ'ŭ, kăŭmă'hă o kā
nā'ăŭ.

sorry, mī'nămī'nă, mi'hī.

sort, 'ă'nŏ: to sort, waĕ, hŏ'ŏkă'ăwa'lĕ.

soul, 'ūha'nĕ.

sound, kă'nĭ, le'ŏ; (confused), wălă'ăŭ;
(strait), kōwā; (firm), pa'ă; (healthy), kī-
nă' 'o'lĕ; (as opinion), 'o'ïai'ŏ mao'lī: to
sound, kă'nĭ, hŏ'ŏkă'nĭ; resound, kŏ'ē'lĕ.

soup, kŭ'pă, kăĭ.

sour, (acid), 'ă'wă'ă'wă; (morose), nanăŭ,
kĕ'ĕmo'ă.

source, kŭ'mŭ; (spring), punăwăĭ.

south, he'mă, kūku'lŭ he'mă; southeast, hĭki-
năhe'mă; southwest, kŏmŏhănăhe'mă.

souvenir, meă hŏ'ŏmană'ŏ.

sow, pua'a kŭmŭlăŭ: to sow, lūlū'

space, wā, kōwā, (ke) ākeă.

spade, 'ŏ'ŏ kopă'lā'.

Spain, Kepanī'ă.

Spaniard, Panĭo'lŏ.

spare, (frugal), pāki'kŏ; (thin), wīwī; (as
tire), kŏĕ; (as time), kă'ăwa'lĕ: to spare,
(forbear), 'aŭ'ă; (be merciful), āhŏnu'ĭ.

spark, hŭnăa'hĭ.

sparkle, li'lĕli'lĕ, hŭlă'lĭ.

sparrow, mă'nŭ lī'ĭlī'ĭ.

speak, 'ōle'lŏ, 'ĭ; (converse), kămă'ĭli'ŏ; (address), hă'ĭ'ōle'lŏ.

Speaker of House, lu'nă hŏ'ŏmă'lŭ.

spear, (dart), ĭ'hĕ; (pike), pŏlŏlū'.

special, kūĭkawā, waĕ.

specie, (coin), kālā pa'ă: species, 'ă'nŏ.

specimen, meā hō'ï'kĕ.

spectacle, nanāïnă.

spectacles, măkăa'nïa'nï.

speculation, (financial), hŏ'ŏpŭ'kăpŭ'kă; (con-
jecture), no'ŏno'ŏ wa'lĕ.

speech, 'ōle'lŏ, (address), hă'ï'ōle'lŏ.

speed, holŏmāmā; to speed, holŏnu'ï, 'āwïwï.

spell, (time), wā, mănā'wă ï'kï; (charm), hă'nă
hŏ'ŏmă'nămă'nă: to spell, pĕ'lă; (relieve),
hŏ'ŏma'hă măï.

spend, hŏ'ŏlï'lŏ a'kŭ; (wastefully), u'hău'hă.

sphere, pōpō, poĕpoĕ; (station), kūlă'nă.

spice, huă 'ă'lă, meă hŏ'ŏmi'kŏ āï.

spider, nă'nănă'nă, lă'nălă'nă.

spill, (overflow), hanï'nï; (upset), hŏ'ŏkăhŭ'lï.

spin, (as rope), mi'lŏ; (as a top), nini'ŭ.

spine, ïwïkŭămŏ'ŏ; (thorn), kŭkū'.

spiny, wă'năwă'nă.

spirit, (soul), 'ūha'nĕ; (ghost), lă'pŭ; (courage), 'ă'nŏ koă.

spit, ku'hă; sand spit, laĕ o'nĕ.

spite, hŏ'ŏmăŭha'lă, 'ō'pū'ï'nŏ.

splendid, nă'nï kămăhă'ŏ.

split, (as wood), kākā; (into factions), mokuahă'nă; (divide), māhe'lĕ.

spoil, (plunder), wăïwăï pi'ŏ: to spoil, (as
vegetables), pălăhū'; (as meats), mĕ'lŭmĕ'-
lŭ; (to rob), hăŏ, păka'hă.

sponge, 'ūpï, hŭ'ăhŭ'ăkăï: to sponge, holoï;
(be a parasite), hŏ'ŏpïlïmĕă'ăï.

spoon, pu'nă.

sport, pă'a'nï, lĕ'ălĕ'ă.

spot, kĭ'ko, 'onĭ'ŏ; (dirt), pā'ĕ'lĕ; (place), kăŭ-
    wă'hĭ: (to soil), hŏ'ŏpăŭma'ĕ'lĕ; (detect),
    hāki'lŏ, kĭ'ŭ.

spout, kānŭ'kŭ; nŭ'kŭ: to spout, pūăpūa'Ĭ.

sprain, maŭĬ.

spray, (liquid), ĕ'hŭ, ĕhŭkăĭ; (branch), lālă.

spread, (feast), 'ăhă'ăĭnă: to spread, lă'hă;
    (as cloth), hālĭ'Ĭ, hŏho'lă; (as news), hŏ-
    'ŏlă'hă.

spring, hŏ'lŭ; (water), punăwăĭ; (season),
    kăŭ kŭpŭlăŭ; (to leap), lĕ'lĕ; (pounce on),
    po'Ĭ, popŏ'Ĭ; (germinate), kŭ'pŭ, no'pŭ;
    (bubble up), pūă'Ĭ.

sprinkle, (rain), u'ă ĭ'kĭ: to sprinkle with hand,
    pĬ, pīpĬ; (to hose), kĭkĬ.

spur, kēpā; (lateral), lālă; (of fowl), kākă'lă:
    to spur on, hŏ'ĕ'ŭ'ĕ'ŭ.

spy, kĭ'ŭ: to spy, hŏ'ŏmākākĭ'ŭ.

squadron, māhe'lĕ 'aŭmo'kŭ.

square, kuĕă, hŭĭnăhă'; (just), hŏ'ŏpo'nŏ, kăŭ-
    lĭ'kĕ.

squash, ĭ'pŭ pū, pălă'ăĭ: to squash, hŏ'ŏpăkū'.

squat, poŭpoŭ: to squat, kiĕlĕlĕĬ.

squeak, 'ŭĭ'ŭĭ'.

squeeze, (trouble), pĭlĭkĭ'ă: to squeeze, (as in
    a clamp), 'umĭkĬ; (as in milking), 'ŭwĭ';
    (press down), kăŏ'mĬ.

squid, hĕ'ĕ.

stab, hoŭ.

stable, ha'lĕ holŏholŏ'nă; (firm), 'ŏ'nĭpă'ă,
    pa'ă.

stack, ahu'ă; smokestack, pu'kă ŭa'hĬ.

stadium, kăhŭ'ă pā'a'nĬ.

staff, hŏ'ŏkŏ'ŏ; (official), nā kōkŭ'ă; (flag),
    pa'hŭ hăĕ; (music), o'ă.

stage, (platform), 'āwăĭ; (period), wā; The
Stage, 'oĭhă'nă kĕă'kă.

stagger, hīkākā, künĕ'wănĕ'wă.

stain, (dye), kŏ'hŭ; (blot), pā'ĕ'lĕ, kīnā': to
stain, pe'nă, kŏ'hŭ.

stairs, alăpĭ'ĭ, 'ānŭ'ŭ.

stake, (stick), pa'hŭ; (wager), wăĭwăĭ pi'lĭ,
pŭ'ŭ.

stale, kăhi'kŏ, manana'lŏ.

stalk, kŭ'mŭ: to stalk, hŏ'ŏmo'hŏ.

stall, (market), wă'hĭ kū'āĭ: to stall, (stick
fast), mamăŭ; to stall off, hŏ'ŏpănĕ'ĕnĕ'ĕ.

stammer, 'u'ŭ'.

stamp, (imprint), hō'āĭlo'nă pă'ĭ; (postage),
pŏ'ŏle'kă: to stamp, pă'ĭ; (with foot), he'hĭ,
ke'ĕ'hĭ.

stand, (table), pākaŭkaŭ lĭ'ĭlĭ'ĭ; to stand, kū.

standard, haĕ; (criterion), (ke) ā'nă, pa'ămăŭ.

star, hōkū'.

starboard, 'ăŏ'ăŏ 'ākaŭ.

starfish, pĕ'ă.

starch, pi'ă.

stare, nānā po'nŏ, hăkăpo'nŏ.

start, puo'hŏ; (to begin), hŏ'ŏmă'kă: to be
startled, pū'i'wă.

starve, măkĕ'āĭ, hō'ŏ'kĭ'āĭ.

state; moku'āĭnă; The State, Kē Aŭpu'nĭ;
(condition), 'ă'nŏ; "in state," hă'nŏhă'nŏ:
to state, hă'ĭ, hōăkā'ka.

statement, hă'ĭ'nă, 'ōle'lŏ.

station, kăhŭ'ă; (rank), kūlă'nă; (railway),
ha'lĕ hŏ'ŏlŭ'lŭ; (police), halĕwăĭ: to station, hŏ'ŏno'hŏ.

stationary, pa'ă.

stationery, kălă'nă.

statistics, nā he'lŭ.

statue, kĭ'ĭ, kĭ'ĭ kalāĭĭ'ă.

stay, (prop), kŏ'ŏ; (rope), kăŭlă kŏ'ŏ: to stay, (stop), no'hŏ, kă'lĭ; (to prop), kŏ'ŏ, pāĭpāĭ.

steady, (fixed), pa'ă, (regular), măŭ; (reliable), kūpa'ă; (sober), 'o'nă 'o'lĕ: to steady, hŏ'ŏkūpa'ă.

steak, 'ĭ'ŏ kōă'lă.

steal, 'āĭhu'ĕ, la'wĕ wa'lĕ.

steam, ma'hŭ.

steamer, mokua'hĭ.

steel, kĭ'lă: to steel, hŏ'ŏpa'äki'kĭ'.

steep, nĭ'hĭnĭ'hĭ: to steep, hŏ'ŭ'.

steer, pĭ'pĭ pŏ'ă: to steer, u'lĭ, hŏ'ŏkĕ'lĕ.

stem, kŭ'mŭ; (as of vessel), ĭ'hŭ, mu'ă.

stenographer, kakăŭ poko'lĕ.

step, footstep, kăpŭa'ĭ: to step, he'hĭ; (as a mast), kūku'lŭ.

step-father, makuăka'nĕ kolĕă.

steps, alăpĭ'ĭ, (ke) 'ānŭ'ŭ.

sterling, 'o'ĭai'ŏ, maolĭ.

stern, ho'pĕ; (severe), 'o'ole'ă.

stevedore, pŏ'ŏlă'.

stew, meă 'āĭ ku'pă.

steward, kuĕ'nĕ.

stick, lā'ăŭ: to stick, sticky, hŏ'ŏpi'lĭ, pĭpi'lĭ.

stiff, 'o'ole'ă, mālo'ĕlo'ĕ; (as breeze), ĭkăĭkă.

stifle, 'u'mĭ, 'u'u'mĭ.

stifling, (close), ĭkĭĭ'kĭ.

still, (apparatus), mĭkĭ'nĭ pŭ'hĭ wăĭ'ō'nă: (quiet), māli'ĕ; (yet), a hi'kĭ i kē'ĭă wă.

stilt, stilts, kŭkŭlŭaĕ'ŏ.

stimulant, meă hŏ'ŏhŏĭhŏĭ.

stimulate, hŏ'ĕŭ'ĕŭ.

stimulus, kŭ'mŭ hŏ'ŏlă'lĕlă'lĕ.

sting, meă kĭ′kĭ; (scorpion's), huĕ′lŏ 'ă′wă:
　to sting, (wasp, etc.), kĭ′kĭ, 'ō; (with bite),
　'ă′kĭ.

sting-ray, hĭhĭmă′nŭ.

stingy, pĭ, 'aŭ′ă, kulĭpă′ă.

stink, pĭlăŭ, hŏho′nŏ.

stir, (commotion), hăŭnaĕlĕ: to stir, (mix),
　kăwĭ′lĭ; (rouse), hōa′lă, hŏ'ĕŭ'ĕŭ.

stitch, hŭ′mŭhŭ′mŭ, hŏ′nŏ: stitch in side,
　'umĭ'ĭ.

stock, waĭho′nă; (capital), kŭmŭpa'ă; live
　stock, pūă' holŏhŏlo′nă: (as of gun), pŏ'ŏ
　lă'ăŭ: to stock, hŏ'ŏpĭ′hă, hŏ'ŏlă'kŏ.

stockings, kakĭ′nĭ.

stomach, 'ŏpū′.

stone, pŏha′kŭ: to stone, haĭlŭ′kŭ; throw single
　stone, pe′hĭ i kā pōha′kŭ.

stool, no′hŏ lĭ'ĭlĭ'ĭ; footstool, ke'ĕhĭ′nă.

stoop, kūlŏŭ.

stop, (to end), hŏ'ŏpăŭ, hŏ'ō′kĭ; (to stand),
　kū: "stop!" 'uō′kĭ!

stopper, 'ŭmo′kĭ, popŏ'ĭ.

store, (shop), ha′lĕ kū'ăĭ; (warehouse), waĭ-
　ho′nă: to store, hŏ'a′hŭ.

storm, 'ĭ′nŏ, 'o'olokū': to storm, (attack), hŏ-
　'ū′kă.

stormy, (weather), 'ĭ′nŏ'ĭ′nŏ; (assembly), hăŭ-
　naĕlĕ.

story, (narrative), ka'aŏ; (fib), hŏ'ŏpŭ′nĭpŭ'nĭ;
　(of house), pă′pă olu′nă.

stout, (plump), pŭ'ĭpŭ'ĭ; (strong), ĭkăĭkă.

stove, kăpŭa′hĭ.

straight, pololeĭ.

straightforward, hŏ'ŏpo′nŏ.

strain, (racial), ma'mŏ: to strain, hŏ'ŏmālŏ'ĕ-
  lŏ'ĕ; (as rope), li'ŏli'ŏ; (to filter), kănă'nă,
  kă'kă.

straits, kōwă; (need), pĭlĭkĭ'ă.

strand, ma'a'wĕ; (shore), kăhăkăĭ, (ke) o'nĕ:
  to strand, ĭ'lĭ.

strange, 'ē, 'ă'nŏ'ē, kupăna'hă.

stranger, mălĭhĭ'nĭ, kănă'kă 'ē.

strangle, (throttle), 'u'mĭ, 'u'u'mĭ; (choke),
  pū'u'ă.

strap, kăŭlă 'ĭ'lĭ.

stratagem, păpăhă'nă hŏ'ŏhălu'ă.

straw, măŭ'u malo'ŏ.

strawberry, 'ohelŏpă'pă.

stray, 'ăŭwă'nă, ho'lŏho'lŏ wa'lĕ.

streak, 'onĭ'ŏnĭ'ŏ; (of light), kūkū'nă.

stream, kăhăwăĭ: to stream, kă'hĕ.

street, alănu'ĭ.

streetcar, kă'ăŭwi'lă.

strength, strenuous, ĭkăĭkă.

stretch, hŏ'ŏmālŏ'ĕlŏ'ĕ; (spread), hōhō'lă; (as
  the hand), kĭkŏ'ŏ, 'o; be stretched, mŏlĭ'ŏ.

stretcher, mănĕ'lĕ.

strict, hŏ'ŏpo'nŏ lo'ă, hŏ'ŏpololeĭ.

strife, 'ā'ŭ'mĕ'ŭ'mĕ, mokuahă'nă; (fight), hăkăkă'.

strike, (to punch), kŭ'ĭ; (whip), hahaŭ; (cease
  work), olŏha'nĭ; (as clock), kă'nĭ; (as
  flag), kŭ'ŭ.

string, kuăĭnă; (fish line), (ke) a'hŏ.

strip, 'āpă'nă lŏ'ĭ'hĭ: wĕ'hĕ; (peel), maĭ'hĭ;
  (lay barren), hŏ'ŏnĕ'ŏnĕ'ŏ.

stripe, 'onĭ'ŏnĭ'ŏ, kă'hăkă'hă lolo'ă.

strive, (endeavor), hŏ'ŏïkăĭkă; (contend), 'ā'ŭ'mě'ŭ'mě, hăkăkā'; (be factional), mokuahă'nă.

stroke, (blow), hahaŭ, hi'lĭ; (pen), kă'hă; (business), pu'kă; (oar), kū ă'nă; to stroke, kă'hĭ 'o'lŭ'o'lŭ.

strong, ĭkăĭkă, pŭ'ĭpŭ'ĭ; strong-smelling, hoho'nŏ.

struggle, 'ā'ŭ'mě'ŭ'mě, hākōkō.

stubborn, pa'ākikĭ', nu'hă.

student, haŭmā'nă.

to study, hŭ'lĭ nă'ăŭaŏ.

stuff, meă; (baggage), ukă'nă; (trash), 'ŏpă'lă: to stuff, hŏ'ŏnŭ'ŭ 'ăĭ; hŏ'ŏpĭ'hă.

stumble, 'ōkŭ'pě.

stump, kŭ'mŭkŭ'mŭ: to stump, (electioneer), pāĭpāĭ; (overreach), hŏ'ŏpiŏ; to be stumped, kūnănă.

stun, (deafen), kŭ'lĭkŭ'lĭ; (knock out), hŏ'ŏpăŭ kā 'ĭ'ke.

stupid, lōlō, hūpō.

sturdy, ĭkăĭkă, pŭ'ĭpŭ'ĭ.

sty, pă pua'a; (on eyelid), u'leu'le.

style, 'ă'nŏ; good style, hĭ'ěhĭ'ě: to style, kă'pă.

subdue, (conquer), hŏ'ŏpi'ŏ; (tame), hŏ'ŏlă'kălă'kă.

subject, (denizon), măkă'ăĭnă'nă, kŭ'pă; (topic), kŭmŭhă'nă: (subordinate), māla'lŏ: to subject, hŏ'ŏma'lŭ.

submarine, (boat), mo'kŭ lŭ'ŭ.

submit, (yield to authority), aě i kā le'ŏ mă'nă; (obey), hŏ'ŏlŏ'hě; (surrender), hā'ă'wĭ pi'ŏ.

subscribe, kakăŭ ĭnŏă; (to paper), la'wě nūpě'pă.

substance, meă; of remark, 'ĭ'ŏ;

substantial, (solid), pa'ă; (prosperous), kŏ'ĭ-kŏ'ĭ, kū'o'nŏ'o'nŏ.

succeed, (replace), pă'nĭ; (accomplish), kō.

success, holŏmu'ă.

such, o ĭ'ă 'ă'nŏ, lĭ'kĕ mē.

suck, 'o'mŏ.

sucker, (shoot), 'ohā', pōhu'lĭ; (fool), hūpō.

sudden, hikĭle'lĕ, 'ĕmŏ'ŏ'lĕ.

sue, (in law), hŏ'ŏpĭ'ĭ; (beg), nonoĭ hă'ăhă'ă.

suffer, (undergo pain), 'ĕ'hă'ĕ'hă; (allow), aĕ.

sufficient, la'wă.

sugar, kōpă'ă; sugarcane, kō; sugarmill, wĭ'lĭ kō.

suggest, hŏ'ŏpŭ'kă mană'ŏ, ku'hĭ.

suit, (clothes), pa'ă lo'lĕ kŏ'mŏ; (action at law), hĭhĭ'ă; (courtship), 'ĭ'mĭ ma'lĕ.

suitable, kūpo'nŏ.

sulky, nūnu'hă, mūmu'lĕ.

sulphur, kūkaĕpĕ'lĕ.

sum, hŭĭ'nă nu'ĭ: to sum up, he'lŭ.

summary, hō'ŭ'lŭ'ŭ'lŭ: (prompt), hăkălĭ'ă 'o'lĕ.

summer, kăŭ wĕ'lā.

summit, wēkĭ'ŭ, pi'kŏ.

summon, kăŭo'hă, kāhĕă.

sun, lā: to sun, kăŭlă'ĭ.

sunbeam, kūkū'nă.

sunburn, papă'ă lā.

Sunday, Lā Pu'lĕ, Kāpa'kĭ, La Hō'ă'nŏ.

sunrise, pu'kă ă'nă o kā lā.

sunset, napŏ'ŏ ă'nă o kā lā.

sunshine, lă'ĕlă'ĕ o kā lā.

superintend, hŏ'ŏpo'nŏpo'nŏ.

superintendent, lu'nă.

superior, meă kǐ'ĕkǐ'ĕ a'ĕ; (higher), mālu'nă
a'ĕ; (surpassing), 'oǐ a'ĕ.

superstition, mană'ŏ hūpō; (idolatry), hŏ'ŏmă-
năkǐ'ǐ.

supervisor, lu'nă kiă'ǐ.

supper, pa'ǐ'nă ă'hǐă'hǐ.

supplement, pakŭ'ǐ.

supply, la'kŏ: to supply, hŏ'ŏlă'kŏ, hŏ'ŏlă'wă.

support, (prop), kŏ'ŏ; (livelihood), mālă'mă:
(to hold up), paĕpaĕ, kŏ'ŏ; (nourish), hā-
năǐ.

suppose, mană'ŏ wa'lĕ.

suppress, hŏ'ŏpăŭ, kinăǐ; (as emotion), 'u'mǐ.

supreme, mă'nă kǐ'ĕkǐ'ĕ, kǐ'ĕkǐ'ĕ lō'ă.

sure, 'o'ǐai'ŏ lō'ă, maopŏ'pŏ lō'ă; (secure).
pa'ă lō'ă.

surf, na'lŭ.

surf-board, pă'pă hĕ'ĕnă'lŭ.

surface, 'ǐ'lǐ.

surgeon, kaŭkă kă'hă.

surgeon-fish, ma'ǐ'ǐ'ǐ.

surname, ǐnŏă 'oha'nă.

surplus, pākĕ'lă, kĕ'ŭ.

surprise, hă'ŏhă'ŏ, kahahā'.

surrender, hāă'wǐ pi'ŏ, hāă'wǐ lǐ'lŏ.

surround, hŏ'ŏpŭ'nǐ, pō'ăǐ.

survey, (land), ā'nă'ăǐnă; (view), nānă po'nŏ.

survive, o'lă.

suspect, suspicion, hŏ'ŏhūoǐ.

suspend, hŏ'ŏlĕ'wă; suspend by neck, kă'ă'wĕ,
lǐ; (as judgment), kāpăĕ ǐ'kǐ.

suspense, pilǐhu'ă, pihoihoǐ.

swallow, mŏ'nǐ; (to gulp), ă'lĕ.

swamp, nenĕ'lŭ; (salt marsh), (ke) alǐ'ă: to
swamp, pǐhŏ'.

swarm, huhu'ï: to swarm, mumu'lŭ.

sway, hŏ'ŏmă'lŭ ă'nă: (to totter), lŭ'lĭlŭ'lĭ.

swear, hŏ'ŏhĭ'kĭ; (blaspheme), kŭ'ă'mŭ'ă'mŭ.

sweat, hoŭ.

sweater, kuĕ'kă.

sweep, pūlu'mĭ, kāhĭ'lĭ.

sweet, (tasty), 'o'nŏ; (melodious), nă'hĕnă'hĕ;
      (fragrant), 'a'ă'lă.

sweetheart, ĭ'pŏ.

swell, (sea), 'ă'lĕ'ă'lĕ: to swell, pe'hŭ, māhu'ă-
      hu'ă.

swift, māmā lō'ă, kĭkĭ'.

swim, 'aŭ.

swing, lĕlĕkōa'lĭ: to swing, lĕ'wă, lĕ'wălĕ'wă.

switch, (whip), lā'ăŭ hi'lĭ; R. R. switch, hāŏ
      alăkă'ĭ.

sword, păhĭkăŭă.

swordfish, 'ă'ŭ.

sympathy, (ke) alo'hă, ālo'hă me'nĕme'nĕ.

symptom, 'oŭ'lĭ; (in diagnosis), kūlă'nă.

syrup, mălăkĕ'kĕ, wai.

system, hŏ'ŏno'hŏno'hŏ po'nŏ ă'nă.

T

table, pă'pă; (stand), pākaŭkaŭ.

tablet, (writing), pă'pă kakăŭ; (medicine),
      hūaă'lĕ.

tack, kŭ'ĭ lĭ'ĭlĭ'ĭ; hard tack, pele'nă: to tack,
      hŏ'ŏpĭ'ĭ.

tact, (ke) ākăhaĭ, no'ĕaŭ.

tag, hŏ'ăĭlo'nă: to tag along, hahăĭ māho'pĕ.

Tahiti, Kăhi'kĭ.

tail, (beast), huĕ'lŏ; (bird), pu'ăpu'ă; (fish),
      hĭ'ŭ; (kite), kakăĭapō'la.

tailor, kēlălo'lĕ.

take, nā lōa'a: to take, la'wĕ; (to seize), ho'-
    pŭ; (to capture), hŏ'ŏpĭŏ; (to obtain),
    lōa'a.

tale, ka'aŏ, mō'ole'lŏ; (count), helu'nă.

talent, kālĕ'nă, no'ĕaŭ, ăkămăĭ.

talk, kămă'ĭli'ŏ; loud talk, wălă'ăŭ: to talk
    foolishly, 'ŏlĕ'ŏlĕ'; (to gabble), 'ŏ'hĭ'ŏ'hĭ.

tall, kĭ'ĕkĭ'ĕ, lō'i'hĭ; tall and thin, pīlălă'hĭ.

tame, lă'kă; (flat), hŏĭhŏĭ 'o'lĕ: to tame, hŏ-
    'ŏlă'kă.

tan, (bark), hi'lĭ; sun-tan, haŭlĭ i kă lā: to
    tan, hŏ'ŏlŭ'ŭ 'ĭ'lĭ.

tangle, hĭhĭ'ă: to tangle, kāhĭ'hĭ.

tank, pahŭwăĭ, luăwăĭ.

tap, (water), pĭŭ'lă wăĭ: to tap, (rap), kīkĕ';
    (broach), hoŭ.

tape, le'kĭ, molĭ'nă.

tar, kă.

tardy, lo'hĭ.

target, hō'ăĭlo'nă.

tariff, pă'pă đu'tĕ wăĭwăĭ, pă'pă 'aŭhăŭ.

taro, kă'lŏ.

taro-patch, lŏ'ĭ.

task, păŭkŭ' hă'nă, u'kŭ păŭ; (lesson), hăă-
    wi'nă.

tassel, kŭ'ŭwe'lŭ.

taste, good taste, mikĭoĭ: to taste, hō'a'o.

tasty, 'o'nŏ, mĭ'kŏ.

tattoo, (drum), hŏ'ŏkă'nĭ pa'hŭ: to tattoo, ka-
    kăŭkă'hă.

tax, 'aŭhăŭ: (to accuse), 'ahĕ'wă.

taxi, kă'ă hŏ'ŏlĭ'mălĭ'mă.

tea, (beverage), kī; (meal), pa'ĭ'nă ă'hĭă'hĭ.

teapot, ĭpŭkī'.

teach, ā'ŏ: teacher, kŭmŭă'ŏ, kŭmŭku'lă.

team, hŭ'ĭ.

tear, wăĭmă'kă; (rip), năhaĕ: to tear, ŭhaĕ;
tear to pieces, haĕhaĕ.

tease, hŏ'ŏhĕ'nĕhĕ'nĕ: to tease, (banter), hă-
năwă'lĕ; (vex), hŏ'ŏnaŭ'kĭŭ'kĭ, hŏ'ŏhĕ'nĕ;
(importune), nē.

telegram, kelĕkăla'mă.

telephone, kelĕpo'nă.

telescope, 'ohĕnānā.

tell, hă'ĭ; (count), he'lŭ: bank teller, lu'nă
he'lŭ kālā.

temper, 'ă'nŏ; good temper, 'o'lŭ'o'lŭ; bad
temper, 'a'ă'kă.

temperate, pāki'kŏ.

temperature, wĕ'lă ame kē a'nŭ.

temple, luăki'nĭ, ha'lĕ lă'ă, heĭaŭ.

temporary, kūikawă'.

tempt, temptation, hō'a'o, hŏ'ŏwă'lĕwă'lĕ.

ten, 'ŭ'mĭ, he 'ŭ'mĭ: tenth, kā 'ŭ'mĭ.

tenant, hoă'aĭnă, moă hŏ'ŏlĭ'mălĭ'mă ha'lĕ;
(serf), lōpā'.

tend, măla'mă, lă'wĕlă'wĕ.

tendency, hilĭnă'ĭ, (ke) āu.

tender, (ship's), mo'kŭ lă'wĕlă'wĕ; (legal), kālā mā kē kānăwăĭ; (bid), pă'lăpă'lă kŏ'hŏ:
(soft), pă'lŭpă'lŭ, no'lŭ; tender-hearted, lokomāĭkă'ĭ: to tender, hăă'wĭ.

tenement, nā lu'mĭ hŏ'ŏlĭ'mălĭ'mă.

tent, ha'lĕ lo'lĕ, ha'lĕ pĕ'ă.

term, (time), māhe'lĕ mănă'wă, wă; (expression), 'ōle'lŏ, huă'ōle'lŏ: to term, kă'pă:
terms, kānăwăĭ.

terminate, hŏ'ŏpăŭ, hō'ŏ'kĭ.

terminus, hopĕ'nă alăhaŏ.

termite, hŭ'hŭ, 'ukŭlā'ăŭ; (winged), naŏnaŏ-
le'lĕ.

tern, nŏĭŏ.

terrace, 'ānŭ'ŭ, honu'ă pă'pă.

terrible, wĕ'lĭwĕ'lĭ.

territory, kĕlĭko'lĭ; (land), 'ăĭnă; (province),
panălā'ăŭ.

terror, wĕ'lĭwĕ'lĭ, hŏ'pŏhŏ'pŏ.

test, (trial), hō'a'o; (standard), ā'nă.

testament, (will), kăŭo'hă, pă'lăpă'lă hŏ'ŏĭlĭ'nă.

testify, hō'ĭ'kĕ.

testimony, 'ōle'lŏ hō'ĭ'kĕ.

text, (of discourse), pŏ'ŏ'ōle'lŏ, kŭmŭmană'ŏ;
(of book), 'ōle'lŏ i pă'ĭĭ'ă.

than, māmu'ă o; "This is bigger than . . . ,"
nui keia mamua o, (lit.: Big this before ..).

thank, māhā'lŏ; hŏ'ŏmaĭka'ĭ.

Thanksgiving Day, Lā Hŏ'ŏmaĭka'ĭ, Lā 'Aĭ-
pĕlĕhū', Lā Hōalo'halo'hă.

that, (that one, generally), kēlā', ĭ'ă, ŏĭ'ă, 'u'ă
. . . lā; (that of yours), kenā'; (who, which),
ăĭ: in order that, i; (because), nō kā meă.

the, (singular), kā, kē; (plural), nā.

theater, keă'kă.

theft, thief, 'ăĭhu'ĕ.

their, (dual), kō laŭă; (plural), kō lākoŭ.

them, ĭā lăŭă, ĭā lākoŭ.

themselves, lăŭă ĭ'hŏ, lākoŭ ĭ'hŏ.

then, (at that time), ĭ'ă wā, ĭ'ă mănā'wă;
(therefore), alăĭlă.

thence, măĭ lăĭlă ă'kŭ.

theory, kŭmŭmană'ŏ.

there, malăĭlă, maō', iō': there! aĭă la!

therefore, nolăĭlă, nō ĭ'ă meă.

thermometer, meă ā'nă wĕ'lă.

they, (dual), lāŭă; (plural), lākoŭ.

thick, māno'äno'ä; (not clear), pōwe'hĭwe'hĭ; (intimate), pi'lĭ; (crowded), pa'äpū'.

thief, 'äĭhu'ĕ.

thigh, 'uhā'.

thimble, kŏ'mŏ, kŏ'mŏ hŭ'mŭhŭ'mŭ.

thin, la'hĭla'hĭ; (in flesh), wīwī.

thing, meă.

think, mană'ŏ; (reflect), no'ŏno'ŏ.

thirst, thirsty, măkĕwăĭ.

thirteen, 'ūmĭkūmamako'lŭ; thirteenth, kă 'ŭmĭkūmamako'lŭ.

thirty, kănăko'lŭ; thirtieth, kē kănăko'lŭ.

this, kē'ĭă, 'u'ă . . . nĕĭ.

thistle, puăka'lă.

thorn, kŭkū', meă 'o'oĭ.

thorny, wă'năwă'nă.

thorough, olăhonū'ă, pa'ă po'nŏ.

thoroughfare, (ke) alănŭ'ĭ.

though, ĭ'nā' pa'hă, 'oĭaĭ nă'ĕ.

thought, mană'ŏ, no'ŏno'ŏ.

thoughtful, (intelligent), no'ŏno'ŏ, mikolĕlĕhu'ă; (considerate), mali'ŭ.

thousand, kăŭkă'nĭ, tăŭsă'nĭ: thousandth, kē kăŭkă'nĭ.

thrash, hahaŭ, hi'lĭ.

thread, lo'pĭ; (of discourse), kŭ'mŭ hă'ĭă'ŏ.

threat, threaten, hŏ'ŏwĕ'lĭwĕ'lĭ.

three, ko'lŭ, eko'lŭ, 'ako'lŭ: third kē ko'lŭ.

thrill, kăpălĭ'lĭ kā hoŭpŏ.

thrive, (prosper), hŏ'ŏkūo'nŏo'nŏ; (grow), u'lŭ po'nŏ; (as plants), lu'pălu'pă.

throat, pū'ŭ.

throb, kŏ'nĭ, kăpălĭ'lĭ.

throne, no'hŏ ălĭ'ĭ.

throng, pū'ŭ'lŭ'ŭ'lŭ kā'năkă: to throng, kūpĭ-
    pĭ'pĭ, ākŏ'äkŏ'ă.

through, (finished), păŭ po'nŏ: (between), mā,
    māwaĕnă: (by reason of), nŏ kā meă; (by
    means of), mā o.

throw at, nŏŭ; throw away, kilŏĭ, kiŏ'lă, hŏ-
    'ŏlĕĭ.

thrust, hoŭ, 'ŏ.

thumb, mănămănăli'mă nu'ĭ.

thump, kŭ'ĭkŭ'ĭ.

thunder, hēki'lĭ.

Thursday, Pō'ahā'.

thus, pe, pēneĭ.

tick, 'ŭ'kŭ; (sound), kŏ'ŏ'lĕ.

ticket, kikĭ'kĭ; (political), pālo'kă.

tickle, hŏ'ŏmānĕ'ŏnĕ'ŏ; (gratify), hŏ'ŏlĕ'ălĕ'ă.

tidal wave, kăĭ mĭmi'kĭ, kăĭ'ĕ'ĕ.

tide, kăĭ, (ke) āŭ; (high), kăĭ nu'ĭ; (low),
    kăĭ malŏ'ŏ, kăĭ mă'kĕ; (ebb), kăĭ e'mĭ;
    (flow), kăĭ pĭ'ĭ.

tie, (knot), hipŭ'ŭ; family tie, pĭ'lĭ; tie-vote,
    kŏ'hŏ lĭ'kĕ; neck-tie, lĕĭ'ă'ĭ: to tie, hikĭ'ĭ,
    nākĭ'ĭ; (to equal), hŏ'ŏhālĭ'kĕ; (in games),
    pă'ĭ a pă'ĭ.

tight, pa'ă; (as money), kakă'ĭkă'hĭ; (drunk),
    'o'nă.

till, (money), pa'hŭ kālā: to till, mā'hĭ: (un-
    til), ā, ā hi'kĭ.

tiller, kănă'kă māhĭ'ăĭ; (rudder), hoĕu'lĭ.

timber, lā'ăŭ.

time, wā, mănā'wă; (era), (ke) aŭ.

timid, hŏ'ŏpĕ'ĕpĕ'ĕ, hi'lāhi'lă.

tin, kĭ'nĭ.

tint, (color), kŏ'hŭ: to tint, hŏ'ŏlŭ'ŭ.

tiny, măkăli'ĭ.

tip, pi'kŏ, wēkī'ŭ; tip of tongue, lăŭălĕ'lŏ; (as in races), hăĭlo'nă: to tip, hăă'wĭ manawăle'ă.

tire, (ke) a'pŏ hŭi'lă: to tire, lu'hĭ.

tissue, (biological), ĭ'hŏ, 'ĭ'ŏ; (paper), pĕ'pă la'hĭla'hĭ.

title, (rank), ĭnŏă hă'nŏhă'nŏ; (heading), pŏ'ŏ; (right), kūleă'nă.

to, (towards, unto), i, lă', lŏ': (sign of infinitive), e.

toad, pŏlo'kă.

toady, hŏ'ŏpĭlĭmeă'ăĭ.

toast, pala'oă papă'ă: to toast, kŏă'lă; drink a toast, ĭ'nŭ hŏ'ŏmāhă'lŏ.

tobacco, pă'kă.

toboggan, pă'pă hŏlu'ă: to toboggan, hĕ'ĕ hŏlu'ă.

today, kē'ĭă lă.

toe, mănămănăwāwaĕ.

together, pū.

toilet, (dressing), kāhi'kŏ; (water-closet), wă'hĭ hŏ'ŏpăŭpĭlĭkĭ'ă.

tolerate, āhŏnu'ĭ, hŏ'ŏmanawanu'ĭ.

toll, 'aŭhăŭ: to toll the bell, hŏ'ŏkă'nĭ i ka pĕ'lĕ.

tomato, 'ohi'ă ha'ŏlĕ.

tomorrow, apŏpô.

ton, kă'nă.

tone, kă'nĭ o kă le'ŏ.

tongue, (ke) ălĕ'lŏ, (ke) elĕ'lŏ.

tonight, kē'ĭă pō, i kē'ĭă pō.

too, (also), nō hŏ'ĭ; too much, nu'ĭ lo'ă.

tool, meă hă'nă, meă pa'ăhă'nă.

tooth, ni'hŏ.

toothpick, (ke) 'ō ni'hŏ.

top, wĕlǎŭ, wēkī'ŭ, pi'kŏ; spinning top, hū.

torch, lǎ'mǎ, lǎmǎkū'.

torment, (pain), 'ĕ'hǎ nu'ĭ; (harassment), meǎ
    hŏ'ŏpĭlĭkĭ'ǎ nu'ĭ: to torment, hŏ'ŏma'ǎŭ,
    hǎ'nǎ 'ĭ'nŏ.

torpedo, mīkĭ'nĭ hŏ'ŏpǎhū'.

torrent, wǎīkǎ'hĕ nu'ĭ.

toss, kiŏ'lǎ, hŏ'ŏlĕĭ.

total, (sum), hŭĭ'nǎ: (all), pǎŭ lo'ǎ, holo'ŏkoǎ.

touch, hŏ'ŏpā', pi'lĭ.

tough, 'o'olĕ'ǎ, ūǎū'ǎ.

tour, hŭǎkǎ'ĭ kǎ'ǎpŭ'nĭ: to tour, he'lĕ mǎka'ĭ-
    ka'ĭ.

tourist, mǎka'ĭka'ĭ.

tournament, paĭŏ pā'a'nĭ.

tow, (fiber), ma'awĕ: to tow, kǎŭwō'; tow a
    ship, hŏ'ŏkŏ'lŏ mo'kŭ.

towards, i, ĭō', mā.

towel, kāwe'lĕ.

tower, 'ālĕ'ŏ, pu'o'ǎ; watch tower, ha'lĕ kiǎ'ĭ.

town, kaŏnǎ, kūlǎnǎkǎŭha'lĕ.

toy, meǎ pā'a'nĭ: to toy, (handle), mi'lĭmi'lĭ;
    (dally), kŏlŏ'hĕ.

track, mehe'ŭ, alǎnu'ĭ: to track, a'lŭa'lŭ.

tract, 'ǎĭnǎ; (paper), pu'kĕ lĭ'ĭlĭ'ĭ.

tractor, meǎ kǎŭwō'.

trade, (commerce), kāle'pǎ; (handicraft), 'oĭ-
    hǎ'nǎ hǎnǎli'mǎ: to trade, kāle'pǎ, kū'ǎĭ
    a'kŭ kū'ǎĭ mǎĭ.

trade-wind, maka'nĭ kǎmǎ'ǎĭnǎ.

tradition, 'ōle'lŏ mǎĭ nǎ kū'punǎ mǎĭ, mō-
    'ole'lŏ.

traffic, (s t r e e t), nĕ'ĕ ǎ'nǎ i kē alǎhe'lĕ;
    (trade), kāle'pǎ.

tragedy, hǎ'nǎ wĕ'lĭwĕ'lĭ.

trail, mehe'ŭ: (to drag), kăŭwō' māho'pĕ; (trace), hŏ'ŏkŏ'lŏ.

trailer, kă'ă kăŭwōi'ă.

train, (railway), ka'ă'hĭ; (retinue), po'ĕ ukă'lĭ; (dress), hŭ'ă: to train, (teach), ā'ŏ; (break in), hŏ'ŏlă'kălă'kă; (accustom), hŏ'ŏmă'ămă'ă; (as vines), hŏ'ŏŭ'lŭ po'nŏ.

traitor, kūmakaiă.

tramp, kue'wă, 'aĕ'ă wa'lĕ: to tramp, he'lĕ wăwaĕ.

trample, he'hĭ.

transact, hă'nă, hŏ'ŏkĕ'.

transfer, hŏ'ŏlĭ'lŏ; (carry), hă'lĭhă'lĭ.

translate, unu'hĭ, unu'hĭ 'ōle'lŏ, māhe'lĕ 'ōle'lŏ.

transparent, a'nĭa'nĭ, moakā'kă.

transport, (ship), mo'kŭ la'wĕ 'ohu'ă; (emotion), lĭ'lŏ lō'ă: to transport, hă'lĭhă'lĭ, la'wĕ.

trap, 'upi'kĭ, păhĕ'lĕ.

trash, 'ōpă'lă.

travel, kă'ăhĕ'lĕ, hŭăkă'ĭ.

tray, pā pāla'hăla'hă.

treachery, kūmakaiă, kĭ'pĭ.

tread, he'hĭ; tread water, hŏ'ŏpīnă'hă.

treason, kĭ'pĭ i kē aŭpu'nĭ.

treasure, wăĭwăĭ: to treasure, hŏ'ŏmană'ŏ, mălă'mă.

treasurer, pu'ŭkū'

treasury, waĭho'nă kālā.

treat, meă e hŏĭhŏĭ ăĭ kă nă'ăŭ: to treat, hă'nă; (doctor), lāpăăŭ; (entertain), hŏ'ŏhăŭ'olĭ; (discourse), wĕ'hĕwĕ'hĕ kŭmŭmană'ŏ; (negotiate), kūkă.

treaty, kŭ'ĭka'hĭ.

tree, lă'ăŭ, kŭmŭlā'ăŭ.

tremble, hă'ălŭ'lŭ.

tremendous, 'a'olĕ o kă'nă măĭ, wĕ'lĭwĕ'lĭ kā
   nu'ĭ.

trench, ăŭwā'hă: to trench, kupā'.

trepang, beche-de-mer, lo'lĭ.

trespass, (entry), kŏ'mŏ he'wă; (offense), hĕ'-
   wă, ha'lă.

trial, (endeavor), hō'a'o; (suffering), pōpilĭki'ă; court trial, hŏ'ŏkŏ'lŏkŏ'lŏ.

triangle, hŭĭnăkŏ'lŭ.

tribe, (family), 'oha'nă, (descendents), ma'mŏ.

trick, (feat of skill), hă'nă ăkămăĭ; (fraud),
   'apŭ'kă; (habit), hă'nă mă'ă; (in cards),
   hŭ'lĭ, kimă'kĕ: to trick, kŏlŏ'hĕ, hŏ'ŏpŭ'nĭpŭ'nĭ.

tricky, mă'ălĕă, 'āpĭ'kĭ.

trifle, meă lĭ'ĭlĭ'ĭ; to trifle, pā'a'nĭ wa'lĕ.

trigger, kĭ'kŏ o kā pū.

trigger-fish, hŭ'mŭhŭ'mŭ.

trim, 'ăŭlĭ'ĭ, mikĭoĭ: to trim, (prune), pă'ĭpă'ĭ;
   (hair), 'ă'kŏ; (cloth), 'o'kĭ; (ship), hŏ'ŏ-
   po'nŏpo'nŏ; (adorn), hŏ'ŏnă'nĭ.

Trinity, Kē Kăhĭko'lŭ.

trip, hŭăkă'ĭ: to trip, 'ŏkŭ'pĕ; (step nimbly),
   he'lĕ mikĭoĭ.

triplets, pūko'lŭ.

trolley-car, kă'ăŭwi'lă.

troops, pū'ă'lĭ ko'ă.

trophy, maka'nă, hō'ăĭlo'nă nō kā lănăki'lă.

tropic, pō'ăĭ.

tropical, wă'hĭ maha'nă.

tropic-bird, kōa'ĕ.

trot, holŏkŭkū.

trouble, pĭlĭki'ă.

trousers, lo'lĕ wăwaĕ.

truce, kŭ'ĭka'hĭ kŭĭkăwă'.

truck, kă'ă kălă'kă, kă'ăukă'nă.

true, truth, 'o'ĭai'ŏ.

trump, hŭ'lĭ: to trump, kămaŭ, kimă'kĕ; to trump up, 'ĭmĭha'lă.

trumpet, pū kă'nĭ; (speaking), olĕ'.

trumpet shell, pū, olĕ'.

trunk, (tree), kŭ'mŭ; (clothes), pa'hŭ lo'lĕ; (elephant's), ĭ'hŭ.

trust, păŭlĕ'lĕ, hilĭnă'ĭ: (to extend credit), hŏ'ălĕ'.

trustee, kăhŭwălwăl.

trusty, păŭlĕlĕĭ'ă.

try, hŏ'a'o.

tub, kă'pū.

tube, 'o'hĕ, pălpū.

tuberculosis, hōkĭ'ĭ, (ke) akĕpăŭ.

Tuesday, Pŏ'alu'ă.

tuft, pūpū.

tug, (boat), mokua'hĭ hŏ'ŏkŏ'lŏ mo'kŭ: to tug, hu'kĭ ĭkălkă.

tumble, (to overturn), kŭlă'ĭ, hŏ'ŏhĭ'nă; (fall), hio'lŏ, hĭ'nă; (roll), 'olŏkă'ă.

tumbler, kĭ'ă'hă.

tumult, hăŭnaĕlĕ, ulŭao'ă.

tune, le'ŏ me'lĕ: to tune, hŏ'ŏpo'nŏpo'nŏ.

tunnel, (ke) ă'nă i paŏ ĭ'ă.

turkey, pĕlĕhŭ'; (country), Kūle'kĕ.

turn, hŭ'lĭ ă'nă; (spell), wă: to turn, hŭ'lĭ; (to wind), wĭ'lĭ; (to change), lŏ'lĭ; turn from, 'aŭĭ; turn on hinges, 'olĕ'pĕ.

turnstone, akeke'kĕ.

turtle, 'ĕă, ho'nŭ.

tutor, kŭmŭă'ŏ: to tutor, ă'ŏ.

twelve, 'ŭmīkūmamalu'ă: twelfth, kā 'ŭmīku-
     mamalu'ă.
twenty. ĭwăkālu'ă: twentieth, kā ĭwăkālu'ă.
twice, pālu'ă.
twig. lālā 'u'u'kŭ: (to notice). 'ī'kĕ.
twilight, (ke) ălăŭ'lā; (morning), pa'wă, wă-
     nă'ăŏ; (evening), li'ŭlā'; wănăpŏ'.
twin, măhoĕ.
twine, kuăĭnă: to twine. wreathes, 'ōwăĭ; (as
     vines), hĭ'hĭ, hŏ'ŏhĭ'hĭ.
twist, wi'lĭ, hī'lŏ, mi'lŏ.
two, lu'ă, elu'ă, 'alu'ă.
type, 'ă'nŏ; (symbol), hō'ăllo'nă; (printer's),
     huă kepăŭ.
typewriter, kakăŭ kĭ'kŏkĭ'kŏ.
typhoid, fi'vă nu'ĭ, fi'vă hī kŏ'kŏ.
tyrant, meă hŏ'ŏkăŭmă'hă wa'lĕ.

U

ugly, (unsightly), pūpu'kă, nukŏ'kĭ; (ill-
     natured), 'ĭ'nŏ'ĭ'nŏ.
ukelele, 'ŭkŭlĕ'lĕ.
ultimate, ho'pĕ lō'ă.
ultimately, māho'pĕ lō'ă.
umbrella, māmă'lŭ, loŭ'lŭ.
umpire, ŭwaŏ.
unable, hĭ'kĭ 'o'lĕ.
unanimous, lōka'hĭ.
uncle, anăkă'lā, makuăka'nĕ hanăună.
uncommon, (rare), kakă'ĭkă'hĭ; (unusual),
     'ănŏ'ē'.
unconscious, pă'ŭ kā 'ĭ'kĕ păŭ kā lo'hĕ, lĭ'lŏ
     kā no'ŏno'ŏ.
uncover, wĕ'hĕ.
under, māla'lŏ, ĭla'lŏ.

underneath, māla'lŏ ĭ'hŏ.

underpants, palĕmă'ĭ.

undershirt, palĕ'ĭ'lĭ.

undersigned, kā meă nō'nă kā ĭnŏă māla'lŏ ĭ'hŏ.

understand, hŏ'ŏmaŏpŏ'pŏ, maopŏ'pŏ, 'ĭ'kĕ.

undertake, hō'a'o.

undertaker, kănă'kă hŏ'ŏlĕ'wă.

undo, wĕ'hĕ, wĕ'hĕ hoŭ; (reverse). hŏ'ŏkā-hu'lĭ.

undoubtedly, pēlā' ĭ'ŏ nō.

uneasy, pihoĭhoĭ, ma'hă 'o'lĕ.

unexpected, mahŭ'ĭ 'o'lĕ ĭ'ă; (sudden).hikĭ-le'lĕ.

unfortunate, pō'ĭ'nŏ.

unfriendly, makonā', lăŭnă 'o'lĕ.

unfurnished, ku'lĕku'lĕ, hŏ'ŏlă'kŏ 'o'lĕ ĭ'ă; (bare), 'ōlo'hĕlo'hĕ.

unhappy, kăŭmă'hă.

unicorn-fish, kă'lă.

uniform, mākălĭ'kĕ: (invariable), 'ă'nŏ lĭ'kĕ.

union, hŭ'ĭ, hŏ'ŏhŭ'ĭ ă'nă; The Union, Ame-lĭ'ka Hŭĭpŭĭ'ă.

unite, hŏ'ŏhŭ'ĭ, hŏ'ŏkŭ'ĭkŭ'ĭ.

unity, lōka'hĭ.

universe, (ke) āŏ holŏ'ŏkoă.

universal, mā nā wă'hĭ a păŭ.

university, ku'lă nu'ĭ.

unjust, kăŭlĭ'kĕ 'o'lĕ, 'ĕ'wă'ĕ'wă.

unknown, 'ĭ'kĕ 'o'lĕ ĭ'ă.

unless, kē 'o'lĕ.

unlike, lĭ'kĕ 'o'lĕ.

unlikely, 'ā'o'lĕ pa'hă.

unlucky, pākală'kĭ, păŏă.

until, ā, ā hi'kĭ.

unusual, mǎ'ǎ mǎǔ 'o'lě, ē.

up, ĭlu'nǎ, mālu'nǎ.

upper, mālu'nǎ a'ě.

upward, ĭlu'nǎ a'ě.

upon, mǎ, mālu'nǎ; (at), i.

upright, kūpololeĭ, kūpo'nǒ; (honest), hǒ'ǒpo'-nǒ.

upset, (to overturn), hǒ'ǒkǎhǔ'lǐ; (a boat), pǐhǒ'.

upstairs, mālu'nǎ.

urge, kǒĭ, hǒ'ǒkĭkĭ'nǎ; (invite), kō'nǒ.

urine, mǐ'mǐ.

us, (dual), ĭā' kāǔǎ, ĭā' mǎǔǎ; (plural), ĭā' kākǒǔ, ĭā' mākǒǔ.

use, (value), wǎĭwǎĭ; (service), lǎ'wělǎ'wě ǎ'nǎ: to use, lǎ'wělǎ'wě.

useful, wǎĭwǎĭ, mǎkěpo'nǒ.

usual, meǎ mǎǔ.

utmost, ho'pě lō'ǎ, mē kā ĭkǎĭkǎ a pǎǔ.

utter, (complete), pǎǔpo'nǒ: to utter, 'ěkě'mǔ, hǎ'ĭ.

utterance, 'ōle'lǒ.

V

vacant, vacancy, hǎ'kǎhǎ'kǎ.

vacation, wā hǒ'ǒma'hǎ.

vague, pǒwe'hǐwe'hǐ.

vain, hǎ'ǎkěĭ, hǒ'ǒkǐ'ěkǐ'ě: in vain, mǎkěhe'wǎ.

valley, āwǎ'wǎ, kǎhǎwǎĭ.

value, wǎĭwǎĭ; (price), kǔ'mǔ lǐ'lǒ.

valuable, wǎĭwǎĭ.

valve, (ke) pǎ'nǐ.

van, (vehicle), kǎ'ǎ; van of army, hǔnǎlě'wǎ.

vanish, na'lǒ, maha'nǐ.

vanity, (pride), hă'ăhe'ŏ; (idle show), hŏ'ŏ-
    kă'hăkă'hă.

vapor, (steam), ma'hŭ; (fog), 'o'hŭ.

variable, lo'lĭ wa'lĕ, lolĕlu'ă.

variety, kēlā' me kē'ĭă 'ă'nŏ.

various, kēlā' me kē'ĭă.

vary, lŏ'lĭ a'ĕ.

vast, (great), nu'ĭ lo'ă; (boundless), pale'nă
    'o'lĕ.

vegetable, meă'ăĭ lăŭnahĕ'lĕ.

vegetation, meă u'lŭ.

veil, u'hĭ; (for face), 'uhĭmă'kă.

vein, (ke) āŭ; (blood-vessel), a'ă kŏ'kŏ; (ore),
    āŭ mekā'lă.

velvet, wĕlĕwĕ'kă.

ventilate, hŏ'ŏkŏ'mŏ ĕă; (expose), hō'ĭ'kĕ
    ākeă.

venture, (risk), hŏ'a'o; (dare), 'ă"ă.

verandah, lānaĭ.

verdict, 'ōle'lŏ hŏ'ŏho'lŏ.

verify, hō'ŏ'ĭă, hō'ŏ'iaĭ'ŏ.

verse, (section), paukū'; (poetry), me'lĕ.

vertical, kūpololeĭ.

very, lŏ'ă, maolĭ.

vessel, (ship), mo'kŭ; (container), ĭ'pŭ, 'ă'pŭ.

vest, pūlĭ'kĭ.

veteran, ko'ă kăhi'kŏ, pa'ăhă'nă kăhi'kŏ.

veto, hŏ'o'lĕ.

vex, hŏ'ŏnaŭ'kĭŭ'kĭ, hŏ'ŏulŭhu'ă.

vice, (sin), he'wă; (crime), ha'lă; (wicked-
    ness), 'ĭ'nŏ, 'ăĭă'; (substitute), pă'nĭ, ho'pĕ.

vicinity, kă'hĭ kokŏ'kĕ.

vicious, (sinful), pu'nĭ i ke 'ĭ'nŏ; (defiling),
    haŭmi'ă; (mean), 'ĭ'nŏ, hūhū'.

victim, (sacrifice), meä käŭma′hä ĭ′ä; (prey),
    (ke) pi′ŏ; (dupe), meä hŏ′ŏpŭnĭhĕĭ ĭ′ä.
victory, lănäki′lä.
view, nanäĭnä: to view, nänä.
vigilant, kiä′ĭ, mäkäa′lä.
vigor, (strength), ĭkäĭkä; (force), mä′nä.
village, kaŭha′lĕ.
vine, lä′äŭ hĭ′hĭ; grape vine, kŭmŭwaĭnä.
vinegar, pĭnĭ′kä.
vineyard, mäläwaĭnä.
violate, (as promise), hä′kĭ; (ravish), pŭ′ĕ;
    (break forceably), lĭ′mä nu′ĭ.
violent, (as wind), ′ĭ′nŏ; (as man), wĕ′lĭwĕ′lĭ
    kä hūhū′, hehe′nä.
violet, wäĭŏle′kä.
violin, pi′lä, wäĭŏlĭ′nä.
virgin, pŭ′ŭpä′ä: (new), hoŭ; (chaste), hŏ′ŏ-
    pä′ ′o′lĕ.
virtue, (rectitude), po′nŏ; (legal force), mä′nä.
visé, ′äpo′nŏ, hō′apo′nŏ.
visible, ′ĭkĕmä′kä ĭ′ä.
vision, (eyesight), ′ĭ′kĕ o kä mä′kä; (appari-
    tion), (ke) akäkŭ′; vision with eyes closed,
    hĭhĭ′ŏ.
visit, (social), läŭnä; (tour), mäka′ĭka′ĭ.
visitor, hoäläŭnä, mäka′ĭka′ĭ.
vital, (of life), kū i ke o′lä; (of importance),
    wäĭwäĭ po′nŏ, ′ä′nŏ nu′ĭ.
vocabulary, pä′pä ′ōle′lŏ, pu′kĕ unu′hĭ ′ōle′lŏ.
vocal, pi′lĭ i kä le′ŏ.
voice, le′ŏ.
volcano, pĕ′lĕ, mäŭnä pĕ′lĕ; (crater), luäpĕ′lĕ.
volume, (book), pu′kĕ; (quantity), nu′ĭ.
voluntary, mä′kĕmä′kĕ ĭ′hŏ.
volunteer, kōkŭ′ä wa′lĕ.

vomit, lua'ĭ.

vote, (ballot), pālo'kă: to vote, kŏ'hŏ.

voter, meă kŏ'hŏ pālo'kă.

voucher, pă'lăpă'lă hŏ'ĭ'kĕ hŏ'ŏlĭ'lŏ.

vow, hŏ'ŏhĭ'kĭ.

vowel, huăpă'lăpă'lă leŏkă'hĭ.

voyage, (by sea), ho'lŏ mōa'nă; (by air), lĕ'lĕ.

vulgar, (coarse), pĕ'lăpĕ'lă; (unrefined), kuă-
      'ăĭnă.

W

wade, 'ăŭhĕ'lĕ.

wag, kănă'kă hŏ'ŏmăkĕ'ă'kă: to wag, 'ŏ'nĭ'ŏ'nĭ.

wage, (pay), u'kŭ: wage war, hŏ'ŭ'kă kăŭă.

wager, pilĭ.

wagon, kă'ă.

wail, ŭwē', kūmake'nă.

waist, pūha'kă: waistcoat, pūlĭ'kĭ.

wait, (pause), kă'lĭ, kăkă'lĭ; (attend), lă'wĕ-
      lă'wĕ.

waiter, kuĕ'nĕ, meă la'wĕla'wĕ.

wake, (ship's), (ke) a'wĕa'wă; (vigil), kiă'ĭ lĭñ
      pāpa'ŭ: to wake, a'lă.

walk, he'lĕ wăwaĕ.

wall, pā; (of house), păĭă; stone wall, pā pŏ-
      ha'kŭ.

wallet, 'ĕ'kĕ kālā.

wander, 'aĕ'ă, 'ăŭwă'nă; (be a tramp), kue'wă;
      (be delirious), pūpu'lĕ.

want, ne'lĕ, 'ĭlĭhŭ'nĕ: (to desire), mă'kĕmă'kĕ.

war, kăŭă.

ward, (person), meă hŏ'ŏkă'hŭ ĭ'ă; (room),
      keĕ'nă; (precinct), 'āpă'nă: to ward, pa'lĕ.

warden, kă'hŭ mālă'mă, lu'nă kiă'ĭ.

wardroom, keĕ'nă hŏ'ŏkĭ'pă.

warm, maha′nă; lukewarm, pūmaha′nă; (ardent), hŏĭhŏĭ.

warn, ā′ŏ̆.

warrant, (of arrest), pă′lăpă′lă hŏ′pŭ: to warrant, hō‘ŏ′ĭai‘ŏ.

warrior, koă.

warship, mo′kŭ kăŭă, manŭwā′.

wash, holoĭ.

washer, mĭkĭ′nĭ holoĭ, pĭ′hĭpĭ′hĭ păĭpŭ.

wasp, (yellow), hŏpĕ‘ō; (black), nălŏpă′kă.

waste, (desert), wăŏăku′ă, ‘ăĭnă nĕ′ŏ̆nĕ′ŏ; (refuse), ‘ōpă′lă; (prodigality), ŭ′hăŭ′hă: to waste, hŏ‘ŏmăŭ′năŭ′nă.

watch, ŭwa′kĭ: to watch, kiă′Ĭ.

water, (fresh) wăĭ; (salt), kăĭ: to water, hŏ‘ŏkă′hĕ wăĭ.

waterfall (or cascade), wăĭlĕ′lĕ; (trickle), wăĭ păĭhĭ; "down-side up" falls, wăĭpuhi′ă.

watermelon, ĭpŭha′ŏlĕ, ĭpŭ′ăĭmă′kă.

waterproof, (coat), kukăwĕ′kĕ: (impervious), kŏ′mŏ ‘o′lĕ kă wăĭ.

waterspout, wăĭpŭ‘ĭlă′nĭ; (blow-hole), pŭ′hĭ.

wave, (shore), na′lŭ; (ocean), ‘ă′lĕ: to wave, (as hand), pe a′hĭ; (as flag), wĕ′lŏ.

wavy, ‘ănŭ‘ŭnŭ‘ŭ.

wax, pila′lĭ; beeswax, kŭkaĕna′lŏ; earwax, kŏkŭ′lĭ.

way, (path), (ke) a′lă, alăhe′lĕ; (manner), (ke) ‘ă′nŏ, ‘ăŏ‘ăŏ: to be under way, nĕ‘ĕ, kŏ′lŏ.

we, (I and thou), kă′ŭă; (I and he), măŭă; (I and all you), kăkŏŭ; (I and all they), măkŏŭ.

weak, (tender), pă′lŭpă′lŭ, (sickly), năwa′lĭwa′lĭ; (without strength), ĭkăĭkă ‘o′lĕ.

wealth, (riches), wăĭwăĭ; (affluence), la'kŏ.

wean, (as a child), uku'hĭ; (alienate), hŏ'ŏhŭ'lĭ.

weapon, meă kăŭă, meă hō'ĕ'hă.

wear, (as dress), 'ă'ă'hŭ, kŏ'mŏ; wear away, hō'e'mĭ; wear well, pa'ă.

weary, lu'hĭ, mālu'hĭlu'hĭ.

weather, kūlă'nă o kā lā; (good), wā măĭkă'ĭ; (storm), 'ĭ'nŏ.

weave, (plait), ulă'nă; weave cloth, mi'lŏ.

web, meă i ulanăĭ'ă; spider's web, pūnawĕ'lĕwĕ'lĕ.

wed, wedding, ma'lĕ.

wedge, ŭ'nŭ.

Wednesday, Pō'ako'lŭ.

weed, nahe'lĕhe'lĕ: to weed, waĕlĕ.

week, pu'lĕ, hĕpĕko'mă.

weep, hālo'ĭlo'ĭ; (wail), ŭwē'.

weigh, (find weight), kăŭpăŏnă; (consider), no'ŏno'ŏ; weigh anchor, hŭ'kĭ i kē helĕu'mă.

weight, kăŭmă'hă, kŏ'ĭkŏ'ĭ.

weird, 'ă'nŏ lă'pŭ, 'ĕ'ĕhĭ'ă.

welcome, (ke) alo'hă, kĭ'pă alo'hă: to welcome, hŏ'ŏkĭ'pă 'o'lŭ'o'lŭ.

welfare, pōmaĭka'ĭ.

well, luăwăĭ; (artesian), luăwăĭ a'nĭa'nĭ: (healthy), mă'ĭ 'o'lĕ: to well up, pŭă'ĭ: (rightly), po'nŏ.

west, kŏmŏhă'nă: western, 'ăŏ'ăŏ kŏmŏhă'nă.

wet, pu'lŭ, kăwăū'.

whale, kohŏlā', pala'oă.

wharf, ŭwa'pŏ, ŭa'pŏ.

what, heahă? (that which), kā meă; what! kăĭ!

whatever, (all that), kēlā' me kē'ĭă; (at all), nō.

wheat, hŭi'kă, pala'oă.

wheel, hŭi'lă, pokăkă'ă: to wheel, kă'ă.

wheelbarrow, hŭi'lă pală'lă.

when, (how soon?), ahĕă? (how long ago?), ĭnăhĕă? (at the time), i kā wā.

whence, (from which?), măĭ hĕă măĭ? nōheă? (from that which), măĭ kă'hĭ.

whenever, i kā wā, aĭă a.

where, (?), māhĕă? (at which place), mā kă'hĭ; (whither?), ihĕă? i kăhĭ hĕă?

wherever, mā nā wă'hĭ a pău.

whether, (of two), owăĭ o laŭă; whether or not, ĭ'nā' pa'hă . . . ĭ'nā' 'ā'o'lĕ pa'hă.

which, (?), hĕă? kā meă hĕă? (that), ăĭ ["the thing which he saw," ka mea ana i 'ĭke ai].

whichever, kēlā' pa'hă kē'ĭă pa'hă . . . ăĭ.

while, wā, mănā'wă: (pass time), hŏ'ŏha'lă mănā'wă: (during), 'oĭaĭ, i kā wā.

whip, hahaŭ, hi'lĭ.

whirl, kăkă'ă, nini'ŭ.

whirlpool, mĭmĭ'lŏ.

whirlwind, pūahi'ŏhi'ŏ, 'ĕ'ă.

whiskey, wăĭ'ō'nă, wekekĕ'.

whisper, hāwă'năwă'nă.

whistle, (steam whistle, auto horn, etc.), oĕoĕ: to whistle, hŏ'ŏkĭ'ŏkĭ'ŏ; (as wind), hū.

white, kĕ'ŏkĕ'ŏ, kĕ'ă.

who, (?), wăĭ? owăĭ? (the one that), kā meă . . . ăĭ.

whole, holŏ'ŏkoă.

wholesale, kū'ăĭ nu'ĭ.

wholesome, (sound), kūpo'nŏ; (healthy), hŏ-'o'lă.

why, (reason), kŭ'mŭ: Why? Nō kē ă'hă? "Why indeed!" Nō kē ăhă' lă!

wicked, (sinful), 'ăĭă', he'wă; (bad), 'ĭ'nŏ.

wide, (broad), lăŭlā'; (extensive), ākeă.

widow, wăhinĕkanĕma'kĕ.

wife, wăhi'nĕ, wăhi'nĕ ma'lĕ.

wig, lăŭŏ'hŏ kŭ'ĭ.

wild, (untamed), hihĭ'ŭ, 'ahĭ'ŭ, la'kă 'o'lĕ; (angry), hūhū'.

wilderness, wăŏăku'ă, wăŏnăhĕ'lĕ.

will, (testament), kăŭo'hă; (determination), mană'ŏ.

willing, 'o'lŭ'o'lŭ.

win, (at games), ĕŏ; (conquer), lănăki'lă; (succeed), pu'kă; (get), lōa'a.

wind, maka'nĭ: to wind, wi'lĭ.

windmill, wi'lĭ maka'nĭ.

window, pukă'a'nĭ'a'nĭ.

windshield, pa'lĕ maka'nĭ.

windward, ĭlu'nă, kŏ'ŏlăŭ, mană'ĕ.

wine, waĭnă.

wing, (of bird), 'ehĕ'ŭ, pekĕke'ŭ; (of house), pakŭ'ĭ, măhe'lĕ; (of army), măhe'lĕ, lālā: to wing, (wound), pā; (to fly), lĕ'lĕ.

wink, 'ĭ'mŏ, 'ăwĭhĭ.

winner, meă pu'kă, meă ĕŏ.

winter, kăŭa'nŭ, hŏ'ŏĭ'lŏ.

wipe, kăwe'lĕ, holoĭ.

wire, ŭweă.

wireless, ŭweă'o'lĕ.

wise, nā'ăŭaŏ, no'ĕaŭ.

wish, mă'kĕmă'kĕ, (ke) ā'kĕ.

wit, (knowledge), 'ĭ'kĕ.

witch, kŭpu'ă; (seeress), wăhĭ'nĕ kĭ'lŏkĭ'lŏ.

witchcraft, (divination), kĭ'lŏkĭ'lŏ; (lethal sorcery), hŏ'ŏpĭ'ŏpĭ'ŏ, 'ană'ănā'.

with, mĕ, pū.

withdraw, (take back), la'wĕ hoŭ; (to retire),
    hŏ'ĭhŏ'ĭ, hă'ălĕ'lĕ.

wither, măĕ, mĭmi'nŏ.

withhold, 'aŭ'ă, kao'hĭ.

within, ĭlo'kŏ, mălo'kŏ.

without, (outside), māwa'hŏ, ĭwa'hŏ; (not
    having), mē . . . 'o'lĕ.

witness, (testify), hŏ'ĭ'kĕ; (see), 'ĭ'kĕ.

witty, hŏ'ŏmăkĕă'kă.

wizard, kŭpu'ă; (diviner), kĭ'lŏkĭ'lŏ.

woe, pŏpilĭki'ă nu'ĭ, kăŭmă'hă nu'ĭ, wălănĭ'ă:
    woe! ăŭwē!

wolf, 'ĭlĭŏhăĕ.

woman, wăhi'nĕ; women, wă'hinĕ.

wonder, hă'ŏhă'ŏ.

wonderful, kupăĭăna'hă, kămăhă'ŏ.

wood, lā'ăŭ; firewood, wăhi'e; driftwood, pĭ-
    hă'ā'; sandalwood, 'ĭlĭă'hĭ, lă'ăŭ'ă'lă: woods,
    ulŭlă'ăŭ.

wool, hŭ'lŭ.

woolen, hŭ'lŭhŭ'lŭ.

word, 'ōle'lŏ, huă'ōle'lŏ.

work, hă'nă.

workmanship, 'ă'nŏ o kā hă'nă.

works, workshop, wă'hĭ hă'nă.

world, āŏ: The World, Kē Aŏ Néĭ, kā honu'ă
    nĕĭ.

worm, (of screw), năŏ; earthworm, kŏ'ĕ; cut-
    worm, pŏ'kŏ; army worm, pĕ'ĕlu'ă; (per-
    son), lăpŭwa'lĕ.

worry, kăŭmă'hă, pihoĭhoĭ o kā nă'ăŭ.

worse, 'oĭ ă'kŭ kă 'ĭ'nŏ.

worst, 'ĭ'nŏ lŏ'ă.

worship, hŏ'ŏmă'nă, hăĭpu'lĕ.

worth, wăĭwăĭ ĭ'ŏ.

worthy, kūpo'nŏ, kŏ'ĭkŏ'ĭ.

wound, 'ĕ'hă, pălăpū': to wound, hŏ'ĕ'hă.

wrap, (cover), u'hĭ; (shawl), kīheĭ: to wrap,
    wăhĭ'.

wreath, lĕĭ: to wreathe, hŏ'ŏlĕĭ, kăŭ lĕĭ.

wreck, shipwreck, ilĭmŏ'kŭ; (misfortune), pŏ-
    'ĭ'nŏ: to wreck, hŏ'ŏpo'ĭ'nŏ; (as a ship), i'lĭ.

wrench, hăŏ wi'lĭ: to wrench, (sprain), māŭĭ;
    (force), wi'lĭ.

wrestle, hăkōkō.

wrestler, meă hăkōkō.

wretched, (miserable), kăŭmă'hă, lŭ'ŭlŭ'ŭ;
    (worthless), 'ĭ'nŏ'ĭ'nŏ.

wriggle, paka'ŭwĭ'lĭ.

wring, 'ūwĭ'.

wringer, mikĭ'nĭ 'ūwĭ' lo'lĕ.

wrinkle, mĭ'nŏmĭ'nŏ.

wrist, pūli'mă.

write, kakăŭ, kakăŭ lĭ'mă.

wrong, he'wă, po'nŏ 'o'lĕ.

Y

yacht, mo'kŭ hŏ'ŏho'lŏ lĕ'ălĕ'ă.

yam, u'hĭ.

yard, (measure), ĭwĭlĕĭ, ĭă'; (enclosure), pă.

yarn, (story), ka'aŏ; (fiber), lo'pĭ hŭ'lŭhŭ'lŭ.

yawn, hamă'mă.

year, măkăhi'kĭ.

year-book, pu'kĕ măkăhi'kĭ.

yeast, hū, hū pala'oă.

yell, 'ūwă', hŏ'o'hŏ.

yellow, me'lĕme'lĕ, lĕ'nălĕ'nă.

yelp, 'ăŏ'ăŏă.

yes, (in full assent), aĕ; (with reservations),
    ē; (indifferent), ū; (unwilling), 'ū.

yesterday, inĕhĭnĕĭ.

yet, (nevertheless), akā' nă'ĕ; not yet, 'ā'o'lĕ
   i kĕ'ĭă wā.

yield, hu'ă lōa'a: (to produce), hŏ'ŏhu'ā;
   (agree), aĕ.

yoke, ku'ă pĭ'pĭ, 'aŭă'mŏ: to yoke, kăŭlu'ă.

you, (thou), 'oĕ; (you two), 'ōlŭ'ă; (all you),
   'ōukoŭ.

your, (singular), kāŭ, kōŭ; (dual), kā 'ōlŭ'ă,
   kō 'ōlŭ'ă; (plural), kā 'ōukoŭ, kō 'ōukoŭ.

yourself, 'oĕ ĭ'hŏ nō, etc.

young, opĭ'ŏpĭ'ŏ, hoŭ, u'ĭ; (as fruit), mă'kă.

youngster, ke'ĭkĭ.

youth, opĭ'ŏ.

youthful, u'ĭ, opĭ'ŏ.

Z

zeal, mană'ŏ ĭkăĭkă.

zero, 'o'lĕ.

zigzag, kĭkĕ'ĕkĕ'ĕ.

zone, (geographical), kā'ĕĭ; (biological), wăŏ;
   (city), māhe'lĕ.

Hawaiian-English
Vocabulary

The original plan of this work was an English-Hawaiian vocabulary, with the Hawaiian words correctly pronounced and the English equivalents as applied at the present day. Such has been completed in the preceding portion.

Later, the publisher earnestly requested a complementary Hawaiian-English vocabulary, which is supplied in the following pages. The limitations of the linotype machines available threatened to delay the work unnecessarily, so the full pronunciation of the Hawaiian words (already given in the preceding portion) is not repeated. It is sufficient to remember that in most Hawaiian words, the accent falls on the syllable next to the last, and hence, needs no representation in the list. However, it is used to indicate exceptions, or vowels unusually long.

A

a, of, to, at.

(ke) a', jaw.

(ke) 'a, broken lava.

'a, to burn.

'a'a', conflagration: burning, raging: to kin-
    dle; burn fiercely; rage.

(ke) 'a'a', broken lava; stony.

'a"a', dwarf: short and stocky; silent, lonely;
    stuttering.

'a"a, a dare: to dare, tempt; to venture.

(ke) a'a, small roots; veins or arteries, etc.

'a'aho, lath; lattice.

'a'ahu, cloak, outer garment: to put it on.

'a'ai, cancer: eating, spreading.

'a'aki, to bite; nibble as fish.

(ke) a'akoko, vein; blood vessel.

'a'ala, pleasant odor.

(ke) a'alolo, nerve.

'a'ama, black rock-crab; theft.

'a'aniu, fiber cloth at coco-palm leaf butt.

'a'apo, quick to learn; to catch and retain

'a'aua, coarse skin or complexion.

ae, yes, consent.

a'e, oblique directive; separately.

'a'e, to step over an object; to break a tabu;
    to go onto.

'aea, to raise head; to rise out of water.

'ae'a, wandering; to wander.

'ae'ae, finely comminuted material; face pow-
    der.

aelo, rotten, as applied to eggs.

aeko, eagle.

aeko, eagle.

(ke) aha, what? why?

aha, braided cord of coir, hair or intestines, prayer based on braided coir, assemblage of priests, edge or border, measure in single line.

ahaaha, to pant heavily.

'aha'aina, great feast.

'aha'i, break off and take away.

'ahahui, company, society.

'aha'olelo, council, legislature.

(ke) ahe, breeze, wind.

ahe', person avoiding another on account of fear.

'ahe', cough.

ahea, when? in the future.

aheahe, light breeze.

'ahe'ahe', hacking cough.

ahele, hand snare.

aheleia, trapped.

'ahewa, punishment, blame, censure.

'ahewaia, condemnation.

(ke) ahi, fire.

(ke) 'ahi, albicore.

(ke) ahiahi, afternoon, evening.

'ahi'ahi, defame; bring to disrepute; tattle.

'ahina, gray color.

'ahinahina, slate color.

'ahiu, fierce, wild.

'aho, lath; batten for thatch.

(ke) aho, fish line; breath, patience, resolution, kindness: to have breath.

(ke) ahonui, endurance; patience: patient.

(ke) ahu, heap, storage.

'ahu, clothing mat, canoe mat.

(ke) ahua, bank; ford: to be raised on a platform.

(ke) ahu'awa, sedge used for fiber.

'ahui, bunch.

'ahuiwaina, bunch of grapes.

(ke) ahulau, epidemic, pestilence.

ahupua'a, land division, estate.

'ahu'ula, feathered cloak.

ahuwale, conspicuous, in plain sight.

ai, relative particle.

(ke) ai, coition.

'ai, food: to eat, consume, destroy.

'a'i', neck.

aia, there.

aia, behold!

'aia', irreligious, unprincipled.

'a'ia'i, brilliant white; clearness of glass.

'aie', indebtedness: to owe.

'aihamu, to eat waste food; to destroy by
    sorcery.

'aihue, thief: to steal.

'a'i'kala, collar.

(ke) aikane, friend.

'aikola, "Serves you right!"

'aiku', to eat informally.

'a'iku', wry-neck, stiff neck; high collar.

aila, oil, lard, grease; to smear with it.

ailaea, ailea, gasoline.

'ailolo, an expert, graduate.

'aina, food, eating, dining; refuse; land.

'ainaho'oilina, inherited estate.

'aiwaiu', infant.

aka, particle prefixed to imply care.

aka', but, if not.

(ke) aka, shadow; reflection.

'aka, to laugh, deride.

'aka'aka, laughter: to laugh.

'aka'akai, bulrush, onion.

(ke) akahai, meekness: modest; gentle.

(ke) akahele, to go, or going, carefully; to beware.

'akahi, one; first: once.

akaka, clear, plain, luminous.

akakale'a, manifest.

akake', reckless; intrusive.

(ke) akaku', apparition.

'akala, raspberry: pink.

(ke) akamai, wisdom, ingenuity: skillful.

'akau, right hand; north; right.

(ke) ake, liver; ambition; eagerness: to desire.

(ke) akea, broad, open space: publicly.

(ke) akeakamai, philosophy, philosopher.

'ake'ake'a, to obstruct, block.

(ke) akema'ma', the lungs.

akena, agent; to boast, brag.

'aki, to bite, cut with teeth, backbite.

'aki'aki, to nibble; to slander.

akimilala, admiral.

'ako, to clip, cut, pluck.

'akoakoa, assembled: to assemble.

'ako'ako'a, coral; the horned coral.

(ke) aku, bonito.

aku, verbal directive.

(ke) akua, God, or gods.

(ke) ala, road, path, way: to awake, arise.

(ke) 'ala, fumes: spicy, perfumed, aromatic; to anoint with perfume.

'ala', round smooth stone.

'alae, mud-hen.

'alaea, red ochre.

(ke) alahaka, step-ladder.

(ke) **alahele**, itinerary.

(ke) **alahao**, railroad.

alai, obstruction: to hinder.

alaila, then.

alaka'i, leader: to guide.

'alala, to cry as young animals.

alaalai, **alailai**, to hinder, cross, obstruct.

'alana, church offerings: to offer same.

'alani, orange.

(ke) **alanui**, highway, road.

'alapahi, slander: to slander.

alapi'i, ladder, steps, stairs.

(ke) **alaula**, twilight morning and night; first
   dawn.

(ke) **ale**, to swallow whole; to gulp.

'ale, wave, billow.

'ale'ale, moving, tossing as sea waves.

(ke) **alelo**, tongue.

alekohola, alcohol.

alemanaka, almanac.

'ale'o, watch tower; look out.

(ke) **alia**, salt marsh or bed.

'alia, to wait, restrain.

alepapeka, alphabet.

'alihi horizon: rope for net weights and sink-
   ers.

alihikaua, commander-in-chief.

(ke) **ali'i**, chief, king.

alimakika, arithmetic.

alina, scar; disgrace.

(ke) **alo**, front; face; presence.

aloalo, hibiscus.

'alo, to elude, dodge, evade.

(ke) **aloha**, affection, sympathy, greeting.

(ke) **alohi**, a shining; glitter, brilliancy.

(ke) alohilohi, luster, sparkle etc.

alopeka, fox.

(ke) alu, to combine forces for action.

'alu, muscles of eye: to relax, hang down; ruffle up.

alualu, pursue; to hunt; to follow.

'alu'alu, flexible skin; fetus; loose, wrinkled; slack, as rope.

(ke) 'alualua, rough road; multiplication table.

(ke) aluka, crowd; indiscriminate heaping up.

'alunu, see 'anunu.

(ke) ama, float for canoe outrigger.

'ama'ama, mullet.

(ke) amama, ancient "amen."

'amana, gallows.

(ke) amala, blacksmith, armorer.

amene, amen.

'ami, hinge; joint; reciprocal and hula motion; inch-worm.

(ke) amio, eddy of water; current of air.

(ke) amo, shoulder burden: to carry so.

ana, present participle: pronoun, "of him."

(ke) ana, a cave.

(ke) ana, measure, model or pattern.

'ana, pumice.

ana'aina, to survey land.

'ana'ana', sorcery.

'ana'anapu, repeated flashing: to flash, as lightning.

'anae, full sized mullet.

(ke) anahonua, geometry.

'anai, to rub, to grind, polish, blot out; to lay a curse.

(ke) anaina, an assembly: to congregate.

anana, a fathom.

'anapa, a flash, sparkle; to glitter.

anatomia, anatomy.

(ke) anawaena, diameter.

'ane'ane, nearly, almost.

anei, at this time; just now; a word indicating a question.

ane'i, here.

anela, angel.

'anemoku, peninsula.

ani, gentle breeze: to blow softly; to draw net on surface; to beckon.

'ania, smooth and even.

(ke) aniani, glass: transparent.

(ke) anini, awning.

ano', at present time, now.

(ke) ano, dread; reverence; sense of invisible presence, good or evil.

(ke) 'ano, likeness; meaning; quality; kind.

'ano'ano, seeds, progeny.

'ano'e', unlike: to be different.

(ke) anu, anuanu, cold.

(ke) anuenue, rainbow.

anuhe, caterpillar.

'anunu, (also 'alunu), usury; grafter; greedy; covetous.

(ke) ao, day. daylight; The Earth; cloud; enlightenment, knowledge.

(ke) a'o, tuition: to teach.

'ao, dried taro. sweet potato, or breadfruit.

'aoa, 'ao'aoa, howl, of dog.

'ao'ao, side.

'a'oe, 'a'ohe, 'a'ole, 'a'ohe, the negative.

(ke) a'ohoku', astronomy: to teach it.

(ke) aouli, the firmament, sky.

'apa,'apa'apa, slow, careless; interfering; blocking progress.

apa', roll, bundle, bolt of cloth.

'apana, portion, part.

apala, apple.

apau, (properly a pau), all.

'apiki, scoundrel: tricky, crafty.

(ke) apo, ring, band, bracelet: to span, embrace.

'apo, 'apo'apo, to catch, grasp, seize.

'apono, to approve.

'apono'ia, adopted, accepted.

'apopo, tomorrow.

'apu, coconut shell cup; small bowl.

(ke) apuapu, a file, rasp.

'apuepue, hardly; with difficulty.

'apuka, cheating, forgery, a swindler, embezzler.

(ke) au, current, eddy or circular motion in water, train of thought; gall, bile.

(ke) au, period, reign.

au, I.

au, yours, thine.

a'u, of me.

(ke) a'u, swordfish.

(ke) 'au, handle, shaft.

'au, to swim.

'au'a, closeness: stingy: to withhold.

'auamo, bearing stick, yoke; to carry on shoulder.

a'uane'i, soon.

auau, to walk fast.

'au'au, a bath: to wash.

aue', auwe', Alas! Dear me! Oh my! Expression of grief.

'auhau, a tax; a tribute; doctors' fees; dues: to assess.

'auhea, where?

'auhe'e, to flee.

'auhele, to wade; to swim about.

'aui, case in grammar: to decline, pass by.

'auina, descent, slope, decline.

'auka', bar, as of soap, gold, etc.

'auku'u, the bittern, the heron.

'auli'i, petite, neat, nice.

'aulima, firestick for hand.

'aumakua, ancestral spirit; reliable person.

'a'ume'ume, contention, strife: to pull back and forth.

'aumoana, sea farer.

(ke) aumoe, lateness at night; sleep time.

'auna, great number; flock, as of birds.

'aunaki, nether stick for rubbing fire.

(ke) aupuni, government.

'auwa'a, fleet of canoes.

'auwaalalua, nautilus.

'auwae, the chin.

auwaha, furrow, ditch, channel.

'auwai, ditch.

'auwana, to wander, go astray.

auwe', aue', Alas!

(ke) awa, passage through reef; modern, "harbor."

'awa, the narcotic, Piper: bitter.

'awa'awa, sour, bitterness, to taste.

'awahia, sour, bitterness, of feeling.

'awai, pulpit; rostrum.

(ke) awakea noon.

(ke) awalau, channel or harbor of many inlets, i.e., Pearl Harbor.

'awapuhi, ginger.

(ke) awawa, valley.

'awe,'awe'awe, squid's tentacles.

(ke) aweawe, wake of vessel; trail of smoke: tenacious; adhesive.

'awe'awe'a, indistinct; not clearly apprehended.

awelike, average.

'awihi, a wink, to wink with one eye as in flirting.

'awi'wi', to hasten, hurry.

D

Demokalaka, Democrat.

E

e, call for attention.

e, by: sign of future tense.

'e', different, other, new, strange: previously: adversely.

ea, call of attention.

ea', assent or question—"Aye," "Eh what?"

(ke) ea, breath; life; air; breeze.

'ea, turtle; thrush in mouth.

'e'a, cloud of dust; whirlwind; dust or spray windblown.

eaea, medicine; offensive odor of sea or swamp.

eaha, What? How?

'e'e, to embark, go aboard.

'e'ehia, reverence: fearful, solemn.

'e'eke, to shrink from anything.

'eha, physical injury, pain, ache: sore: to suffer.

'eha'eha, pain, mental distress: sad.

ehako', dove.

'eheu, wings, winged.

'ehia, how much? how many?

eho, stone pillar; stone god.

'ehu, sand-colored; reddish light-colored na-
    tives.

(ke) ehu, ehukai, spray.

ehuehu, violence.

'ei, 'eia, here; here is.

eka, acre

'eka, dirty, foul.

'eka', hand of bananas.

ekalesia, church organization.

'eke, bag, pouch, pocket.

'eke'eke, displeasure; nervousness: fussy;
    over-exacting.

'ekemu, to speak; to respond.

'ekeu, wing.

eki, ace.

'eku, to root, turn up earth.

'elaueki', bayonet.

'elele, messenger; delegate.

(ke) elelo, tongue.

'ele'ele, dark, black.

'elelu' roach.

'elemakule, old man.

elepani, elephant.

'eleu, efficient, capable; active, alert, lively.

'eli, to dig.

emepela, emperor.

emi, emiemi, recession: cheap: to decrease, re-
    cede, debase, sink, flag.

emikua, to back up.

'emo'ole, instantly, sudden, prompt.

'ena'ena, heat: hot; properly heated.

enemi, enemy.
enikini, steam engine.
enuhe, caterpillar.
eo, wager won: winning.
epane, apron.
'eu, full of mischief or fun: to rise from a
    sitting position; to move along.
euanelio, the gospel.
'ewa'ewa, biased, unjust, unequal.
(ke) ewe, navel string; place of one's birth;
    ancestral trait.

F

fea, bazaar.
falu', influenza.

H

ha, four.
ha, to expel breath.
ha'a, causative prefix.
ha'a, the Hawaiian dance; dwarf.
ha'aha'a, low; lowly, meek, humble.
ha'aheo, proud, haughty, magnificent: to
    strut.
ha'akei, proud, haughty: to scorn.
ha'alele, to desert, forsake, cast off.
ha'alulu, to tremble, totter, shudder, quake.
ha'anou, to hold breath by intense effort.
ha'ano'u, to exaggerate in speach.
ha'anui, a boaster: to boast.
haawe, a back burden: to carry on back.
haawi, to give.
haawina, a gift, a portion; a lesson.
hae, flag; bark of dog: fierce; vicious.
haehae, to tear, to rend.
ha'ele'ele, blackish, brown.

ha'ha', to feel with hand.

hahai, to follow.

haha'i, a breaking: to tell on, report.

hahana, very warm from exercise, fever or heat of the day.

hahau, to whip; to play cards on table.

ha'i, to narrate, tell, confess.

ha'i, a break, to be broken.

ha'i, another.

ha'ia'o, sermon, discourse.

ha'iha'i, undulation of voice: to break.

haikaika', to mock, make faces.

haikea, pale.

haiki, narrow, pinched.

ha'ili'ili, to curse, revile; blaspheme the gods.

hailona, omen; sign; lot in casting lots.

hailuku, to stone; to destroy; to hit with a weapon.

ha'ina, declaration, answer, statement.

hainaka', handkerchief.

ha'i'olelo, a preaching, address.

haipule, piety: religious: to worship.

haka, hole; ladder; henroost; spiritualistic medium.

hakahaka, blanks; want: hollow as eyes; empty.

hakaka' fight; to quarrel.

hakalia, delay, slowness; space of time.

hakapono, to watch earnestly, stare, gaze.

hakeakea, faded: to fade.

haki, easily broken: to be broken.

hakihaki, brittle; to be broken in pieces.

hakilo, to spy, watch narrowly.

hakina, piece, fragment.

ha'ko'ko', wrestling: to wrestle.

haku, a lord, core: to weave, compose.

haku'aina, landowner.

hakui, food cooked with hot stones.

haku'i, echo: to reflect sound.

hakumele, poet.

hala, sin: wicked: to sin; to miss.

hala, Pandanus.

halahi', to miss a mark; whiz; miscarry.

halakahiki, pineapple.

halana, to overflow, flood.

halawai, a meeting: to meet.

hale, house, home.

haleali'i, palace.

halehalawai, meeting house.

haleku'ai, store.

halelana, floating house; house boat; Noah's
    Ark.

halelu' psalm.

halepa'ahao, jail, prison house.

halepapa'a, storehouse, barn.

halepule, prayer house; church; chapel.

hali,halihali, carry in hand; fetch.

hali'a, premonition, hunch; sudden remem
    brance.

hali'ali'a, beloved; remembered with affection.

hali'i, to spread out, on or over.

halike, to equalize; resemble.

haliu, to turn and look or listen.

ha'lo', to peep around or under.

halo'ilo'i, watering of eyes; tears welling in
    eyes.

haloko, pool.

halulu, roar of water, wind, trucks, airplanes,
    etc.

haluku, thuds accompanying quarrel or playing in house; bangs on walls.

hamama, open: to open, yawn.

hamale, hammer: to hammer.

hamau, silent; to hush.

hamo, anointed; to smear; rub lightly.

hamole, round and smooth; hairless, bald.

hamu, meal fragments.

hamumu, hamumumu, hum.

hana, work, labor; to make, do.

hana, to be or become warm.

hana, bay, in place names.

hana', middle post of house gable end.

hanai, feed, nourish, support, adopt.

hanalima, labor: hand-made.

hanapa'a, steady employment.

hanau, birth: to be born.

hanauna, a generation: relatives of the same.

hanawale, to do gratuitously; to pick on others.

haneli, a hundred.

hanini, spill, overflow, pour out.

hano, to use as a syringe; inject.

ha'no', asthma.

hanohano, glory, honor, pomp: distinguished.

hanopilo, hoarse.

hanu, breath: to breathe, to smell.

hanuhanu, to sniff a scent.

hanupanupa, choppy as of the sea.

hanupilo, offensive breath, halitosis.

hao, iron: a robber: to plunder, to grasp greedily.

ha'oha'o, wonder, marvel.

haole, white, foreign.

hapa, fraction, part.

hapaha', quarter.

hapai, lift up, carry: pregnant.

hapaku'e, impediment in speech: deformed.

hapala, to daub, paint; smear, blot, defile, defame.

hapalua, half; half a dollar.

hapapa, shallow soil; superficial: to grope with the hands.

hapapulima, autograph.

hapuku, to grab hastily; to gather.

hau, dew, snow, ice, frost; a certain breeze.

ha'u, to snort; to puff tobacco smoke.

hauka'e, filthy, smudged: to deface, blot out.

haukalima, ice cream.

haukapila, hospital.

ha'ukeke, shiver with cold, quiver.

haulani, restive, on the go; unconventional.

ha'ule, lost; dropped: to fall; stumble; (poetically), to die.

hauli, dark, swarthy; brown.

haumana, student, apprentice.

haumia, impurity, defilement, (spiritually).

hauna, fishy smell; stinking, rank.

haunaele, commotion; panic; riot, roughhouse: to flee in war.

hau'oli, joy.

haupa', eat greedily.

haupia, pudding of arrowroot and coconut milk.

hauwala'au, gabble.

hawai, aqueduct, flume.

Hawai'i, Hawai'i.

hawanawana, to whisper.

hawawa', inexperience: awkward, clumsy.

he, a or an.

he, young caterpillar; grave.

hea, which? what?

heaha, what?

heʻe, squid, octopus: to flee, flow, melt.

heʻeholua, tobogganing; to toboggan.

heʻenalu, surfing; to ride on the surf.

heʻhe', boil, running sore.

hehena, madness: insane.

hehi, to tread; trample, stamp, step.

hehu, to uproot, dig up.

hei, net, snare, stratagem, string figure, decoration, ornament.

heʻiʻ, papaya.

heiau, large place of worship.

heihei, a race: to race.

heiheilio, to race horses.

hekau, stone anchor; towline; hawser.

hekili, thunder.

hele, to go, move, walk.

helehelena, face, features.

helelei, scattered; broken or crumbled.

helepela', Begone!

heieuma, anchor.

helu, memorial recitation: to count; to scratch in the earth like a fowl.

heluhelu, read; recount; recite.

heluna, numbering, a number, amount.

hema, the left; south.

hemahema, awkward, clumsy, inexpert: to want.

hemo, loose, separated, untied.

hemolele, holy, perfect.

henehene, disdain, mockery, derision, sneer.

hepekoma, week.

heu, heuheu, fuzz, down or fine hair.

hewa, fault, defect, error, mistake.

hiʻa, netting shuttle: to make fire by rubbing.

hia'a', wakeful.

hiaku, to fish for aku.

hiamoe, sleep.

hiapo, first-born.

hiehie, impressive appearance, good style, pride: dignified.

hihi, tangle of weeds, rank growth of grass, vines etc.

hihia, entanglement; law case: difficult.

hihimanu, stingray.

hihi'o, to see in a vision or a dream.

hihiu, wild, untamed, barbarous.

hi'i, to hold in arms, to nurse.

hi'ipoi, to tend and feed child or person; fondle.

hi'ka'ka', to reel, stagger.

hiki, to be able, accomplish, arrive; to rise, as the sun.

hikie'e, fixed couch or lounge.

hiki'i, a binding: to tie.

hikilele, mental shock: to startle.

hikina, east; arrival.

hikiwawe, to be quick: quickly.

hiku, seven.

hilahila, shyness; shame: bashful.

hili, bark for dyeing: to plait, tie on, whip, smite.

hilina'i, trust, confidence: to lean on.

hilo, spin, twist, braid.

himeni, hymn, song: to sing.

hina, hinahina, gray.

hina, to fall down.

hina'i, basket.

hinu, oil, ointment, grease.

hinuhinu, bright, shining, polished.

hio, a mountain wind; whistling wind in house: to break wind.

hioʻ, leaning, oblique: to slant.

hiʻo, restless; boisterous.

hiʻohiʻona, appearance.

hiʻolani, to lie at ease, lounge; (poetically), to sleep.

hiolo, collapse, as a house; lansdlide.

hiʻona, features, appearance.

hipa, sheep.

hipuʻu, knot, fastening: to tie a knot.

hiu, to fling, throw violently.

hiʻu, tail of fish.

hiwahiwa, precious, esteemed.

hiwi, summit.

ho, asthma; hoe: (as imperative verb), transfer, remove.

hoʻ is a common abbreviation for the causative prefix **hoʻo,** when preceding a vowel.

hoa, companion; club: to beat with a club.

hoʻaʻ, to kindle, inflame.

hoaʻa, to become confused; blunder.

hoaʻai, guest; dining companion.

hoaʻaina, tenant.

hoʻaʻano, to bluff.

hoahana, partner, fellow workman.

hoahanau, blood relative.

hoʻahewa, condemn, blame, find guilty.

hoʻahu, lay up, collect, gather.

hoaʻiaʻi, white, clear, shining.

hoʻaiʻeʻ, to extend credit, charge indebtedness.

hoʻailona, sign, mark, signal, target, lot cast.

hoʻakaka, to explain thoroughly.

hoʻakea, enlarge, extend.

hoʻakoakoa, to assemble, collect, muster.

ho'ala, to rise, arouse.

hoalauna, neighbor, visitor, close friend.

hoaloha, friend.

ho'alohaloha, to court; to bless; to give
thanks; to pay respects to.

ho'alu'alu, to loosen: to slack a rope.

ho'amana, to empower.

hoana, grindstone: to grind.

ho 'a'no, reverance: holy.

ho'ano'e', to change.

hoanoho, neighbor.

ho'anuanu, to freeze.

ho'ao, ancient marriage.

ho'a'o, to try, taste, undertake.

hoapaio, antagonist, opponent.

ho'apono, approve.

ho'auhe'e, to disperse, put to flight.

ho'auhuliana, revolution.

hoe, paddle.

ho'ea, risen: to be in sight; to arrive.

ho'eha, to injure, give pain.

ho'eha'eha, injure, give pain, harass, vex.

ho'emi, to lessen, reduce, rebate, debase; drive
back.

ho'eu'eu, to rouse to action, rally, drive in
work; to stir up.

hoeuli, rudder.

hoewa'a, to paddle a canoe.

hohe, coward.

hoho', to snore, snort.

hohoa, to strike, beat.

hohola, to unfold, spread, extend, radiate.

hohono, strong smelling.

hohonu, deep.

ho'i, to go back: also, besides.

hoihoi, joy, hopefulness: glad, brisk.

ho'iho'i, to restore, bring back.

ho'ike, witness, exhibit: plain: to make known.

ho'ike'ike, to make known, display.

ho'ino, to harm, abuse, persecute, insult.

ho'ino'ino, to disfigure, deface; slander.

hoka, chagrin: thwarted.

hoka'e, to smudge.

hokai, to disturb.

hokele, hotel.

hoki, mule.

hoki'i, tuberculosis.

hokiokio, to whistle.

hoku', star.

hokulele, meteor.

hokuwelowelo, comet.

hola, hour.

hole, to groove.

holehole, to peel, to strip off.

holo, to run, move, sail.

holoholo, to walk about; sail about.

holoholona, animals.

holohau, to skate.

holoholo'olelo, gossip, slander.

holoi, to clean, wash, scrub.

holokahiki, Hawaiian sailor voyaging to foreign lands.

holoku', gown, "Mother Hubbard."

holo'okoa, entire, whole.

holokuku', to trot as a horse.

holoma'ma', holonui, speed.

holomua, progress.

holowa'a, box, chest, cradle.

holu, spring: flexible.

holua, a sled for tobogganing.

homai, Bring here! Give here! This way!

home, home.

honi, salutation: to kiss, touch noses, smell.

hono, bay, cave, sheltered spot in the sea.

honu, turtle.

honua, flat land, The Earth.

ho'o, causative prefix. Note: This prefix is
   often shortened to **ho'** before a vowel. Thus
   the word next below, namely **ho'o'**, is in
   full **ho'o-o'**. Ho'ahu, on a previous page is
   in full, **ho'oahu**.

ho'o', to reach in.

ho'oha'aha'a, to humiliate, abase, debase.

ho'oha'i, to flirt.

ho'ohaiki, to contract, shrink.

ho'ohala, to cause to miss, to pass, while away.

ho'ohalahala, to refuse assent, complain, protest.

ho'ohalike, to resemble, make similar, copy.

ho'ohalikelike, resemblance, similarity: to
   equalize.

ho'ohalua, to ambush, lure, spy.

ho'ohanohano, to elevate to rank; to honor.

ho'ohauhili, to cause confusion in speech.

ho'ohaumia, to pollute, defile.

ho'ohaunaele, to incite a riot.

ho'ohehe'e, melt, soften, cast.

ho'oheihei, to race.

ho'ohelelei, to scatter, as sowing; throw away.

ho'ohenehene, ridicule, mock, jeer, mimic, tease.

ho'oheu, to bleach, as clothes.

ho'ohihia, to perplex, vex, complicate, entangle.

ho'ohiki, to make affidavit, to swear.

ho'ohikiwawe, to accelerate.

ho'ohilahila, to be timid; humiliate.

ho'ohinuhinu, to polish.

ho'ohiolo, to demolish, as building.

ho'ohiwahiwa, to honor; to adorn.

ho'oho, to shout, cry out.

ho'ohoihoi, charm, delight, entertain, encourage.

ho'oholo, decision in court: running free, as a horse: to run, sail, settle, determine, appraise.

ho'ohua, reproduce.

ho'ohuahualau, to obtain information by indirect questioning.

ho'ohuhu', to make angry, provoke; to pretend anger.

ho'ohui, to introduce socially.

ho'ohuikau, complicate, complex.

ho'ohuli, to turn around, change, alienate.

ho'ohuoi, suspicion.

ho'oia, to prove.

ho'oia'o, to prove, allege, take acknowledgment.

ho'oikaika, to strengthen, encourage.

ho'oili, to put on conveyance, transfer, export.

ho'o'ili'ili, to collect in store, gather in heaps.

ho'oilina, inheritance, heir.

ho'okuleana, to entitle; to give right of usage or possession.

ho'oilo, winter.

ho'oipo, ho'oipoipo, to woo, court, make love.

ho'oka'a, to pay a debt; discharge obligation.

ho'oka'awale, separate.

ho'okae, treat contemptuously, scorn.

ho'okahakaha, showy, dandified, display.

ho'okahe, to pour out, irrigate.

ho'okahi, one, alone, only.

ho'okahuli, overthrow, overturn, confound.

ho'okala, to sharpen, grind.

ho'okama, to adopt, as a child.

ho'okamakama, prostitution, fornication.

ho'okamani, to pretend; hypocrisy, sham.

ho'okamaniha, to be rude, unsocial, or un-
feeling.

ho'okanaka, manly; to act like a man.

ho'okano, to be proud, haughty.

ho'okapu, to prohibit, consecrate.

ho'okapukapu, to exalt, glorify; make a pre-
tence at consecration.

ho'okau, to place.

ho'okaulana, to make famous, celebrate.

ho'okaulike, to balance.

ho'oka'ulua, to slacken, procrastinate, hesitate.

ho'okaumaha, to lay burden on, grind, oppress, wear.

ho'oke', to crowd together, push one aside.

ho'oke'ai, to abstain from food, fast.

ho'okele, to steer, conduct; steersman.

ho'oke'oke'o, make white, bleach.

ho'oki'eki'e, pride: to elevate, lift up, be proud.

ho'okikina, to hurry, command, boss; make
dogs fight.

ho'okina, to persist.

ho'okina', to mar, maim.

ho'okipa, to entertain, welcome.

ho'oko', to fulfill, carry out contract.

ho'okoe, to reserve, set aside.

ho'okohu, presumption: to appoint, empower.

ho'okokoke, to approach.

ho'okolo, to crawl along, crouch; to track,
trail.

ho'okolokolo, to try in court.

ho'okomo, to insert, enter, put into.

ho'oku'e', to oppose, clash.

ho'oku'eku'e, to push, to elbow.

ho'oku'eku'emaka, to frown, scowl.

ho'oku'emaka, a frown.

ho'oku'i, to join, connect, annex, weld.

ho'oku'ikahi, to unite, reconcile, make treaty.

ho'oku'iku'i, to unite, join by sewing, splice.

ho'oku'ina, a joining, uniting, seam in garment.

ho'okuke, to drive off, banish, expel, shoo.

ho'oku'ku', a fitting, measuring; to compete.

hookulike, conform.

ho'okumu, to begin, originate, establish.

ho'okupa'a, to confirm an agreement, persist, be steady, establish.

hookupono, to fit, qualify.

ho'okupu, a contribution: to contribute; to cause growth.

ho'oku'u, dismiss, release, absolve, free.

ho'ola, safety, salvation: to heal, recover.

ho'ola'a, to consecrate, set apart.

ho'olaha, to spread out, advertise, extend, publish.

ho'olaka, ho'olakalaka, to tame.

ho'olako, to supply, enrich, provide.

ho'ola'la', to plan.

ho'olale, to cause stir, hasten, incite.

ho'olalelale, to get ready quickly; to hasten generally.

ho'olana, to cause to float, launch, give attention, cheer up.

ho'olaule'a, to celebrate, appease, calm, reconcile, satisfy complainant.

ho'olauna, to give introduction; be good friends.

ho'olawa, to finish; have enough; supply.

ho'olawe, to carry, take from, deduct.

ho'ole, to deny, refuse assent.

ho'ole'ale'a, to amuse, charm, assuage, gratify.

ho'olei, to throw away, reject, fling; to put on a garland.

ho'olewa, a funeral and service: to bear or carry a corpse.

ho'olilo, to cause transfer, change, spend, be lost.

ho'olimalima, to lease, hire, make a bargain.

ho'olohe, to cause to hear; listen, obey, submit.

ho'olo'ihi, to prolong, extend.

ho'ololi, to change, alter, reverse.

ho'olualua'i, to chew the cud; to induce vomiting.

ho'oluhi, make weary, oppress.

ho'oluliluli, drink shaker: to stir up, agitate, rock as in cradle.

ho'olu'olu, to quiet, comfort, pacify.

ho'olu'u, to immerse; to dye, color; dip into.

ho'olu'u'ili, to tan hides.

ho'oma'a, to accustom, practice; gain skill by practice.

ho'oma'alili, to cool or compose oneself.

ho'oma'ama'a, to make familiar by use; practice; acclimate.

ho'oma'au, to bully, tease, persecute, torment.

ho'oma'ema'e, to clean.

ho'omahie, to flirt, as a child.

ho'omahola, to spread out, as clothes; expand as flower.

ho‘omahuahua, to enlarge, magnify, increase.

ho‘omahu‘i, fashion: to ape, mimic, imitate.

ho‘omaika‘i, Thanksgiving; honor, favor: grateful: to make good, correct, bless, thank, praise.

ho‘oma‘ino, to revile, abuse, make sad.

ho‘oma‘ino‘ino, to slander, deride.

ho‘omaka, to begin, commence a work.

ho‘omakakiu, watchful: to lurk, lie in wait, watch jealously.

ho‘omakaukau, to prepare, qualify.

ho‘omaka‘uka‘u, to terrify.

ho‘omakauli‘i, thrifty, careful, provident: to economize.

ho‘omake‘aka, witty; comic: to excite laughter.

ho‘omalamalama, to cause light, illuminate; enlighten.

ho‘omalili, to appease.

ho‘omalimali, to soothe; to flatter; gratify; gain by flattery.

ho‘omalo‘elo‘e, to strain.

ho‘omaloka, unbeliever: impious: to be dull; disbelieve.

ho‘omalo‘o, to make dry, wither; season, as lumber.

ho‘omalu, to make peace; rule over, protect.

ho‘omaluhiluhi, to exhaust, i.e., tire.

ho‘omalule, to be limp; metamorphose.

ho‘omalumalu, to overshadow, obscure, darken, cloud over.

ho‘omana, to worship, ascribe divine honors.

ho‘omanaki‘i, idolatry.

hoomanamana, heathen worship: to practice sorcery.

ho'omana'o, to remember.

ho'omanawale'a, to give alms, contribute to charity.

ho'omanawanui, patience: to endure.

ho'omane'one'o, to make itchy; to tickle.

ho'omaopopo, to assure, make certain.

ho'oma'ona, to satiate.

ho'omau, to be constant; persist; perpetuate.

ho'omau', to moisten, soak.

ho'oma'aue', to mimic speech.

ho'omauhala, to hold a grudge, cherish revenge.

ho'omaunauna, wasteful: to spend uselessly.

ho'omo'a, to cook.

ho'omoana, camping place: to encamp.

ho'omohala, ho'omohola, evolution: to unfold, as a blossom; spread.

ho'omoho, to stalk.

ho'ona', appease.

ho'ona'auao, to instruct.

ho'onana, to take purgative.

ho'ona'na', to quiet, comfort, console.

ho'onanea, to put at ease, relax; to be absorbed in occupation.

ho'onani, to glorify, honor, adore, exalt; decorate.

ho'onaueue, vibration; shaking of earthquake: to rock, shake to and fro.

ho'onaukiuki, to irritate, provoke, exasperate.

ho'onele, to deprive, make destitute.

ho'oneoneo, to desolate, ravage.

ho'onoa, to free from kapu; abolish; cause to cease.

ho'onoho, to install, seat, regulate, locate.

ho'onu'u, to eat heartily, devour.

ho'opa', to touch, handle, hit.

ho'opa'a, to make fast.

ho'opa'ahao, to imprison.

ho'opa'ana'au, to memorize.

ho'opa'apa'a, argument or quarrel.

ho'opae, to run canoe up on beach.

ho'opahu', to explode, blast.

ho'opahupahu', fire crackers: to sound successively, throb violently.

ho'opa'i, to fine, punish, revenge.

ho'opailua, to nauseate: abhor; loathe.

ho'opakele, to deliver, rescue, cause escape.

ho'opalahalaha, to widen, extend.

ho'opalau, to betroth.

ho'opa'lau, to commit perjury.

ho'opalupalu, to soften, mollify.

ho'opane'e, to postpone.

ho'opa'pa', repartee: to feel as a blind person.

ho'opapa, corner shelf: to overlay.

ho'opau, to finish, cease, consume, cancel.

hoopaupilikia, to relieve nature.

ho'ope', to anoint, perfume; to break fine, mash.

ho'ope'pe', to pound, crush, break by blows; to cringe, to approach with fear.

ho'opiha, to fill.

hoopihoihoi, to excite.

ho'opi'i, to accuse in court, appeal, inform.

ho'opi'ipi'i, to beat against the wind; to stir or rouse to anger.

ho'opili, to stick to, cling to, apply.

hoopilihua, to perplex.

ho'opilikia, to get into difficulty; bother.

ho'opilimea'ai, to toady.

ho'opi'o, to arch, bend, curve, crook.

ho'opi'opi'o, to practice sorcery.

ho'opi'pi', to smoke, as hams.

hoopipili, to glue, paste.

ho'opohae, to tear open for examination.

hoopohihihi, to bewilder, puzzle.

ho'opo'ino, to injure, mar, deface.

ho'opokole, to shorten, contract.

ho'opololei, to straighten, correct, aim.

ho'opono, honor, uprightness: honest: to rec-
    tify, put in order; to have a good charac-
    ter.

ho'oponopono, to superintend, regulate; make
    up deficit.

hoopowehiwehi, to confuse, make obscure.

hoopuehu, to scatter, disperse.

ho'opu'iwa, to frighten suddenly; astonish.

ho'opuka, to emerge, appear, publish; per-
    forate.

ho'opukapuka to merchandise, speculate; con-
    tradict.

ho'opulu, to fertilize land.

ho'opunana, to make a nest.

ho'opuni, to surround; deceive.

hoopunihei, to decoy, trap.

hoopuniwale, to fool; to be easily fooled.

ho'opunipuni, deceit, treachery; to lie.

ho'ouka, ho'uka, to attack; to load animal or
    boat.

ho'oulu, to sprout, make grow; stir up

ho'ouluhua, to weary, vex, oppress, bore.

ho'ounauna to order, command, boss; send
    on   errand.

ho'owaha, to insult.

ho‘owahawaha’, to treat with contempt, ridicule, despise.

hoowalewale, to tempt, deceive, ensnare, bewitch, charm.

ho‘owali, to mix, blend; with ‘ai, "food," to digest.

ho‘oweliweli, to alarm, terrify, menace, threaten.

hope, last, ending, late, rear, substitute.

hopena, ending, conclusion.

hope‘o’, wasp, "yellow jacket."

hopohopo, fear, dread.

hopu, hopuhopu, to seize, grasp, catch, scramble.

hopuna‘olelo, sentence; pronunciation.

hou, sweat: new, recent, fresh, additional: to stab, poke at.

ho‘u’, to soak, dip in liquid.

ho‘ulu‘ulu, to collect, assemble; cause increase; add.

hu, ferment, yeast, leaven: to swell up as leaven; whistle as wind.

hua, fruit, egg, seed, result, testis.

hu‘a, train of dress: to froth.

hua‘ai, edible fruit.

huaale, hua’le, a pill, tablet, medicine.

huahuwa’, envy.

hua‘i, to dig out of ground, uncover oven.

hu‘akai, hu‘ahu‘akai, sponge, sea-foam.

huaka‘i, large company traveling.

huamoa, hen's egg.

hua‘olelo, a single word; expression.

huapalapala, letter of alphabet.

huapo‘o, side of the head.

huawaina, grapes.

hue, gourd, water calabash.

hu'e, to cause to flow out; unload; remove.

huelo, tail of beast or reptile.

huewai, long-necked gourd for water.

huhu, clothes-moth; termite.

huhu', anger, displeasure.

huhui, a swarm.

hui, union: to unite, come together, assemble.

hu'i, cold, chilly, ache, rheumatic pain.

huihui, mixed, mingled, united.

hu'ihu'i, cold, chilly.

huikala, to cleanse, purify; pardon.

huikau, disarrangement; confusion.

huila, wheel.

huila palala, wheel-barrow.

huina, a number, meeting point, angle.

huinaha', a square, quadrilateral.

huinakolu, triangle.

huipu', to mix together, unite, blend.

hukakai, tasteless, unpalatable.

huki, to draw, pull; deviate.

hula, dance and song: eye twitching: to dance
    to rhythmic song.

hula', to raise with lever; expel, eject.

hulahula, the foreign dance: twitching: to
    flutter.

hulali, shining surface, reflector: to glitter;
    be muddy.

huli, to turn, seek; change opinions.

hulilau, calabashes or gourds (large size).

hulilua, shifty; turning both ways.

hulipahu, second mate of vessel.

hulu, feathers, wool, hair in general.

huluhulu, wool blanket, blanket: hairy.

hului, to draw together; to grab all.

hulumanu, plumage.

hume, to bind on loins; put on malo.

humu, humuhumu, to sew cloth, to sew.

huna, minute particle, grain.

huna', to conceal, disguise, pretend.

hunahuna, crumbs.

hunahuna' to secrete, hide.

huna'kele, native burial, secret burial: to so
    bury.

hunalewa, van of an army.

hunapa'a, rear of an army.

hune, poverty: poor.

hunoai, parent-in-law.

hunona, child-in-law.

hu'pe', nasal mucus.

hu'po', savage, ignorant; fool.

hu'wa', envy.

hulo', hurrah!

i, sign of imperfect tense, potential, and im-
    perative moods.

i, to, towards, in, etc., and connecting verb
    with object.

'i, to speak, say.

ia, he, she, it.

ia, this, (present); that, (absent).

ia, sign of passive.

ia', to, before proper names and pronouns.

ia', yard.

i'a, fish.

'ia', as long as, while.

'iaha, to what? for what?

'iako, canoe outriggers.

i'aloa, preserved corpse; mummy.

'ie, made of canvas, cotton, linen; braided
    material; woody vine (Freycinetia), wov-
    en basket: flexible.

i'e, tapa mallet.

Iehova, Jehovah.

'ie'ie, Freycinetia: decorated with its leaves.

i'ekuku, tapa mallet.

ihe, javelin, war dart, spear.

iheihe, a fish.

ihi, strip off bark or skin, flay, peel.

'ihi, 'ihi'ihi, holy, sacred, majestic.

iho, soft tissue or pith, earth axis, axle: self:
    to descend: downwards; at that time, then,
    just, already.

ihoiho, heart of tree; candle.

ihu, nose, snout, bill.

ii', sour, mouldy.

'i'ini, to yearn, crave, desire.

ikaika, power: strong, energetic.

'ike, knowledge: to know, see.

'ikemaka, visible; to witness.

iki, small, little.

'ilalo, below.

ilamuku, executive officer, marshall.

ili, descent of property: to strand a ship.

'ili, skin, hide; bark, surface, area

'ilihia, fear, awe, reverence: shocking.

'ilihune, poor, destitute; in need.

iliili, to pile irregularly.

'ili'ili, pebbles; pieces in **konane.**

'ilikai, sea surface.

'ilikea, light colored skin.

'ilikona, wart.

ilimoku, shipwreck.

ilina, cemetery.

'ilio, dog.

'iliohae, a wolf.

'iliwai, water hose: horizontal.

ilo, maggot.

iloko, within.

iluna, above, upward.

'imi, seek, look for.

'imo, 'imo'imo, to wink, twinkle; ('imo, with one eye; 'imo'imo, with both).

imu, ground oven.

imua, before, in front of.

ina', if, provided that.

'ina, sea-urchin. .

inahea, when? (of past time).

inaina, anger, malice.

'inamona, a relish; kukui roasted and pounded with salt.

inehinei, yesterday.

'iniha, an inch.

'ini'iniki, to pinch repeatedly.

'iniki, nip off, pinch.

'inika, ink.

'ino, sin; wickedness; storm: bad: very.

inoa, name.

'ino'ino, badness; worthless; to be sad.

inu, a drink, to drink.

io, hawk.

i'o, true, real; certainly.

'i'o, flesh; one's person; gist.

ioio, to taper.

'io'io, to chirp, peep.

inikua, insure.

'iole, rat.

ipo, sweetheart.

ipu, gourd, melon; cup, mug; dish.

ipuahi, censor.

ipuʻaimaka, ipuhaole, watermelon.

ipuʻala, muskmelon.

ipuʻawa, the bitter gourd.

ipuhao, iron pot; kettle.

ipuholoi, wash basin.

ʻipuka, door, passageway.

ipukai, dish or bowl for fish or meat.

ipukiʻ, tea-pot.

ipukukui, lamp.

ipupaka, tobacco pipe.

iubileʻ, jubilee.

itamu, item.

iuka, inland.

iwa, nine.

iwaena, between, among.

iwaenakonu, middle, center.

iwaho, out, outside.

iwi, bone; close relative.

iwikaʻele, keel of ship.

iwikuamoʻo, backbone; chief's near relative
    and attendant.

iwilei, shoulder bone, collar bone; a yard.

iwipoʻo, skull.

K

ka, ke, the definite article.

ka! exclamation of surprise, etc.

ka, of, or belonging to.

ka, to bail water; to dash, radiate.

ka, tar.

kaʻa, a roller, wheel or wheeled vehicle: to
    roll.

kaʻaahi, kaʻahi, railroad train.

kaʻahele, a journey: to travel about.

ka'akaua, a chariot.

ka'alelewa, flying clouds: to drive with the wind.

ka'ao, legend, fable; to recite, narrate.

ka'apuni, going or traveling around.

ka'au, forty.

ka'auila, street car.

ka'awili, to writhe in pain.

ka'e, brink, border.

ka'elewa'a, unfinished canoe or boat.

kaena, to boast, glory, brag, be conceited.

kaha, to draw, make a scratch, cut open.

kahaha!, expression of surprise; to wonder.

kahakaha, to scarify; engrave.

kahakai, the sea shore; shore belt.

kahawai, stream, river, ravine.

kahe, to flow.

kahea, to call.

kaheka, shore pool; salt pan.

kahekoko, hemorrhage.

kahi, a place: some.

kahi, a comb: to cut, shave, scrape.

kahihi, to entangle, choke with weeds.

kahiki, foreign country.

kahiko, ancient, aged.

kahiko, garments; furniture: to adorn, dress, invest.

kahikolu, The Trinity.

kahili, a fly-brush, a broom; royal standard.

kahinu, to rub with oil; anoint.

kahi'umi'umi, to shave the beard.

kahoaka, soul of living person.

kahu, guardian: to bake in ground; kindle fire.

kahua, foundation, encampment.

kahuli, to turn over; to be changed, be upset.

kahuna, expert practitioner; (modern application), sorcerer.

kahunapule, priest, parson.

kahuwaiwai, trustee.

kai, the sea, sea water, brackish; gravy.

ka'ika'i, to carry in hands; to take up, carry.

ka'i, to lead, direct, attract.

kai'e'e, tidal wave.

kaikaina, a man's younger brother; a woman's younger sister.

kaikamahine, daughter; girl; niece.

kaikea, sap, sapwood; fat of hogs etc.

kaikua'ana, a man's older brother; a woman's older sister.

kaikuahine, a man's sister.

kaikunane, a woman's brother.

kaiku'ono, gulf, bay.

ka'ili, to snatch; take by force; jerk fish line; labor for breath.

kaimana, diamond.

kai mimiki, tidal wave.

kaka, to rinse.

kaka', the common duck.

ka'ka', to beat, whip; split wood.

kaka'a, to roll, turn over and over; spin as a top.

kakahiaka, morning.

kakaiapola, kite tail.

kaka'ikahi, few, scarce, rare.

kakaka, cross bow.

kakala, spur of cock; anything sharp or pointed.

kakala'au, fencing with spears.

kakale, to be thin, watery; to dilute.

kakali, to wait, expect.

kakalina, gasoline.

kakane, to blight.

kakani, to make a noise; be noisy.

kaka'olelo, counselor, adviser.

kakapahi, fencing, sword exercise.

kakau, to write; to tattoo.

kakau'olelo, scribe, clerk, secretary.

kakele, to slip, slide.

kaki, to charge a debt.

kaki', khaki.

kakela, castle.

kakiana, sergeant.

kakolika, catholic.

kakia, to nail.

kakini, stocking: dozen.

kaki'o, the itch.

kakiwi, to layer slips; to plant graftings.

kako'o, to support, uphold, assist.

kakou, we, (inclusive plural of three or more).

kala, government proclamation; end of house;
    surgeon fish: to proclaim; to absolve,
    pardon.

ka'la', money; silver; dollar.

kala'e, clear, calm.

kalai, to hew, to cut.

kalai'aina, political economy.

kalaimoku, counselor.

kalaipohaku, mason; stone cutter.

kalaima, crime.

kalaiwa. driver, chauffeur.

kalakala, rough, rude, harsh; like a rasp;
    thorny.

kalana, county.

ka'lana, sieve; stationery; to strain.

kalani, gallon.

kalapu, club.

kalaunu, crown.

kalea, whooping cough: to choke.

kalekona, dragon.

kalawina, Presbyterian.

kalele, to lean on for support.

kaleleleo, accent.

ka'lena, talent.

ka'lepa, a peddler; merchant: trading.

kalepalepa, to flap, as sails or flag.

ka'lewa, a swing: to float; to lie off and on; carry weight suspended between two.

kali, to wait.

kalima, cream.

kalo, taro.

kalikiano, Christian.

kalikimaka, Christmas.

kalua, double

ka'lua, to bury; to bake underground.

kaluha', water weeds.

kama, child.

kama'a, shoes, sandals.

kama'aina, native born.

kamaha'o, wonderful, astonishing.

kama'ilio, to converse.

kamala, booth, hut, shed.

kamali'i, children.

kamaloli, snail.

kamana', carpenter.

kamaniha, rude, coarse, sullen.

kamano, salmon.

kamelo, camel.

kamumumu, rumble, clatter; crunchy.

kamokoi, to fish with rod.

kana, a ton.

ka'na, his.

kanaha' forty.

kanaka, a man; a human being.

ka'naka, people, men.

kanake', candy.

kanakolu, thirty.

kanaloa, a certain deity.

kanalua, doubtful.

ka'nana, same as ka'lana.

kanapi', centipede.

kanawai, a law.

kane, male; husband.

kanea, loss of appetite.

kanemake, widow.

kanemale, married man; bridegroom.

kani, sounding; a singing, report of gun.

kanikau, a dirge: to mourn.

kanikela, counsul.

kaniuhu', sorrow, grief: to sigh, complain.

kano, a handle for a tool; tree trunk.

kanu, to bury or plant.

ka'nuku, funnel for liquids.

kao, goat; skyrocket; scow.

kaohi, to withhold, detain, restrain.

kaokao, syphilis.

ka'oko'a, separate, neutral.

kaola, house-beam; bar or fence rail.

kaolele, sky rocket; fireworks.

kaomi, to press down, squash; suppress emotion.

kaona, import; implication.

kaona, town.

kapa, cloth beaten, cloth, bed clothes; bank, shore, margin: to designate by name; to nickname; to term.

kapae, to turn aside; pervert; stow away.

kapakahi, one sided; crooked; partial.

kapakai, sea shore.

kapakapa, assumed name, alias: fictitious.

kapala, a writing, priting: to blot out.

kapalili, to tremble, palpitate, throb, flutter.

kapalulu, to flap the wings, shake, quail.

kapena, captain.

kapeku, to splash water, as in driving fish.

ka'pi', **ko'pi'**, to sprinkle; to salt.

kapiki, cabbage.

kapili, to join, unite; to plaster.

ka'pi'pi', **ko'pi'pi'**, to sprinkle.

kapikala, capital.

kapolena, canvas.

kapo'o, depression; enter or sink into out of sight.

kapu, tub: forbidden; sacred.

kapukapu, dignity.

kapua'i, footprint, sole, foot measure.

kapua'hi, fire place.

kapulu, dirty, careless, gross.

kau, summer season; period: to place, hang, alight.

ka'u, yours.

ka'u, mine.

kaua, war, battle.

ka'ua, we, inclusive dual: to detain; invite to stay.

kauhale, village, neighborhood

kauhuhu, ridgepole.

kauka, doctor.

ka'ukama, cucumber.

kaukanawai, to establish laws.

kaula, rope.

ka'ula, a prophet.

kaulahao, iron chain.

kaula'i, to hang out to dry.

kaulana, fame: celebrated.

kaulawaha, bridle.

kaulia, to be suspended; hung on cross.

kaulike, to balance; make alike.

kaulua, double, as canoes etc.

ka'ulua, to hesitate; delay.

kaumaha, weight, weariness; sacrifice.

kauna, four.

kauo', kauwo', draw, drag along.

kauoha, dying charge, command: to order;
    to commit to another.

kaupaku, roof; to thatch.

kaupaona, scales for weighing: to weigh.

kaupalena, to limit, to bound.

kaupili, mutual love; to be united.

kaupo'ohiwi, to shoulder, as weight or arms.

kauwa', servant, slave.

kauwahi, something, some place, some part.

kawaha, vacant, hollow.

kawau', dampness; moisture from fog.

kawele, towel, napkin.

kawelewele, hanging ropes; leader in towing.

kawili, to mix together, blend.

ke, ka, the definite article.

ke, sign of tense.

kea, white.

ke'a, stud animal: to hinder, to bar; to shoot
    arrows,

keaka, theatre.

keakea, white.

ke'ake'a, obstruction.; crossed sticks: to hinder.

kealia, salt marsh; salt pan.

ke'apa'a, chest.

ke'e, crookedness: crooked.

keehi, to trample, stamp with foot.

ke'emoa, crabbed, sour, surly.

keena, room, office, apartment.

keha, to be puffed with pride.

kehakeha, to be proud.

kehau, mist; frosty vapor.

kehena, Gehenna, Hell.

keia, this.

keiki, child.

kekahi, one, some, some one.

kekake, donkey.

keke', cranky, surly: to contend, scold; expose the teeth.

ke'ke', protruding abdomen.

kekea, albino.

keke'e, crooked, incorrect.

kekele, degere, degree.

kela', that.

kele, to reach by sailing; to sail off and on.

kele, kelekele, fat, grease; slippery.

keleawe, copper, brass.

kelekalama, telegram.

kelekalapa, telegraph.

kelepona, telephone.

kelikoli, territory.

kena', that (in possession of person addressed).

kena', to order, command, compel.

keneka, a cent.

kenekulia, century.

kenelala, general.

kenikeni, ten cents, a dime.

ke'oke'o, white; proud, haughty.

kepa, to snap, as teeth; to scrape, as dirt from board.

ke'pa', spur.

kepahi', Japanese.

kepau, lead, rosin, tar.

keonimana, gentleman; polite.

keu, additional; remainder; surplus.

ke'u, surly: to contradict, scold, snap.

ki, the ti-plant (Cordyline): to shoot; squirt.

kia, pillar, post, mast; spike, nail; deer; rod for bird lime: to trap birds.

kia'aina, governor

ki'aha, tumbler, cup, mug.

kia'i, a guard: to watch over.

kiakona, deacon.

kiapolo', devil, demon.

kialoa, long, beautiful canoe.

ki'ei, to look into, peep at.

ki'eki'e, high, exalted, steep, holy.

kiele, fragrant blossom, the shrub and perfume; Gardenia.

kihapai, farm; cultivation patch.

kihe, to sneeze.

kihei, shawl.

kihelei, astride: to straddle.

kihi, outer corner, edge, tip.

ki'i, image, picture, idol, statue: to fetch.

ki'ka', cigar; guitar.

kikaha, to pass without recognition; to soar like the frigate bird.

kikala, the hip, buttocks, rump.

ki'ke', dialogue, repartee: to rap, rejoin.

kike'eke'e, zigzag.

kikania, burr.

kikaliki, cigarette.

ki'ke'ke', knock at door.

kiki, sting.

kiki', rapid, quickly.

kikiki, ticket: to cheat.

kiko, dot, point, small spot: to peck.

kikokiko, spotted, speckled, striped.

kiko'o, a span: to bend the arm, or bow; stretch out hand or wing.

kikowaena, center of circle.

kila, steel; chisel.

kilakila, tall, strong, great, brave, majestic.

kilepalepa, to flap or flutter as flag.

kilika, silk; black mulberry.

kilo, star-gazer, astrologer; to spy.

kilohana, the very best.

kilohi, vanity; pride; to be looking in a mirror; to glance about with pride.

kiloi, to throw away.

kilokilo, enchantment: magical: to tell fortunes.

kilokilohoku', astrologer.

kilou, a hook.

kimo, to nod drowsily; bend in bowing; to pound.

ki'na', blemish, blotch; sin.

kimopo', secret plot to kill: to assassinate.

kinai, to quench; extinguish as fire.

kini, 40,000; tin; gin; zinc.

kinipo'po', baseball; ball-playing.

kinipo'po' peku, football.

kino, body.

kinohi, the beginning; origin; Genesis.

ki'o, dirty puddle; dregs: to excrete.

kio'e, to dip up, scoop, skim.

kioea, curlew; tall and thin person.

kiola, to lay down for inspection; throw away; overthrow.

ki'owai, puddle, pond.

kipa, kindness, hospitality: to turn in and lodge.

kipaku, to drive away, banish, expel.

kipapa, a pavement: to pave.

ki'pe', bribe: to pelt with stones.

kipi, rebel; sedition: to revolt.

kipikua, pickaxe.

ki'po', break box open; smash.

kipuka, an opening; snare for birds; poncho.

kipulu, fertilizer.

kiu, spy.

kiure, jury.

kiwi, horn.

ko, sugar cane: to be fulfilled; become pregnant; drag, tow.

koa, soldier: to be brave.

ko'a, horned coral; coral rock.

ko'ala, cooked on coals; broiled: to toast.

koali, beach vine; Ipomea.

koe, remainder; excess: to remain; to clean off pulp.

ko'e, angleworm.

koekoe, to mar surface by rasping or scratching.

ko'eko'e, cold and wet; cold food: tasteless.

ko'ele, farm; garden for the chief: to strike, beat, tick as a clock.

koena, remainder.

kohana, naked.

kohi, to dig; check; disunite.

koho, to choose, select, guess.

kohola, reef flats; bare reef.

kohola', whale.

kohu, sap, especially colored; ink or coloring matter; likeness: agreeable; appropriate.

kohu'ole, silly.

kohupono, decent: to choose to do right.

koi, to urge, implore; tempt.

ko'i, adze.

koia, of him.

ko'ikahi, carpenter's plane.

ko'iko'i, heavy, substantial, honorable.

koina, compulsion; pressure to pay.

koke, quickly

koko, blood.

ko'ko', knitted or netted bag.

kokoke, near to, almost; to be near.

kokoleka, chocolate.

koko'olua, assistant, helper.

kokua, help.

kokuli, ear wax.

kole, raw; inflamed.

kolamu, column.

kolea, plover; step-parent; parent-in-law.

koli, a meteor: to pare, whittle.

koliana, accordion.

koli'uli'u, indistinct sound from afar.

kolo, to crawl.

koloa, wild duck.

kolohe, polluting, vile; roguish, playful, mirthful, jolly.

kolohala, pheasant.

koloka, cloak.

kolopa', crowbar.

kolu, three.

kolu', glue.

komikina, commissioner.

komike, committee.

komo, tenon; finger ring, thimble: to enter.

komohana, west.

komolole, to dress.

komowale, to trespass.

kona, south; south-west.

kona, his, hers, its.

konane, bright, clear; Hawaiian checkers.

koni, to throb; to taste, to try.

konikoni, to nibble, as fish; to throb repeatedly.

kono, to solicit, invite.

konohiki, overseer of chief's estate.

konu, suffix used with waena, "center."

ko'o, prop, brace; cock's tail feathers.

ko'oko'o, staff; supporter.

ko'olau, north; windward.

kopa, soap.

kopa'a, sugar.

kopala, corporal.

kopala', shovel.

kope, rake; coffee.

ko'pi', sprinkle with salt.

kou, yours

kou', moist, wet, damp.

ko'u, mine.

ko'wa', space, strait, channel.

kowali, to swing to and fro, as skipping rope.

ku, suitable, adaptable, liable; to arise, stand.

kua, anvil for tapa or for blacksmith: to fell
a tree.

kua, the back.

kua'aina, back country: coarse.

kua'ana, older of brother or sister.

kua'au, basin inside reef.

kuahine, brother's sister.

kuahiwi, mountain summit.

kuahu, altar.

kuai, to rub or grind two together.

kua'i, to remove entrails.

ku'ai, to barter.

kuailo, to explain some enigma.

kuaina, twine, string.

kuala, usuriously.

kuala', dorsal fins of fish.

kualapa, ridge.

kualono, broad ridge; space atop the mountain.

kuamo'o, backbone; frequented path.

kuamuamu, blasphemy: to revile; to curse.

kuapa'a, bondman: severe; laborious.

kuapo, exchange, "swap".

kuata, quart.

kuaua, fall of rain; passing shower.

ku'auhau, genealogy: historical.

ku'e, to push with elbow.

ku'e', be opposed; resist.

kuea, square.

ku'e'e', disagree, bicker.

kueka, sweater.

ku'eku'e, joint, knuckles, elbow.

ku'emaka, eyebrows.

kuene, steward, waiter: to adjust; to prepare or conduct correctly.

kuewa, vagabond.

kuha, spit.

kuhewa, (ma'i kuhewa), heart failure; stroke.

kuhi, to infer, intimate, point out; surmise.

kuhihewa, error in judgment or opinion.

kuhikuhi, to show, point out, designate.

kuhikuhihana, program.

kuhina, regent, premier.

kuhoupo'o, to dive head-first.

kui, pointed instrument, pin, nail, needle, spike.

ku'i, to pound with the end; to punch; to disseminate news; to sound, as thunder; to join.

ku'ia, to stumble; to be hindered.

ku'ihao to forge, work iron.

ku'i'ia, wrought.

ku'ikahi, treaty; union of feeling.

kuikawa', free, unbound, independent, temporary.

ku'ina, sewing, seam.

ku'ipalu, to pulp, pound fine.

ku'ipehi, to attack verbally or physically.

kuka, coat.

ku'ka', to consult.

kukae, excrement.

kukaenalo, beeswax; unbleached muslin.

kukaepele, sulphur; matches.

kuka'i'olelo, chat, conversation.

kukala, to broadcast; proclaim publicly; notify.

ku'ka'la', auction.

kukaweke, rain coat.

kuke, to nudge, push gently.

ku'ke, cook.

kukekuke, push repeatedly with elbow.

kukini, cushion.

kuki'ni, messenger; runner in a race: to run.

kuko, strong desire: to lust.

kuku, to strike, beat.

kuku', thorn, piercing seed.

kukui, candle-nut; lamp; torch.

kukuli, to kneel, crouch.

kukulu, to erect, build, stick up.

kukuluhema, South.

kukulu, to drip.

kukuluae'o, stilts: the stilt bird.

kukuna, rays; radii.

kukuni, to kindle; burn.

kula, gold.

kula, dry land; field; open land.

kula'i, to push, push over.

kulaia, festal, feast day; holiday.

kulana, reputation, station, rank.

kulanakauhale, town, city.

kulanalana, unsettled, unsteady: to reel.

kuleana, a right; ownership; interest.

kulekule, unsettled; unfurnished.

kulele, drive away with a puff.

kuli, knee; deafness: deaf: to be stunned
    with noise.

kulia, one's lot; luck: to strive.

kulihiamoe, to doze.

kulikuli, to stun with noise; Hush! Shut up!

kulike, accord.

kulima waiu', cream.

kulina, corn.

kulipolipo, depth: extremely.

kuloko, domestic affairs; interior.

kulolo, pudding of coconut with taro.

kulou, to bow, bend forward; stoop.

kulu, drop of water; leak from above.

kuluihiamoe, nap: overcome with sleep.

kulukulu, to drop continuously; give talking.

kuluma, customary.

kumama, units in excess (used in counting).

kumakaia, traitor; ambuscade; to betray.

kumakena, mourning in loud voices.

kumano, head of watercourse; reservoir; dam.

kumolemole, smooth and steep, as unscalable precipice.

kumu, bottom, foundation, origin, tree trunk.

kumuaʻo, teacher, instructor; coach.

kumuhoʻohalike, pattern, example.

kumuhana, scheme, topic, subject.

kumukahi, origin; beginning or occasion for any thing.

kumukuʻai, equivalent in barter; price in cash sales.

kumukumu, stumps or roots; to be cut short.

kumulau, a producer, breeder; female with many offspring.

kumumanaʻo, subject, text, theory.

kuʻmuʻmuʻ, to be dull or blunt as a tool.

kumupaʻa, principal, capital; solid foundation.

kumuwaina, grape vine.

kuna, form of itch.

kuna, freshwater eel.

kuʻnaʻnaʻ, to be stumped, at wit's end, to stand gazing about.

kunane, brother of a sister.

kunewa, kunewanewa, weariness, to stagger.

kuni, to kindle; burn, or light.

kunihinihi, edge of precipice; central ridge of hair or helmet.

kunou, to make signs by nodding or beckoning.

kunu, cough: to roast meat on coals.

kunukalea, whooping cough.

kunukunu, to grumble covertly; to groan.

ku'o'i', to limp or stagger; to rock like a vessel.

kuoko'a, standing aloof; independent.

kuokuolo, kuolo, vibrating motion, as in rubbing.

ku'ono, recess in room; nook; bay, gulf.

kuonoono, prosperity: well furnished; supplied.

kuo'o, serious, sober-minded, earnest.

kupa, citizen, resident; soup; cooper.

kupa', dig a trench; dig out canoe.

kupa'a, firm. strong, fixed; to stand fast.

kupaka, to writhe, twist.

kupakako, clerk; supercargo.

kupalu, to stuff with food; to make a favorite.

kupanaha, wonderful.

kupapa'u, corpse.

kupe'e, bracelet or anklet; fetters.

kupenu, to dip; to dye by dipping.

kupikipiki'o', raging of the sea or multitude.

kupiliki'i, to be crowded, confused; be in a jam.

kupina'i, noisy; general crying; echo; mourning.

kupipipi, throng.

kupono, upright, honest, perpenticular; to fit.

kupololei, perpendicular.

kupou, bend forward in drowsing or stumbling.

kupu, to sprout.

kupukupu, ferns.

kupua, sorcerer, wizard.

kupulau, kau kupulau, Spring.

kupuna, grandparent; ancestor.

kupuni, to stand around; surround as an enemy.

ku'u, my, mine: to release, let go.

ku'uku'u, short-legged spider.

kuululu', shiver with cold.

ku'uwelu, tassel, fringe.

L

la, the sun, day.

la, particle following verbs.

La 'aipelehu', La Ho'alohaloha, or Ho'omaika'i, Thanksgiving Day.

la'a, sacred; devoted; to be holy.

laala'au, herbs, shrubs.

la'au, vegetative growth; wood; trees; medicine.

la'au'ala, sandal wood.

la'aulapaau, medicine.

la'aulu, growing season.

la'aumaka'i, policeman's baton.

la'au'o'oi, bramble, briar.

lae, forehead, cape, brow of hill.

la'ela'e, unobstructed view; clear; bright shining as sun.

laha, to be spread out.

lahilahi, thin.

laho, scrotum.

laholio, rubber, elastic.

lahui, assemblage; people; nation: to prohibit, lay a tabu,

la'i, to be calm.

laiki, rice.

laikini, license.
laka, tame, domesticated.
lakeʻe, to be coiled; to be flexed.
lakeke, jacket
laki, luck, lucky.
lakikuʻ, lattitude.
lako, supply, sufficient.
lakou, they (three or more).
lala, diagonal.
laʻlaʻ, branch, bough; member: to parcel out.
lalama, to get into mischief by handling.
lalani, rank, row, line.
lalau, mistake: to go astray.
lalau, seizing.
laʻlau, to seize.
lalelale, haste; to hurry.
lali, greasy, as hands; fat; slippery as mud.
lalilali, greasy; wet.
lalo, down.
lama torch, light; alight; rum.
lana, to float, be buoyant.
lanaʻau, float with current; drift.
lanahu, nanahu, coal, charcoal.
lanai, shed, porch, booth.
lanakila, conquest: to prevail.
lanalana, unstable; buoyant; spider.
lani, sky.
laoa, laowa, be choked by obstruction.
laʻolaʻo, bundle of fuel sticks, fagot.
lapa, flat; ridge, side of ridge.
lapaau, to cure illness.
lapalapa, flat; blaze: to boil.
lapu, ghost.
lapulapu, collect in little heaps.
lapuwale, foolishness, vanity: worthless.

lau, leaf; tip; 400: to produce leaves; to
   reach out for.
laua, they two.
lauhala, pandanus leaf.
laula', broad.
laulaha, to be spread abroad.
laulau, a bundle; wrapper.
laule'a, peace, friendship.
laulima, cooperation.
laumania, smooth, even, plane.
laumeki, to flow or move slowly; recede.
laumilo, to writhe; kill by torture or by
   twisting.
launa, friendly; to associate
launahele, vegetables.
lauoho, head hair.
lauwili, confusion: variable, fickle; deceitful.
lawa, enough, ample.
lawai'a, a fisherman: fishing: to catch fish.
lawakea, white cock; white attire.
lawe, to take, carry, transfer.
lawehala, sinner.
lawehana, workman; laborer; to undertake.
lawelawe, to serve; to handle.
lawepio, to capture.
lawewale, extortion.
le'a, joy, pleasure, gratification.
le'ale'a, to delight in, be merry.
leke, lady.
leha, to turn eyes; glance.
lehei, lekei, to jump, leap over; alight.
lekeona, legion.
lehelehe, lips.
lehelehei, hop as a bird.

leho, cowrie shell.

lehu, ashes; 400,000.

lehulehu, many; a multitude, host.

lei, necklace, wreath; crown; string of beads.

lei'a'i, necktie.

leina, a leap, a spring, a bound.

leka, letter.

lele, to fly, jump.

lelekoali, a swing; to swing.

lelele, to hop, bounce, frisk.

lelelele, running jumps: to skip, run off; fore-
    sake as a wife.

lelepau, to trust in; to credit.

lemu, buttocks.

lemi, lemon, lime.

lena, yellow: to strain as a bow, sight or aim,
    bend.

leo, a voice.

leoha', hoarse.

leopaki, leopard.

lepa, flag, garment border or fringe.

lepe, cockscomb: diagonally

lepela, leper, leprosy.

lepeka, mite (coin).

lepo, dirt.

lewa, atmosphere; visible heavens: to swing;
    float.

lewalewa, to swing frequently; to float;
    dangle.

li, chill from cold, ague, or fear: to hang by
    neck.

lia, fear or dread in visioning a spirit.

li'a, a desire for; a yearning after.

liha, nausea; a nit.

lihi, border, edge.

lihilihi, eyelids, eyelashes; lace.

li'i, little, small.

li'ili'i, small, little, diminutive.

like, to be like.

likiki, receipt.

likini, rigging.

liko, opening as a bud; to swell.

lilelile, bright, shining; to sparkle.

lili, jealous, anger; pride.

lilia, a lily.

liliha, nausea: to be satiated.

liliko'i, passion fruit.

lilina, linen.

lilio, tightly drawn; slant-eyes.

lilo, to become another's; to change; be lost.

lima, arm, hand; five.

limaikaika, to assault, handle roughly, "to strong-arm."

limu, alga.

linalina, a scar on body; to be sticky.

lino, rope; to weave, twist or braid.

lio, horse.

li'o, restless, uneasy.

linoleuma, linoleum.

liona, lion.

lipi, sharp, tapering; axe.

lipine, ribbon.

lipo, deep, bottomless as the ocean.

liu, leakage, bidge water: to leak.

li'ula', dusk; twilight; mirage.

liuliu, prepared; ready.

li'uli'u, for some time.

loa, long, of time or space; very.

loa'a, gain: obtained: to be obtained.

loea, skillful, clever, applied to women.

loha, wither, wilt.

lohe, to hear.

lohea, to be heard.

lohi, slow, feeble.

lo'i, taro patch.

loiele, dull, slow.

lo'ihi, long, in time or distance; tall.

loi, to "size one up."

loiloi, deprecation of appearance or work: to
    sneer.

loina, rule; law.

loio, lawyer.

lokahi, accord, unanimity, unision, agreement.

loke, rose; roast.

loko, pond, lake.

lo'ko, within.

loko'ino, to act vilely; deal malevolently.

lokomaika'i, benevolence, grace, favor, good
    will.

lokowai, fresh water lake; fountain.

loku, heavy rains; tears; anguish, mental
    or physical.

lola, roller: sluggish, inactive.

lole, cloth, particularly foreign; garment: to
    be reversed, changed; to skin an animal.

loli, sea-slug: to turn over, to change.

loli'i, to make ready; provide.

lolo, brain, marrow.

lo'lo', idiot: palsied.

lolohi, very slow; backward: to loiter.

loloiele, stupid, dull.

loloiwi, marrow.

lomi, to press, massage.

loniku', longitude.

lono, report, news: to be heard; to hurl.

lo'ohia, to be overtaken; to come upon, befall, happen.

lopa', farmer, tenant.

lopi, thread.

lou, hook, pain in side: to bend as hook.

loulu, palm.

lu, that thrown away or scattered: to scatter, sow; to shake.

lua, a pit: two.

luaahi, luahi, volcano; hell

luahine, old woman.

lua'i, vomit.

lua'ipele, sulphur; lava.

luakini, temple; church.

lualua'i, the cud.

luana, leisure: satisfied, easy, content: to live idly.

lua'ole, the best; darling; nonesuch.

luapele, crater, volcano.

luapuhi, blow hole.

lu'au, taro leaf; feast.

luawai, well, cistern.

lu'e, to be loosened, scattered.

lu'elu'e, gown.

luhe, wither, droop, fade.

luhi, opperssion, fatigue: tiresome.

luina, sailor, mariner.

luku, slaughter, wholesale destruction.

lukanela, lieutenant.

lula, rule; manners.

lule, to shake.

luli, to vibrate, rock, roll as ship.

luliluli, to wag, totter.

lulu, calm; still, of wind and water.

lulu', donation: scattering: to sow; to shake
    out dust; to winnow; to throw dice; to
    shake fists.

lulua'ina, freckle.

lulumi, to crowd in.

luma'i, to kill by drowning; to duck in water.

lumakika, rheumatism.

lumi, room.

luna, overseer: upper, above.

lunaho'omalu, chairman.

luna'ikehala, conscience.

lunakanawai, judge.

lupe, a kite.

lu'u, to dive, plunge out of sight.

lu'ulu'u, grief: painful, miserable.

luwahine, luahine, old woman.

M

ma, et al.; accompanying; as, Keawe ma, "Ke-
    awe and his group."

ma, to fade, wilt; blush: at, by, through, in,
    unto, alongside of, by means of, according to.

ma'a, experience; habit: accustomed.

ma'a, a sling; to sling.

ma'alahi, nobleness; easily done.

ma'alea, subtlety: prudent, wise, crafty,
    shrewd, sly.

ma'alili, lukewarm, cooled.

ma'alo, to pass by or through; proceed; lose.

ma'ane'i, here, at this place.

ma'au, indifference; persecution.

ma'awe, fiber, strand.

mae, blasted, as fruit; withered.

maea, displeasing odor.

ma'e'ele, cramp: benumbed, numb.

maemae, withered, drooping.

ma'ema'e, clean, pure, chaste.

maewa, swaying.

maha, to rest; to enjoy ease and quiet after pain.

mahalo, wonder: to approve, praise, applaud, thank.

mahana, warm.

mahani, to cool off, as emotions; to pass off or away; to vanish.

maha'oi, bold, impertinent.

mahea, where?

mahele, a portion, division.

mahi, energetic: to cultivate.

mahi'ai, to farm.

mahiki, to vibrate: to peel off as scale; to exorcise.

mahimahi, dolphin, Coryphaena.

ma'hina, the moon, a month.

mahina, cultivated patch.

mahina'ai, field, farm; husbandry.

mahiole, war cap, helmet, officer's cap.

mahoe, twins; name of tree.

mahola, to spread out, extend; expand.

mahole, to bruise, as the flesh; break up.

mahope, behind, after; hindermost.

mahu, steam.
    nearly: from.

ma'hu', hermaphrodite; male simulating female.

mahuahua, to increase, expand, thrive.

mahuka, to flee, escape from; to bolt.

mai, Do not! Come here! Hither; almost,

ma'i, sickness, disease; the private parts.

mai'a, banana.

mai'ao, human finger or toe nail.

maiau, neat, skillful, expert.

ma'ihi, to strip; peel as fruit.

maika'i, good, beautiful.

maile, perfumed vine.

mainoino, inhuman; defacement; atrocity; suffer.

mai'u'u claw; hoof.

maka, face, eye, edge, point, mesh etc.; very hard stone: raw, uncooked; green, unripe.

maka'ainana, commoners, distinct from chiefs.

maka'ala, watchfulness: to be awake, alert.

makaaniani, spectacles.

maka'e', to be opposed to.

ma'ka'ha', gateway; passage through fish pond walls.

makahiamoe, drowsy.

makahiapo, first born.

makahiki, year.

makai, seaward.

maka'i, guard, constable; to inspect, spy.

maka'ika'i, diversion; visit; to go sight-seeing.

maka'ikiu, detective.

makaki'i, a mask.

makakiu, to be a spy.

makala, to untie, loosen.

makaleho, haughtiness; lust, lasciviousness.

makali'i, very small or fine, diminutive.

makalike, uniform.

makalua, socket for the eye-ball.

makaluku, bent on slaughter.

makamae, precious, valuable; much desired.

makamaka, friend; beloved one.

makamua, first; the beginning.

makana, gift, present.

makeneki, magnet; magneto.

makani, wind.

makapa'a, blind in one eye.

makapo', completely blind.

makapouli, to faint; be dizzy.

makau, to be ready.

ma'kau, fishhook.

maka'u, fear.

makaukau, readiness.

maka'upena, mesh of net.

makawai, small outlets for water; running tears.

make, dead: to die.

make'e, covetous: to have great regard for.

make'ewaiwai, avarice.

makehewa, bad bargain: in vain; to no profit.

makeke, mustard; market.

makemake, desire, wish.

makena, mourning; lamentations; many, often, much.

makewai, thirst: thirsty.

makia, bolt, pin, nail, spike.

makepono, good bargain.

makika, mosquito.

makili, to open a little, as the mind.

makilo, to beg.

makolo, to crawl: ask a favor.

makolu, wide, thick.

makona', implacable, unfriendly.

makou, we, plural exclusive.

maku', dregs, sediment: thick, stiff, like molasses.

makua, a parent: full grown.

makuahine, a mother.

makuakane, father.

maku'e, to elbow; provoke anger; frown.

makulu, to drip.

ma'la, garden; cultivated field.

mala'e, a calm, calmness, pleasant appearance.

malaila, there.

mala'ela'e, clear; serene, as sky; smooth as plain; without obstruction.

malakeke, molasses.

malalo, downward, under, below.

malamamoku, first mate of vessel.

ma'lama, take care, heed.

malama, light; a solar month.

malamalama, light.

malana'i, northeast wind.

malawaina, vineyard.

male, phlegm: to spit.

ma'le, marriage.

malia, perhaps, lest.

malie, quiet, calm, gentle, smooth: to abate.

malihini, stranger.

malimali, soothing.

malino, calm, pacific, smooth.

mali'o, first rays of light.

maliu, to give attention, heed; be civil.

malo, loin cloth.

ma'lo', taut, straight, firm.

malo'elo'e, fatigue: weary, stiff with labor.

malohi, a want of sleep: weary.

maloko, within.

malolo, ebbing of spring tides; day of preparation before sacred day.

ma'lolo, flying fish.

malo'o, dry; dead, of a dried up vegetable.

malu, shady, protected; peace.

malu', secret; without order.

malua, slight depression.

maluhi, tired, weary.

maluhia, safety.

maluhiluhi, wornout; weariness from travel.

malumalu, shade; protection, safety.

maluna, above.

mama, to chew and reject.

ma'ma', light, quick, active, swift.

mamae to wilt, be wilted.

mamala, fragment; small piece broken from a larger.

mamala'olelo, clause (in grammar).

mamalu, a shade, umbrella, defense: covered, shaded.

mamao, far away, distant.

mamau, to stall; to stick fast.

mamo, descendent; war cloak of the mamo feather.

mamua, before, first, formerly.

mamuli, behind, afterwards, by and bye.

mana, authority, power, might.

mana, branch or limb of tree.

ma'na, to feed from mouth.

manai, needle for stringing flowers.

mana'i, windward.

manaka', bored, dull, tame.

manako', mango.

manalo, sweet, as fresh water.

manalonalo, unseasoned, insipid.

manakuke, mongoose.

manamana, a branch: branching.

manamanalima, finger.

manamanawawae, toe.

mananalo, insipid, stale.

manaʻo, to think, wish, will.

manaʻoiʻo, to believe.

manaʻolana, hope.

manaʻonaʻo, to grieve.

manaʻohaʻi, proposition.

manawa, feelings, affections.

manaʻwa, time.

manawaʻino, evil disposition.

manawaleʻa, alms, charity: generous.

manawanui, steadfastness; patience.

manele, sedan chair, litter.

maneʻo, itch; acrid.

mania, smooth, even surface.

mania, dizziness, sensation when filing saws;
    unpleasant noise.

maniania, even, smooth, dull, sleepy, lazy.

manienie, Bermuda grass.

mano, 4000.

maʻno, head of distributing water channels.

manoʻ, shark.

manoanoa, thick, as a board; coarse.

manoʻi, coconut oil scented; perfume.

manu, bird.

manuea, blundering, careless, awkward.

manuahi, gratis.

manukuʻ, pigeon; dove.

manumanu, rough, defective; blunt, not sharp.

manununu, to creak, grate.

manuwaʻ, warship .

mao, to be ended, as a rain storm or tears.

maoʻ, there, yonder.

maʻo, green.

maoa, soreness from rubbing.

maʻoi, bold, shameless, arrogant.

maoli, native; genuine.

ma‘ona, filled, satisfied.

maopopo, plain, clear: to be sure.

mapela, marble.

ma‘pu, fragrance: bubbling, as a spring.

ma‘pu‘, ape.

mapuna, boiling up, as a spring.

mau, constant, continuous, frequent: to be stopped.

mau, a word indicating the plural.

ma‘u‘, moist, wet, damp.

maua, ungrateful.

ma‘ua, we, dual exclusive.

mauhala, unforgiving.

ma‘ui, sprained: to wring.

ma‘ule, to faint.

mauli, last night of moon.

mauna, mountain.

ma‘unauna, wasteful; prodigal.

maunu, bait.

mau‘nu, to moult; shed skin; change from chrysalis.

mau‘u, general name for grass, herbs, rushes.

ma‘u‘u, moist.

mawae, cleft, crack, fissure.

mawaena, among, between.

mawaenakonu, center.

mawehe, to separate, be loosened.

me, with, like.

mea, a thing; material.

mea‘ono, cake.

me‘eau, the itch; mange; blisters on skin.

meha, mehameha, alone, lonely, desolate, forsaken.

meheu, track, trace, foot print, impression; scent followed by dog.

meia, mayor.

mekia, major.

mekekiko, Methodist.

mele, a song; to sing.

melemele, yellow.

meli, honey.

menehune, brownies.

menemene, fearful for one; feelingly.

me'nu', menu.

meka, the mass.

mekala, metal; medal.

meumeu', blunt, dull; rounded on edge.

miana, place to urinate.

miha, to appear dark, as the depths.

mihi, regret; repentance.

mikanele, missionary.

mika, mister.

miki, energetic; readiness.

mikiao, claw.

mikimiki, efficient: to be quick, brisk

mikinilima, mikilima, glove.

mikini, machine.

mikioi, neat; excellence in work; good taste.

mikiona, mission.

mikolelehua, quick minded; skillful; reasoning.

mikomiko, relishable, as food; seasoned; delicious.

mili, to handle, feel, examine.

milimili, curiosity: to view, handle, examine.

milo, to twist; spin, as a thread.

mimi, urine: to urinate.

mimiki, to recede, as undertow.

mimilo, whirlpool.

mimino, to wrinkle, curl up; wither.

minamina, regret for loss or error; sorrow; covetousness.

mineka, mint.

minelala, mineral.

mino, curling up; crown of head; dimple.

mino'aka, smile.

minomino, wrinkle.

minuke, minute.

miomio, to be tapered, compressed; dive in water.

moa, fowl.

mo'a, cooked thoroughly.

moakaka, clear, plain, intelligible.

moana, ocean; to be spread out.

moani, fragrance wafted on the breeze.

moe, bed: to sleep; lie down; dream.

moehewa, to be disturbed; to talk or walk during sleep.

moe'ino, nightmare; unpleasant dream.

moekolohe, adultery, fornication.

moe'uhane, dream.

moemoea', to dream or fantasy.

mohai, sacrifice.

moha'i, to break in two, be broken.

mohala, to open, expand as a flower; to blossom.

moho, candidate.

moi', sovereignty; majesty; king.

mokaki', disorder of room.

mokomoko, a boxer; to box.

moku, land division; ship: to cut, divide in two.

mokuahana, faction: divided, unfriendly.

mokuahi, steam vessel.

moku'aina, state; island.

mokulele, airplane; clipper.

mokulu'u, submarine.

mokupuni, island.

molaki, mortgage.

molalelale, colorless; clear.

mole, tap root; foundation; principle element.

molehulehu, twilight: dim.

molina, tape.

molio, taut: to be stretched.

molowa', lazy.

momi, pearl; jewel.

momona, large, fat; rich, fertile; sweet.

moni, to swallow, consume.

mo'o, lizard, snake; genealogy; track.

mo'olele, dragon.

mo'olelo, history, tradition.

mo'oniho'awa, viper; scorpion.

mo'onui, dragon; alligator.

mo'opuna, grandchild.

mouo, buoy: float.

mu, clothes moth, and other small bugs.

mua, first; previously; foremost.

mu'emu'e, bitter.

muka', a seizing, devouring; smacking of lips.

muki', kissing motion: to suck, to kiss.

muki'ki', to suck in, as smoke or water; to sip.

mukoki, plain, homely.

muku, to be cut short.

mulea, insipid; bitter.

muli, after; behind.

muliwai, lagoon; river.

mumule, silent; sullen; mute.

mumulu, swarming flies, bees, mosquitoes, etc.

mu'o, leaf bud.

mu'umu'u, underslip; loose house dress.

mu'umu'u moepo', night gown.

N

na, definite article, plural: of, for, belonging to.

na', quiet, pacified: to labor for breath, as from asthma.

na'au, intestines; intelligence.

na'auao, enlightenment; wisdom.

na'aupo', ignorance; stupidity.

na'e, but, yet, furthermore.

naenae, to pant for breath; sigh.

naha', bent; broken: to be split, cracked; to act as purgative.

nahae, torn: to tear, rend; break off.

nahaha', broken; brittle: to shatter.

nahelehele, weeds.

nahenahe, mild; melodious.

nahili, awkward, blundering, careless.

nahoahoa, wound on head and related pain.

nahu, to bite.

na'i, conqueror: to acquire by own efforts; take by conquest.

na'ina'i, sour, crabbed; to struggle against opposition.

naio, intestinal worms.

naka, shaking; cracked as earth from heat.

nakaka, split, shattered, cracked.

nakeke, to rustle, rattle.

nakele, soft, slippery, boggy.

naki'i, to tie, bind; to cord.

nakinaki, to bind often, bind fast.

nakolo, echo; hollow sound.

naku, rushes.

naku, to root; to trample.

nakulu, noise of water drops; rumble; echo.

nakulukulu, clatter; pattering.

nalinali, nibble, gnaw.

nalo, a fly: vanished: to be lost.

nalomeli, honey bee.

nalopaka, wasp.

nalu, wave, surf.

nalulu, headache.

namunamu, to nibble, as fish; grumble, mutter.

nana', snarling disposition; fault finding.

nana, for him, his.

na'na', to gaze at, look, examine carefully.

nanahu, lanahu, coal, charcoal.

nanahu, bite (teeth or pain).

nanaina, appearance, countenance.

nanao, insert hands or fingers; think deeply; probe.

nanapono, to watch earnestly.

nanea, leisure: easy, cozy: to repose.

naneha'i, problem in mathematics.

nani, glory, splendor: beautiful.

nao, to probe.

nao, ripples, fine ridges, streaks, thread of screw.

nao wili, drill bit.

na'o, mucus.

naonao, ants in general.

naonao, insert hand; seize.

na'ona'o, phlegm, spittle, mucus.

naonaolele, winged termite; winged ant.

nape, to bend; yielding; swaying, as branches.

napenape, soft, flexible: to be shaken; vibrate rapidly.

napo'o, to set; go down as sun.

nau, to chew, to gnash teeth.

nau, for you, yours.

na'u, of me, mine.

naue, to shake, tremble as earth.

naueue, a moving; earthquake; shock.

naulu, heavy mists; shower of heavy rain without clouds.

naunau, to chew, munch.

naupaka, shrubs of the genus Scaevola.

nawali, sickly, weak, feeble.

nawaliwali, feeble, sick.

nawele fine, like spider-web.

ne, fretting: to be teased; to droop.

ne'e, to move, to change place.

nekelo, a negro.

nei, this; here; this time or place.

nele, want: destitute, deficient.

nelu, fat, fleshy.

ne'ne', goose.

nenelu, miry place, marsh.

neo, nothingness; silence: empty, bare.

neoneo, desolate, solitary; lifeless.

newa, staff, cudgel; policeman's club.

nia, bald; round and smooth as bald head.

niania, calm, shining, smooth, bald.

niao, edge.

niau, easy sailing: to glide.

ni'au, stem of coconut leaflet.

niele, to ask, enquire, interview.

nienicle, to question repeatedly; to pump.

nihi, stealthy.

nihinihi, carefully, quietly.

niho, tooth.

nihomole, a gap in a row; notch.

nihopalaoa, ivory.

ninaninau, to question, examine, probe, interrogate.

ninau, to question.

nini, ointment, balm; petty jealousy.

ninini, to pour out, as liquid.

niniu, to whirl, spin.

nioi, chili pepper plant and fruit.

niu, coconut; palm and fruit.

niuhi, the man-eating shark.

no, of, for.

noa, release from restrictions.

noe, mist, spray.

no'eau, art, i.e. skill: wise, prudent, skillful; acute.

nohea, lovely.

no'hea, whence?

noho, a seat, chair, bench, layer: to sit, to dwell.

nohoali'i, throne.

noho'i, also.

noi, (note: ke noi, the request; ka noi, the one asking), a request: to beg, entreat.

noi'i, to investigate, research; to reflect.

nolaila, therefore.

nolunolu, soft and springy as a mattress.

nona, his, hers.

nonanona, ant.

nono, redness of face, of sunburn, of angry eyes.

nono', to snore.

nonoi, to beg, appeal, borrow.
nonolo, to breathe hard, snore.
no'ono'o, a thought: to think, reflect.
nou, to throw at.
no'u, yours.
no'u, mine.
nounou, to throw stones back and forth.
nu, to groan, shake, sound, roar.
nuha, to sulk, be obstinate, balk.
nuhou recent news.
nui, large, great.
nukoki, plain, homely.
nuku, mouth, snout, bill.
nukunuku, to complain, to rail.
numonia, pneumonia.
nu'nu', dove, pigeon.
nunuha, taciturn, unsocial, stubborn, contrary.
nunui, very large, gigantic.
nunulu, to growl, grunt; to warble.
nupepa, newspaper.

O

o, lest: of or belonging to.
(ke) o, food for journey.
'o, "The 'O emphatic."
(ke) 'o, a piercer, fork: to pierce, dip.
'o, there, yonder.
(ke) o'a, house rafter.
'oa', to burst over, as a stream.
'oaka, flash of light; sun reflection: to open.
'oe, thou, you.
'o'e, sharp darting pain: to prick; to gore.
'oe', 'owe', rustle of leaves; a noise of running
    water: to whiz.

(ke) **oeoe**, whistle or horn of train, steamer or automobile; lengthened neck.

'oha', sprig, sucker, branch.

'ohana, family, clan.

ohaoha, fond recollection, joy, delight.

'ohe, bamboo.

'ohelopapa, strawberry.

'ohena'na', spyglass.

'ohi, to gather up, glean, harvest, collect taxes.

'ohiki, sand crab; to shell, pry up; probe or pierce.

oho, a calling: to call out.

(ke) **oho**, hair of head; leaves.

ohohia, enthusiasm.

'ohu, a fog, mist.

'ohua, dependents of household; passengers.

'ohule, bald.

'ohumu, to murmur, grumble, complain.

'oi, first, most excellent; greater; the best; sharp.

'o'i, to limp.

'oia, yes; it is so.

'oiai, while.

'oiai'o, truth, verity.

'oihana, business; occupation, trade.

'o'ili, to project, appear.

'oiwi, personal appearance; substantial part.

(ke) **oka**, dregs, sediment; sawdust, crumbs, filings, hulls.

'oka, oak tree; oats.

'okana, district; organ.

oki, to end or finish; stop.

'oki, to cut, cut off, cut in two.

'oki'oki, to cut frequently, or in small pieces.

'okipoepoe, circumcision.

oko'a, different, another, separate; whole.

'okole, the anus; posteriors.

'okoleke', pig Latin.

okomopila, automobile.

'okupe, to stumble, trip.

(ke) ola, life; health, recovery: alive: to live.

(ke) ola'i, earthquake.

'olala, lean, poor in flesh.

olalau, demented.

olaola', to gargle.

ole', speaking trumpet.

'ole, no, not; lacking.

'olelo, a word; speech, language: to say.

'olelonane, proverb; riddle.

'ole'ole', indistinct: to chatter.

'olepe, oyster, clam.

'olepe, to turn, as a hinge.

'olepelepe, lattice work· network.

oli, ulioli, to chant.

'oli, 'oli'oli, joy, happiness, exultation

'olinolino, bright, brilliant; to dazzle.

'oliwa, olive; oleander.

(ke) olo, a saw: to saw; to grate.

olohani, to strike work

'olohelohe, destitute, naked, bare of vegetation.

'oloka'a to roll along.

'ololi', narrow.

olona', fibrous shrub, cord.

'olo'olo, calf of leg; to hang loosely; a garment too long.

'olu, supple, flexible; elastic.

'olua, you two.

'olulo, person cast away or shipwrecked.

'olu'olu, cool, agreeable; good natured.

'oma, oven; baking place.

'oma'ima'i, sickly, weak; to ail.

'oma'oma'o, green.

omo, to suck.

'omole, glass bottle.

omomo, to draw into mouth.

'omo'omo, a long loaf of bread or meat.

ona, bird mite; nettling of skin, with pimples.

'ona, owner: drunk.

ona, of him, his.

(ke) one, sand; beach.

onea, destitute of inhabitants.

'onawaliwali, to flag, be weak or poorly.

one'i, here.

oneki, deck.

'oni, to move, stir.

'oni'o, a spot; spotted.

'oni'oni, to dodge; move back and forth; wag.

'oni'oni'o, spotted; striped; streaked.

'onipa'a, firm, strong, fixed, immovable.

(ke) ono, six.

'ono, deliciousness: to relish; desire to taste.

'onohi, eyeball.

'onou, to force, compel; to urge upon.

o'o, ripe (of fruit); mature (of people and
　　animals).

'o"o', digging tool: to crow.

'o'oi, sharp, prickly.

'o'ole'a, unyielding, hard, stiff, exacting, ob-
　　stinate.

'o'olopu', a blister.

'o'opa, cripple: lame.

'o'opu, goby fishes.

'opa', to squeeze.

'opae, shrimp.

'opala, rubbish, litter, garbage.

'opa'opa, wearied; lame from walking.

(ke) 'ope, bundle.

'ope'a, scrotum: to overturn.

'ope'ape'a, bat.

(ke) 'opi, folds, in cloth.

'opili, cramps; torpor.

opio, young.

'opi'opi, to fold up; wrap.

'ōpu, the belly.

'opiuma, opium.

'opua, narrow pointed clouds.

'opu'ino, 'opu'ino'ino, hostile, unfriendly, malevolent.

'opukopekope, malevolent, surly.

'opulepule, light-headed; giddy; moronic.

'opu'u, to bud, sprout, or bloom.

opu'upu'u, coarse.

o'u, yours.

o'u, mine.

'oukou, you, plural.

'ouli, character, description; sign, omen.

'ou'ou, long sharp-snouted.

'owa', to be split, as a board: to crack, as ground.

'owai, to twine into wreathes.

'owai, properly 'o wai, who?

'owaka, a flash.

'owa'owa, divided, cleft.

'owa'owaka, brilliant.

'owau, I.

'owau, a cat.

'owe', see 'oe'.

'owili, a roll, a bolt; to roll up, coil.

'owelawela, warmth of fever.

P

pa, a distributive particle.

pa, barren, as a female.

pa, a wall; an enclosure: to divide out; to fence.

(ke) pa, flat dish, plate, pan.

pa'a, tight, fast, secure; steadfast: a pair; a suit.

pa'a'a, banana skin.

pa'ahana, energetic worker; implements, utensils.

pa'ahao, convict; prisoner.

pa'a'iliono, cube.

pa'akai, salt.

pa'akiki', hard, compact, difficult.

pa'amau, standard.

pa'ani, play of games; sport.

pa'apu', crowded, overwhelmed; deluged with work.

pa'apa'a'ina, brittle.

pae, cluster, group; margin or border: to be cast ashore; to land.

pa'e, to strike on ear.

pa'ele, negro; blot, dirty spot.

pae'aina, paemoku, archipelago.

paepae, platform, pavement, threshold.

paepae, to bear up, support.

paepaekomo, axle.

pa'ewa, pa'ewa'ewa, bent; biased; erroneous.

paha, perhaps.

paha', four-fold.

pahale, house lot; yard.

paha'oha'o, mystery.

pahe'e, sliding; to slip.

pahele, noose; snare; ambush.

pahemahema, ignorant; ungrammatical.

pahemo, to be loosened; to slip in walking.

pahi, knife, sword.

pahikaua, sword.

pahoa, dagger.

pahoehoe, smooth shining lava.

pahole, to peel off; "bark the skin."

pahonohono, to sew up; patch.

pahu, drum, barrel, box, chest, ark, coffin;
stake in ground for mark: to push.

pahu', to burst, explode.

pahuhopu, a point or goal.

pahu'olelo, phonograph.

pahupahu, billiards.

pahupahu', fire crackers.

pahu'ume, bureau; drawer.

pahuwai, water barrel; tank.

(ke) **pa'i,** a printing: to strike with open
hand, clap, slap, stamp, print.

paia, sides or inside walls of house.

pa'i'ai, pounded taro.

paihi' (waipaihi), trickling waterfall or cascade.

paikau, to drill, parade.

paiki, suitcase; doctor's satchel; bag.

pa'iki'i, photograph.

paikikala, bicycle.

paila, heap, pile.

paila wahie, cord of firewood.

(ke) **pallaka,** pilot.

pa'imalau, Physalia; Portuguese man-of-war.

paina, pine tree; fine cloth like serge.

pa'ina, meal, dinner: to feed, to board; to
   snap, as a rope.

paio, debate; combat; quarrel.

paionia, pioneer.

paipai, rocking chair: to rock; to encourage,
   urge on; canvass for votes.

pa'ipa'i, to clap, applaud.

paipu, pipe; water pipe.

paka, tobacco; rain drops: to listen and correct pupils' errors; to park.

pakaha, to oppress, cheat, fleece.

pakahi, apiece; one to each.

pakalaki, bad luck.

pakali, decoy.

pakaukau, table; buffet; bar.

paka'uwili, to encircle, entwine; squirm.

pakeke, bucket; pocket.

pakela, excess: to exceed, excel.

pakela'ai, gluttony; luxurious living.

pakelo, to escape, be free from.

pakeneka, percentage.

paki', to spatter.

pa'ki', to throw down; press with iorn.

paki'i, flattened; flat faced.

pakika, smooth: to slip.

pakike', saucy reply: insolent.

pakiko, to be temperate.

pakini, pan.

pakoli', musical scale.

pa'ku', curtains; screen; partition; inner wall.

pakua', pakuwa', commonplace.

paku'i, added on: to engraft, annex, splice.

pala, ripe, mellow soft.

pala'ai, squash, pumpkin.

palaha, to fall flat.

palahaláha, to be flat, spread out.

palahe', rotten: to decay; run after bursting.

palahe'he', pus, matter.

palaho', rotten, putrid.

palai, a fern: to fry.

palaimaka, enemy's pretense of friendship; contempt.

palaka, pulley-block; jacket-shirt: inactive; neglectful of obligations.

palaki, brush.

palakahuki, to decay as vegetation.

palale', speech not easily understood.

palani, brandy; France; French.

palaoa, whale ivory; ivory.

palaoa, bread, flour.

palapala, writing, inscription; The Scriptures.

palapu', wound.

palau, plow.

pa'lau, to lie.

palaualelo, lazy, unoccupied.

pale, sheath; outer garment: to ward off.

pale'ili, undershirt.

palekai, breakwater, bulwark.

palekana, a defense; a savior: rescue; to have escaped trouble.

palema'i, underpants.

palemaka, veil.

palela li'ili'i, keg.

palemakani, windshield.

palemo, to sink down in water; be sunk.

palena, border, limit.

palepale, to fend off; to parry.

palewawae, house slippers.

pali, cliff, precipice.

paloka, ballot.

palolo, clay.

palu, to lick, to lap.

palua, double.

paluna, balloon.

palula, cooked potato leaves.

palule, shirt.

palupalu, weak, feeble, soft.

pama, palm.

pana, bow; the pulse: to shoot arrows; to
    flip; to snap fingers.

pana'i, reciprocity; ransom: to return favors.

panala'au, colony.

pa'na'na', compass.

panapua, archery.

panau, gadabout: to be restless.

pane, to answer; utter.

pane'e, to hitch forward.

(ke) pani, stopper; something filling a va-
    cancy: to shut, to close.

panihakahaka, to substitute.

panini, cactus, prickly pear.

(ke) pa'nina, end; finis.

panoa, barren region; desert.

paniolo, cowboy; Spaniard.

(ke) paniwai, dam.

pao, to peck like a bird; to dig from below;
    dig out with chisel.

pa'oa, disappointed, unlucky; heavily perfumed.

paona, pound; weight.

paopao, to beat; to peck repeatedly.

paopao, a maul.

papa, flat surface; board; rank, class, order; table.

pa'pa', to forbid, prohibit.

papa'a, burned to crisp, parched, crusted: to thirst.

papahana, plan, stratagem.

papahele, papahehi, floor.

papahelu, list, score.

papa'i, crabs; small hut.

papale, hat, cap.

papalekapu, cap.

papalina, the cheek.

papalua, to double.

papani, a shutting out; river boom: to shut.

papapa, beans.

papa'u, a bar: shallow.

papipi, prickly pear.

pa'pu', a plain; a fort: clear.

pau, all; finished; entirely.

pa'u, soot; smut· ink-powder.

pa'u', woman's skirt; also for riding or dancing.

paua, mussel.

pauka, powder.

pauku', fraction, portion, piece cut off.

paulele, to trust in, confide.

pauma, pump.

pauma'ele, dirty, defiled, foul.

paupauaho, breathless; desperate from weariness.

pe, thus, so, as.

pe', crushed, flattened; to anoint, be perfumed.

pea, bear; pear; avocado.

pe'a, cross, tabu sign; sail.

pe'ahi, the hand: to fan, brush, beckon with hand.

pe'e, to hide self.

pe'elua, caterpillar.

peheu, flipper, fin; wing.

pehea, how?

pe'a, cross, tabu sign; sail.

pehi, to pelt.

pehu, a swelling; to swell.

pekapeka, to tattle; accuse falsely.

pekekeu, wing.

pekana, pagan, heathen.

peku, to kick.

pela, mattress; bail.

pe'la', thus; in that manner.

pelamoe, mattress; pillow.

pelapela, filthy, stinking, foul, nasty.

pele, a volcano.

pelehu', a turkey.

peleke, brake.

pelekikena, president.

pelena, crackers.

pelo, to flatter; to lie.

pelu, to double over; bend at joint, fold.

pena, paint.

penei, thus, as.

peni, writing implement.

penikala, pencil.

penikila, pen.

pepa, paper.

pe'pe', crushed fine, flattened.

pe'pe', baby.

pepe'ekue, lumbering, clumsy.

pepe'epaka, plug of tobacco.

pepehi, beat severely; kill; murder.

pepeiao, ear.

pewa, tail fin of fish.

pewapewa, side fins and tail.

pi, peas, lentils: close, stingy; to sprinkle.

pia, arrowroot.

pi'alu, be almost blind.

piano, piano.

piha, to be full.

piha'a', driftwood.

piha'ekelo, mynah bird.

pihapiha, fish gills; ruffle.

pihe, loud cry; wailing; lamentation.

(ke) pihi, button.

pihipihi, buckle; large button for ornament.

piho', piholo, to swamp in boat; to founder.

pihoihoi, astonishment, joy, excitement, anxiety; timid.

pihopa, bishop.

pi'i, to ascend, climb.

pi'ipi'i, curl of hair: curly-headed.

pika, pitcher.

pikake, peacock; jasmin.

pikapua, vase.

piki, peach; beet.

pikiniki, picnic.

piko, navel; end; summit.

piku, fig.

pila, fiddle, violin; any musical instrument; bill.

pilalahi, tall and slender.

pilali, gum; wax; resin; bird time; kukui gum.

pilau, strong stench, stink.

pua'i, to flow out as blood, or as a fountain.

puakala, thistle; Mexican poppy.

puʻali, company of soldiers, army, host; compression, isthmus: compressed.

pili, coarse grass; relations: related to: to adhere; to coincide; to bet.

pilialo, bosom friend.

pilihua, sad, perplexed, anxious, dejected.

pilikana, kin, relative, friend.

pilikia, trouble.

pilikua, giant.

pilikoko, relative.

pilipaʻa, adhere, stick.

pilipili, adhering, sticking, connected.

pilipuʻ, united; adjoining.

pilipono, suitable; fitted tightly, tight.

piliwaiwai, betting, gambling.

pineki, peanut.

pinana, to climb; to scramble up.

pinao, dragon fly.

pine, a pin: to pin.

pinepine, frequent.

pinika, vinegar.

(ke) pio, captive, prey; to destroy; be conquered; to be extinguished.

piʻo, arc of circle: bent, arched: to be curved.

piʻoʺoʻ, perplexity; mentally confused.

piopio, peep, as a chicken.

pipi, pearl oyster; beef, cattle.

piʻpiʻ, to spray, to sprinkle; to urinate.

piula, pewter, tin, aluminum, etc.

piwa, fever.

po, night, dark. obscure.

poʻa, castrated.

poʻaeʻae, armpit.

poʻai, circle, hoop: to girdle; to go around.

poale, open, as a sore; hole.

po'alo, to gouge eyes; shell beans.

poe, buoy.

po'e, company, assemblage.

poeko, clever in speech.

po'ele'ele, night time; darkness.

poepoe, round, globular, circular.

poha', Cape gooseberry: burst.

pohai, circle of people: to gather around.

pohaku, stone.

pohakulepo, adobe.

poheoheo, knob.

pohihihi, mystery: obscure, puzzling, complex, entangled.

poho, small concavity; bellowing of sail; palm of hand; chalk; patchwork: to puff out; to patch.

poho', loss or damage: sunken: to sink; to lose money.

poholima, palm of hand.

poholo, to sink; to drop or slip through.

poholua, to lie to, as a ship

pohopoho', marshy; muddy; sinking.

pohu, calm after storm.

pohue, gourd; water calabash, piece of gourd.

pohuehue, Morning Glory vine of the beach.

pohuku, to round off corners.

pohuli, shoot, sucker.

(ke) po'i, cover, close container: to pounce on; to curve and break as surf.

poi, taro paste.

po'ino, bad luck; injury.

poka', bullet, ball; ammunition

poka'a, spool: to wind up.

pokaka'a, wheel of pulley or vehicle: turning, rolling.

pokepoke, chops: to cut in pieces.

poki'i, youngest of family.

poko, cut worm.

poko, pokole, short.

pola, bowl, cup; flap of malo.

polewa, to sway to and fro; be unsteady.

poli, bosom or lap.

polinahe, slender waisted.

polo, polo.

poloai, general invitation.

poloka, frog; toad.

pololei, uprightness; straight.

pololi, emptiness: hungry.

polopeka, professor; expert.

polopolona, musty smell; smell of room long closed.

polu', blue.

poluea, nausea; seasickness.

pomaika'i, good fortune; blessing: prosperous.

pona, puna, joints of sugar-cane, bamboo, etc.

ponalo, blight; plant louse.

poni, purple: to besmear, daub, anoint; be purple.

poni moi', coronation; carnation.

pololei, uprightness: hungry.

poniniu, poniuniu, turning motion; vertigo: dizzy: to spin around.

pono, goodness; uprightness: to be just.

pono'i', own, self.

(ke) po'o, head, summit.

po'o, slight depression on surface: to make same.

po‘ohiwi, shoulder.

po‘okela, champion: exceeding, better; exceptional.

po‘ola’, stevedore.

po‘oleka, stamp.

po‘opo‘o, deep, as pit; sunken, as eyes.

popilikia, difficulty, disappointment, distress, disaster.

popo, rotten; to rot.

po’po’, ball; round loaf; any rounded mass: to gather up; make round.

po’po’, (from apopo), tomorrow.

popo‘i, bung, stopper; curling of waves: to cover; to pounce on.

popoki, a cat.

popolo, berried shrub (Solanum).

popopo, rotten, decayed.

pou, post, supporting column.

pouli, dark, obscure.

pouliuli, very dark, gloomy.

poupou, squat; short and stout.

powa’, robber; pirate; murderer.

powehiwehi, dim, vague, seeing indistinctly.

poweko, clever in speech.

pu, together with.

pu’, shel’ trumpet, horn; gun.

pua, blossom, flower; arrow.

pu‘a’, bundle, fagot; herd, drove; to tie in bundles; to feed from mouth.

pua‘a, hog.

pu‘a‘a, to bundle sticks for kindling.

puahilo, slender; fine as a spider's web.

puahio, puff of wind: to come and go suddenly.

puahiohio, whirlwind.

pua‘i, to flow out as blood or as a fountain.

puakala, thistle; Mexican poppy.

puʻali, company of soldiers, army, host; compression, isthmus: compressed.

pualoalo, hibiscus flower.

puana, pitch of tune: to pronounce a word; introduce the subject or speaker.

puanuanu, to be cold, chilly.

puʻao, womb.

puapua, tail feathers; coat tails.

puapuaʻi, spring or fountain; spout.

puapuamoa, frock coat; skirted coat; cock's tail feathers.

puʻawa, bitterness; awa root.

puʻe, potato hill: to hill potatoes; to onset, attack, ravish, force.

puehu, dispersion, scattering.

pueo, owl.

puhaʻ, to hawk; to belch; breathe as turtle.

puhoʻ, abscess; to burst as a boil.

puhaka, the loin; waist.

puhala, pandanus tree.

puhi, eel: to puff, blow; to burn, smoke tobacco.

(ke) puhina, blow hole.

puhipaka, smoke tobacco.

puia, to spread, as fragrance.

puʻipuʻi, fat, plump, stout, flourishing.

puʻiwa, fright; surprise; amazement.

puka, a hole; doorway, entrance; profits: to pass through, issue, appear; to gain; to win a race.

pukaʻaniʻani, window.

pukalakiʻ, ruffled, as hair; flaring temper; scattering blast of wind.

puke, book.

pukiki', strong, furious, boisterous, stormy; Portuguese.

pukini, pudding.

puko'a, rocks submerged; reef; coral rocks.

pukolu, triplets.

pukonakona, tough, brave; strange (of people).

pukuniahi, cannon.

pula, small particle, as dust; mote in eye.

pule, prayer; incantation: to pray, worship.

pulehu, to roast on coals, broil, burn.

pulelehua, butterfly.

pulewa, swinging at anchor.

puliki, vest: to embrace, clasp; to w r a p around.

pulima, wrist.

pulu, wet, as clothes.

pulumi, broom.

pulupulu, cotton; kindling.

pumahana, warm; lukewarm.

puna, stone coral; lime, mortar; a spring; spoon; joint of cane or bamboo.

punahamo, mortar.

punahele, a favorite, friend.

punahelu, mildew, mould.

punalua, triangular matings.

punana, nest.

punawelewele, spider's web.

pune'e, couch, settee.

puni, a surrounding of fish; termination of a period: to desire; be fond of, deceive: to be around.

punia, cold in head.

puniu, coconut shell; human skull.

puniwaiwai, avarice; covetousness.

punohu, to ascend, as smoke.

punua, fledgling.

pu'o'a, pyramid; house with posts uniting at top.

puoho, to start in fright; to exclaim.

pu'olo, bundle, scrip, bag, container.

pupanapana, pistol.

pu'pu', shells in general; bead.

pupuahulu, bustling, hasty, quick.

pupuka, ugly; worthless.

pupule, crazy; insane.

pupupu, small hut.

pu'u, any round protuberance from a pimple to a hill.

pu'ua, choked or suffocated, as with food.

pu'uhonua, refuge, asylum.

pu'uku', treasurer; stewardship.

pu'ulima, fist; wrist.

pu'ulu, crowd.

pu'ulu'ulu, to huddle, throng; to be thickly massed.

pu'unaue, to distribute, share.

pu'uone, sand heap; dune.

pu'upa'a, virgin; kidneys.

pu'upu'ulima, knuckles.

pu'upu'uwawae, ankles.

pu'uwai, heart.

R

Repubalika, Republican.

U

u, the breast, udder.

'u, grief, sorrow: to weep.

ua, rain; shower.

'ua, sign of perfect tense.

'u'a, vain, useless; to no profit.

uahi, smoke; cloud.

uahoa, hard-hearted; harsh; unyielding.

'uala, sweet potato.

'ualakahiki, Irish potato.

uapo, uwapo, wharf; bridge.

uaua, tough, sinewy, hardy.

ue, to shake.

'uha', thigh.

'uha'uha, prodigality: to waste.

uhaki, to break, snap as stick.

'uhane, the soul.

uhi, yam.

uhi, a veil; covering, cloak; stains or tattoo
    marks.

uhimaka, mask.

'uhini, grasshopper; cricket.

uhola, to spread out, unfold.

uhu', grunting, as of hogs.

uhuki, to pull up by roots; eradicate.

u'i, symmetry: young, strong, beautiful.

uila, uwila, lightning, electricity.

'u'ina, the hamzah, ', "a gutteral break in
    pronunciation between two vowels;" sharp
    report; snap of whip, cracking of fingers.

'ui'uiki, to twinkle as stars; gleam, glimmer.

uka, inland.

ukali, to follow after one.

ukana, baggage, luggage, freight.

'ukele, muddy, slippery.

ukiuki, to be offended, to resent.

uku, wages, pay; fine, tax; to pay.

'uku, louse, small insect.

ukuhi, to dip up; to pour from one container
    to another; to wean.

'ukulele, flea; small guitar.

ukupau, contract.

ula, lobster.

'ula, red, scarlet; red of flame.

'ulala, crazy, demented.

ulana, to weave, plait, braid.

'ula'ula, red, rosy, crimson.

ule, penis.

uleule, sty on eyelid: to hang.

uli, blue, as sky; green, as meadow; dark
    blue: to steer.

ulia, accident.

uliuli, blue, green, dark colored, brown, black.

ulu, growth, grove: to grow; to be inspired.

'ulu, breadfruit.

uluahewa, derangement, mania, delusion.

uluao'a, mob, disturbance; confusion.

uluhua, angry, worried, vexed, frantic.

ulula'au, forest.

ulumoku, fleet.

ulumokukaua, navy.

uluna, pillow.

'ulupa', to shatter, dash to atoms.

uluwehiwehi, jungle; overgrowth of verdure.

umauma, bosom, chest.

'ume, attractive; magnetic: to pull, draw out.

'umeke, bowl.

'umi, to throttle, strangle, stifle.

'umi'i, clamp; pain in the side.

'umi'umi, beard or face hair.

'umoki, cork or bung.

unahi, fish scales: to scale fish.

unaunahi, to scale fish.

une, lever: to pry with a lever.

unu, to wedge, prop; to draw up a dress.

unuhi, to draw out from; translate.

'uoki, Stop!

'upa', scissors, bellows; implement with similar action.

'upa'makani, bellows.

'upa'upa', to open and close mouth as in speaking.

upehupehu, inflammation.

'upena, fish net.

'upiki, a trap, snare, treachery; to snap as trap.

'upi, sponge.

upu, recurring thought.

'u'u, to strip bark or skin; to pull out.

'u'u', a stammering: to groan.

'u'uku, small, little.

'u'umi, to throttle, stifle; to restrain, curb.

uwaki, watch, clock.

uwalo, to cry out.

uwao, peaceful: to intercede, arbitrate, reconcile.

'uwa'uwa', noisy, boisterous.

uwe', to weep.

uwea, wire.

uwea'ole, wireless.

'uwi', to squeeze, as milking; to wring.

uwiki, wick.

uwinihapa, brick.

'uwo', cry out; bellow, roar, growl.

W

wa, space, in time or place.

wa'a, canoe.

wae, to select, choose, sort, separate.

waele, to weed.

waena, the middle: between.

waenakonu, the center.

waha, mouth.

wahahe'e, lie.

waha'olelo, deputy, representative.

wahapa'a, to banter; to scold.

wahi, a place; words cited: some, little, few.

wa'hi, portion broken off for sharing: to break open.

wahi', envelope, sheath: to wrap.

wahie, firewood.

wahine, female.

wahinekanemake, widow.

waho, out, outward, outside.

wai, who?

wai, fresh water, liquid.

waia, disgrace.

waiho, to lay down; to place or set aside; stop; assign.

waihona, place for laying up.

waihonaka'la', treasury.

waikahe, stream; a deluge.

wailana, still water: to banish.

wailele, waterfall, cataract.

wailua, spirit.

waimaka, tears.

waioleka, violet.

waiolina, violin.

wai'ona, strong drink.

waipahe', courteous: gentlemanly.

waipuhia, waterfall blown back by wind.

waipu'ilani, waterspout.

waiu', milk.

waiupakapa'a, cheese.

waiwai, goods, property: costly.

waiupaka, butter.

wakawaka, serrated; sharp: to glitter.

wala'au, gabble, loud talking; babble.

walania, pain; anguish; woe.

walawalala'au, great noise: to shout.

wale, alone, only.

wale, phlegm; acidic saliva; mucus.

walea, accustomed; content; apt: to indulge in ease; be satisfied.

walewale, mucus, slime: allurement; decoy: to be deceived.

wali, soft, fine as paste or flour.

walu, eight.

wawalo, to cry out; make a noise; echo.

walu, to scratch; rub, rasp.

wana, sea urchins.

wana'ao, dawn.

wanana, prophecy.

wanawana, thorny, spiny.

waniki, varnish.

wanila, vanilla.

wao, zone on mountain slopes.

waoakua, wilderness, desert; desolate place.

waonahele, wilderness.

wau, I.

wa'u, a grater: to scrape, scratch, grate.

wa'uwa'u, to scrape; to scratch.

wawa', a tumult: noisy.

wawae, leg, foot.

wawahi, to smash, break to pieces, demolish; to change money.

wawa'u, quarrelsome: to scratch as a cat sharpens claws.

wawe, quickly, soon.

wehe, to open, displace, exhibit, loosen.

wehewehe, to explain, expound.

wekeke', whiskey.

wekiu, top, summit.

wela, heat: hot, burnt; burning.

welau, extremity; tip.

welawela, very hot.

weleweka, velvet.

welelau, end, extremity; most distant **part of** country.

weli, fear; scion or shoot from roots.

weliweli, fear, dread: terrible.

welo, welowelo, to float in the wind.

welu, a rag.

weluwelu, to be torn to pieces.

weuweu, herbage; grass.

wi, famine.

wikiwiki, quick.

wili, to twist; to wind.

wiliki', engineer.

wiliko', sugar mill.

wilipuaʻa, corkscrew.

wi'wi', lean, feeble: to be shriveled up.

wiwo, fear, shame, dread: afraid.

wiwoʻole, fearlessness: bold.